Communications in Computer and Information Science 1406

More information about this series at http://www.springer.com/series/7899

Paramartha Dutta · Jyotsna K. Mandal ·
Somnath Mukhopadhyay (Eds.)

Computational Intelligence in Communications and Business Analytics

Third International Conference, CICBA 2021
Santiniketan, India, January 7–8, 2021
Revised Selected Papers

 Springer

Editors
Paramartha Dutta
Visva-Bharati University
Santiniketan, India

Jyotsna K. Mandal
University of Kalyani
Kalyani, India

Somnath Mukhopadhyay
Assam University
Silchar, India

ISSN 1865-0929   ISSN 1865-0937 (electronic)
Communications in Computer and Information Science
ISBN 978-3-030-75528-7   ISBN 978-3-030-75529-4   (eBook)
https://doi.org/10.1007/978-3-030-75529-4

This Springer imprint is published by the registered company Springer Nature Switzerland AG
The registered company address is: Gewerbestrasse 11, 6330 Cham, Switzerland

Preface

It is a matter of great pleasure for us, as the editors, to share some of our experience in the form of a preface in relation to the proceedings of the Third International Conference on "Computational Intelligence in Communications and Business Analytics (CICBA 2021)", held during January 7–9, 2021. What indeed is an instance of pride, is that the papers appearing in this proceedings meet all the stringent technical filter mechanisms befitting an edited volume published in Springer's prestigious Communications in Computer and Information Science (CCIS) series. Needless to say, compliance with all the requirements as laid down in the publication policy is a highly challenging task, which the authors of these papers fulfilled. No doubt it is an admirable achievement on their part. As the editors of this volume, we wish to avail ourselves of this opportunity to express our heartfelt congratulations to them all.

When the conference was planned about one and half years back, we primarily took it as a challenge because the CCIS approval was not easy to garner. From the beginning, the approval was conditional, and there was every possibility that the publication might never come to fruition. Only after thorough scrutiny, until the last phase of camera-ready submission of all accepted papers, was Springer, as our publishing partner, in a position to unconditionally approve this CCIS series publication. Throughout this time we were apprehensive as to whether we, as editors, would be able to see our initiative through successfully. What further complicated the situation was the COVID-19 pandemic, which impacted researchers and practitioners across the globe and, perhaps, made it more challenging to produce contributions of good technical merit. We sincerely appreciate that our Call for Papers was able to attract no less than 84 submissions, out of which 20 stood up to our rigorous review process for inclusion in the proceedings. We feel particularly moved by the submissions from the prospective authors because unfortunately we could not guarantee publication, and yet they still made the effort to share their work.

Coming to the composition of the papers appearing in the proceedings, we categorized them broadly into four domains: (i) Computational Intelligence (six contributions), (ii) Intelligent Data Mining and Data Warehousing (six contributions), (iii) Computational Forensic (Privacy and Security) (four contributions) and (iv) Data Science and Advanced Data Analytics (four contributions). It is goes without saying that all of these papers are highly commendable in a technical sense.

We were particularly impressed by the way that Springer, as our publishing partner, took a principled stand to ensure the high quality of this proceedings, knowing full well that a delayed CCIS approval would, in all likelihood, hinder the interest of prospective authors. We feel gratified that they put quality over and above commercial considerations. We are proud to have them as our publishing partner. We also hope that in the months and years to come, our collaboration will be further enhanced.

Happy reading!!!

April 2021

Paramartha Dutta
Jyotsna K. Mandal
Somnath Mukhopadhyay

Organization

Chief Patron

Vice-Chancellor   Visva-Bharati University, India

General Chair

Kalyanmoy Deb   Michigan State University, USA

Organising Chair

Alak Datta   Visva-Bharati University, India

Program Committee Chairs

Paramartha Dutta   Visva-Bharati University, India
Jyotsna K. Mandal   Kalyani University, India
Somnath Mukhopadhyay   Assam University, India

International Advisory Board

Amit Konar   Jadavpur University, India
Amiya Nayak   Ottawa University, Canada
Atal Chowdhury   Veer Surendra Sai University of Technology, India
Aynur Unal   Stanford University, USA
Banshidhar Majhi   IIITDM Kanchipuram, India
Carlos A. Coello Coello   CINVESTAV-IPN, Mexico
Edward Tsang   University of Essex, UK
Hisao Ishibuchi   Southern University of Science and Technology, China
L. M. Patnaik   IISC Bangalore, India
Mike Hinchey   University of Limerick, Ireland
Mrinal Kanti Naskar   Jadavpur University, India
P. N. Suganthan   Nanyang Technological University, Singapore
Sajal Das   University of Texas at Arlington, USA
Shikharesh Majumdar   Carleton University, Canada
Sushmita Mitra   Indian Statistical Institute, Kolkata, India

Technical Program Committee

A. Damodaram   Jawaharlal Nehru Technological University, India
Aminul Islam   BIT Mesra, India
Amlan Chakraborty   University of Calcutta, India

Anamitra Roy Chaudhury	IBM Research, New Delhi, India
Angsuman Sarkar	Kalyani Government Engineering College, India
Anirban Chakraborty	IISC Bangalore, India
Anirban Mukhopadhyay	University of Kalyani, India
Anuradha Banerjee	Kalyani Government Engineering College, India
Arindam Biswas	IIEST Shibpur, India
Arindam Sarkar	Belur Vidyamandir, India
Arnab K. Laha	Indian Institute of Management Ahmedabad, India
Arnab Majhi	NEHU, India
Arun Baran Samaddar	National Institute of Technology, Sikkim, India
Arundhati Bagchi Misra	Saginaw Valley State University, USA
Asif Ekbal	Indian Institute of Technology Patna, India
B. B. Pal	University of Kalyani, India
B. K. Panigrahi	Indian Institute of Technology Delhi, India
Barin Kumar De	Tripura University, India
Basabi Chakraborty	Iwate Prefectural University, Japan
Biswapati Jana	Vidyasagar University, India
Chandan Bhar	IIT (ISM) Dhanbad, India
Chandreyee Chowdhury	Jadavpur University, India
Debaprasa Das	Assam University, India
Debarka Mukhopadhyay	Adamas University, India
Debashis De	Maulana Abul Kalam Azad University of Technology, India
Debasish Chakraborty	ISRO Kolkata, India
Debesh Das	Jadavpur University, India
Debotosh Bhattacharjee	Jadavpur University, India
Dhananjay Bhattacharyya	Saha Institute of Nuclear Physics, India
Diganta Sengupta	Techno International Batanagar, India
Dilip Kumar Pratihar	Indian Institute of Technology Kharagpur, India
Ganapati Panda	Indian Institute of Technology Bhubaneswar, India
Girijasankar Mallik	Western Sydney University, Australia
Goutam Saha	NEHU, India
Govinda K.	Vellore Institute of Technology, India
Himadri Dutta	Kalyani Government Engineering College, India
Hyeona Lim	Mississippi State University, USA
Indrajit Bhattacharyya	Kalyani Government Engineering College, India
Indrajit Pan	RCCIIT, India
Indrajit Saha	NITTTR, Kolkata, India
J. K. Singh	Jadavpur University, India
Jaya Sil	IIEST Shibpur, India
Jyoti Prakash Singh	National Institute of Technology Patna, India
K. Suresh Babu	Jawaharlal Nehru Technological University, India
Kakali Dutta	Visva Bharati University, India
Kamrul Alam Khan	Jagannath University, Bangladesh
Kartick Chandra Mondal	Jadavpur University, India
Kaushik Dassharma	University of Calcutta, India

Koushik Dasgupta	Kalyani Government Engineering College, India
Koushik Majumder	Maulana Abul Kalam Azad University of Technology, India
Koushik Mondal	IIT (ISM) Dhanbad, India
Kousik Roy	WB State University, India
Krishnendu Chakraborty	Government College of Engineering and Ceramic Technology, India
Manas Sanyal	University of Kalyani, India
Millie Pant	Indian Institute of Technology Roorkee, India
Mita Nasipuri	Jadavpur University, India
Moirangthem Marjit Singh	NERIST, India
Nabendu Chaki	University of Calcutta, India
Nandini Mukhopadhyay	Jadavpur University, India
Nibaran Das	Jadavpur University, India
Nilanjana Dutta Roy	Institute of Engineering and Management, India
Pabitra Mitra	Indian Institute of Technology Kharagpur, India
Partha Pakray	National Institute of Technology, Silchar, India
Partha Pratim Sahu	Tezpur University, India
Parthajit Roy	University of Burdwan, India
Pawan K. Singh	Jadvpur University, India
Pawan Kumar Jha	Purbanchal University, Nepal
Pramod Kumar Meher	Nanyang Technological University, Singapore
Pranab K. Dan	Indian Institute of Technology Kharagpur, India
Prasanta K. Jana	IIT (ISM) Dhanbad, India
Prashant R. Nair	Amrita Vishwa Vidyapeetham, India
Pratyay Kuila	National Institute of Technology Sikkim, India
Rahul Kala	Indian Institute of Information Technology, Allahabad, India
Rajdeep Chakraborty	Netaji Subhas Institute of Technology, India
Rajeeb De	National Institute of Technology Silchar, India
Ram Sarkar	Jadavpur University, India
Ranjita Das	National Institute of Technology Mizoram, India
Ravi Subban	Pondichery University, India
S. K. Behera	National Institute of Technology Rourkela, India
Samarjit Kar	National Institute of Technology Durgapur, India
Samir Malakar	Asutosh College, India
Samir Roy	NITTTR, Kolkata, India
Samiran Chattopadhyay	Jadavpur University, India
Sankhayan Choudhury	University of Calcutta, India
Santi P. Maity	IIEST Shibpur, India
Sarmistha Neogy	Jadavpur University, India
Satish Narayana Srirama	University of Tartu, Estonia
Satyen Mondal	Kalyani Government Engineering College, India
Siddhartha Bhattacharyya	Christ University, India
Sk Obaidullah	Aliah University, India
Soma Barman	University of Calcutta, India

Soumya Pandit	University of Calcutta, India
Sriparna Saha	Indian Institute of Technology Patna, India
Subarna Shakya	Tribhuvan University, Nepal
Subhadip Basu	Jadavpur University, India
Subir Sarkar	Jadavpur University, India
Subrata Banerjee	National Institute of Technology Durgapur, India
Sudhakar Sahoo	Institute of Mathematics and Applications, India
Sudhakar Tripathi	National Institute of Technology Patna, India
Sudipta Roy	Assam University, India
Sujoy Chatterjee	UNIST, South Korea
Sukumar Nandi	Indian Institute of Technology Guwahati, India
Suman Lata Tripathi	Lovely Professional University, India
Sunita Sarkar	Assam University, India
Swapan Kumar Mandal	Kalyani Government Engineering College, India
Tamaghna Acharya	IIEST Shibpur, India
Tandra Pal	National Institute of Technology Durgapur, India
Tanushyam Chattopadyay	TCS, Kolkata, India
U. Dinesh Kumar	Indian Institute of Management Bangalore, India
Umapada Pal	Indian Statistical Institute, Kolkata, India
Varun Kumar Ojha	University of Reading, UK
Vijay Nath	BIT Mesra, India
Asit Barman	Siliguri Institute of Technology, India
Debaditya Barban	Visva-Bharati University, India

Contents

Computational Forensic (Privacy and Security)

Quantified Analysis of Security Issues and Its Mitigation in Blockchain Using Game Theory

Ashis Kumar Samanta[1]([✉]), Bidyut Biman Sarkar[2], and Nabendu Chaki[3]

[1] Department of Computer Science and Engineering, University of Calcutta, Kolkata, India
aksdba@caluniv.ac.in
[2] MCA Department, Techno International Newtown, Kolkata, India
bidyut.biman.sarkar@tict.edu.in
[3] Department of Computer Science and Engineering, University of Calcutta, Kolkata, India
nabendu@ieee.org

Abstract. Storing data in the Blockchain is indeed one of the good security measures for data. However, blockchain itself could be under different types of security threats. The mining of the block into the longest chain is a constrained task. Typically, the nodes having high investments are selected as potential miners in the blockchain. A miner or a pool of miners is assigned for this mining job. The challenge lies in working with the honest miners against the continuous negative influence of dishonest miners. There have been considerable efforts in the existing literature that tries to overcome such security threats. Game theory is used and incorporated towards this by many researchers. This manuscript aims to analyze different security threats of blockchain mining and the possible approaches that have claimed to overcome these. We also analyzed and correlated some of the selected well-cited solution approaches that uses game theory and presented a comparative performance analysis among those.

Keywords: Block-chain · Smart contract · Data security · Security threat · Game theory

1 Introduction

Security and transparency of data are among the primary aspects behind introducing the blockchain (BC) technology. Using the blockchain technology the distributed, pair to pair ledger is made available to all the authorized users within the network in a secured manner. Blockchain technology is used by blending multiple technologies like pair to pair network, distributed and decentralized network technology, cryptography, etc. [3]. A blockchain may be public or private. The transactions are generated as a block. Subsequently, the blocks are verified before these are appended to the longest chain in the network. Each block contains a block header. The block header contains a hash function. This hash value is the main building key-window of blockchain technology. The hash value of the block itself is one of the main security issues as well as a solution to the network. Transactions done by the users are stored within the blockchain. The writing

© Springer Nature Switzerland AG 2021
P. Dutta et al. (Eds.): CICBA 2021, CCIS 1406, pp. 3–19, 2021.
https://doi.org/10.1007/978-3-030-75529-4_1

responsibility of the block is normally assigned to the selected nodes of the network called miners or set of miner pools. The miners are selected depending upon the various protocols and consensus algorithms. The miners are also interested to write the block into the blockchain for their incentives. The transaction fees paid by the transaction blocks are the main incentives of the miner blocks [12]. The security issues of the blockchain are quite much dependent on the performance of the miners. The question arises that at what extent the miners are trustable. Different protocols and consensus algorithms, used in blockchain, are indeed quite matured to identify any dishonest miner, at the instant of any mining process. However, the major threat to blockchain security could be due to the selection of a dishonest miner pool for the process of mining.

The intensive and the deep study give us a specific idea about the security attack experienced by the blockchain at the time of mining of the block. In this particular paper, we analyzed a different kind of security threats faced by the blockchain and also different approaches to overcome this threat using game theory. We also tried to correlate the result of paper [4] and paper [6] and also analyzed the possible outcomes. The comparative analysis of both the paper is presented at the end.

2 Existing Security Issues in the Blockchain

The prime objectives of blockchain technology are the security, transparency, and trustworthiness of transactions and data. Based on the detailed and intensive study on the blockchain, we infer that blockchain is still suffering from various security issues that are presented below.

2.1 Security Issues

2.1.1 51% Vulnerability Issue

The mining power is assigned to the selected nodes in the blockchain network, based on a consensus mechanism called Proof of Work (PoW). If the strength of a mining pool increases more than 50% of the entire selections, then the said pool becomes the miner controlling pool of the chain. If the dishonest miners achieved a majority of 51%, then the hashing control would be a serious security threat for the chain [6, 9].

2.1.2 Double Spending Issue

The mining process (PoW based) is time-consuming. In case of bitcoin, the average mining time of a transaction block is 10 min or more. The dishonest users of the network generally used the same currency (or cryptocurrency) for multiple transactions. This double-spending attack has a fairly high probability of chances due to the short time interval between the two transactions and a long time interval between the receiving of mining acknowledgment of the transactions [11].

2.1.3 Mining Pool Attack Issue

This kind of attack increases the time interval of assigning mining control to the selected miners. The internal pool is attacked by dishonest miners to collect more rewards. The miner then functions maliciously. In case of an external mining pool, the dishonest miner applies higher hashing power to organize a double attack [7, 8].

2.1.4 Distributed Denial of Service Attacks (DDoS) Issues

In the blockchain, the target of the DDoS attack is to retardate the efficiency and activities of the miner pool so that their operation can be disturbed or made to function at a reduced level [4, 5].

2.1.5 Client-Side Security Threats

The blockchain networks maintain public and private key values to manage user accounts. The loss of private keys is also a threat to client-side security [7].

2.1.6 Forking Issue

The software that supports the blockchain framework usually requires system upgradation from time to time. The upgradations may be in terms of hardware, change in the policy of software, or may change in rules of the blockchain. The existing nodes in the network adopting the new upgraded policy and rules form a new blockchain. The nodes that did not upgrade themselves remain in the old chain. There is a lack of compatibility, mutual agreement, and stability between the old and new versions of the chains. That is also a threat to the entire blockchain system [2].

2.1.7 Private Key Security Issues

The private key of the users is one of the security measures in blockchain technology. It describes the credibility of the user. The loss or theft of private keys is a threat to the user as well as the blockchain, as it is not possible to recover the private key by any alternative measure [2].

2.1.8 Criminal Activity Issues

Blockchain suffers from so many criminal threats like bribing, hacking transactions, and extortion money by incorporating "Ransomware" etc. [2].

2.2 Game Theory

"A game is any situation in which players (the participants) make strategic decisions - i.e., decisions that take into account each other's actions and responses" [1]. All the strategic decisions have connected pay-offs that result in rewards or benefits for the players. The players are the decision-makers of their own and always choose strategies towards optimization of payoffs by utilizing the available sets of strategies. In-game theory, it is also considered that the players are rational and their decisions are also rational. Some of the well-known game types are mentioned below.

1.	Non-Cooperative Game	2.	Cooperative Game
3.	Splitting Game	4.	Mean-Payoff game
5.	Stochastic Game	6.	Cournot Game
7.	Stackelberg Game	8.	Sequential Game
9.	Repeated Game	10.	Coordination Game

3 Literature Review

In paper [3], a dynamic Bitcoin (BTC) mining process is proposed. The mining powers (electricity) are invested by respective miners. In this paper, one block is mined by a particular miner. The proposed process is described by incorporating the game theory. The miner writes the block into the chain wins the game among all miners. The co-operative and non-cooperative strategies are used by the miners for the mining process. Three dynamic components of game theoretical models are proposed to find the solutions. These three components are Social optimum, Nash equilibrium, and myopic Nash equilibrium.

a. Social optimum
The co-operation strategy is taken by each miner separately or in the pool to consume the energy to compute. The incentive (pay-off) is distributed equally among each miner in the pool.
b. Nash equilibrium
The non-co-operation (selfish mining) strategy is adopted to maximize the gain of each miner and the pay-off is calculated accordingly.
c. myopic Nash equilibrium
Multiple players (miners) can participate in this dynamic game to maximize one's pay-off with the negligible influence of the present state of the miners.

The consumed electric power is invested jointly by all the miners to participate in the mining process. The wasting of the electrical power by all the miners excluding the miner that owned the game and writes the block into the longest chain. The wastage of electricity (power) consumed is the main problem definition in this paper during mining as the main threat. The proposed solutions claimed that the profit of the miners at an optimum level in case of a cooperative game strategy.

The miner nodes in the mining pool increase their outputs either by cooperating with the mining pool or by investing additional resources and the addressing of the threat of DDoS in the blockchain is done in paper [4]. How the dishonest mining pools stimulate to degrade the efficiency of the actual mining pools to build the confidence of the next PoW has been analyzed. This is done either by increasing the resource of dishonest minor pool or in some other menacing ways. To analyze the fact, non-cooperative game theory has been chosen. Two different sized mining pools are considered as the two players - S (small) and B(big) pool respectively. The strategical pay-off matrix has been calculated and the best strategy is described through Nash Equilibrium. The result of the paper states that the incentive is much more for attacking B-pool by removing one or more miners from the pool than by attacking the S-pool. (Large pool attack = 63%,

Small pool attack = 17%), i.e. the S-pool makes a higher gain by attacking the B-pool than the gain B-pool makes by attacking S-pool. This paper describes the primary focus of to reduce the performance and hampered the effectiveness by DDoS attack.

1. The operation of the computing mining pool slower down.
2. Encourage individual miners to associate with the dishonest mining pool.

In the proposed model the baseline cost of failure the attack in blockchain mining has been discussed. The impact of the miners of the choice of different investment has also been analyzed.

In paper [5], a long term mining strategy of blockchain through repeated games has been introduced. The objective is to give incentive to an honest miner and simultaneously penalize a dishonest miner. After each iteration of the game, the "reputation" of the miners are measured. This paper primarily addresses the DDoS attack of the type.

1. *Block withholding attack*: where the dishonest miner provides a partial solution of verifications. The total solution is provided to the entire pool with a partial contribution to each and earns the incentive without effective investment.
2. *Selfish mining or Stubborn mining*: a miner (or group of miners) increases their revenue by strategically withholding and releasing blocks to the network. Typically, we expect a miner to announce a block as soon as they find it. If the block is confirmed, they will get the block reward.
3. *Eclipse attack*: the attack aims to obscure a participant's view of the peer-to-peer network, to cause general disruption or disturbed the performance.

A concept of a miner manager is introduced in this model. The miner manager invites the subset of the miner pool for mining. The Nash equilibrium is reached by eliminating the strictly dominating strategy.

In paper [6], a model of sequential game theory is developed to address the DDoS attack on the mining pool. The model describes the short term as well as the long term attacking effects of mining pools. The threshold value of non-attacking incentives and the passive intensive of partial attacking is calculated. The conditions of no-incentive (attack) and incentive (no-attack) are calculated accordingly. This model is calculating the cost (fixed cost as well as variable cost) of the attack. A defensive mechanism is incorporated to calculate the unit cost of attacking. After each round, the miner can migrate from one pool to another according to its regaining strategies. In each round, the miner can go for the attack to lose its incentive as a short term effect. The miner can go for a long-term migration effect to give consistency for the next round, to reach a steady-state of Nash equilibrium. On violating that when one miner is attacking the other one, the Nash equilibrium deviated.

In paper [7], a punishment mechanism is proposed to the devices of edge networks rather than the miner pool of Blockchain. When a request or DoS attack on the server is encountered by a device of edge network, the server may give the output of the request or punish the device. A model is developed for this punishment mechanism through non-cooperative game theory. Both the device and the server can adapt its strategy depending on the history recorded in the blockchain. This model states that to achieve the maximum gain both the players (edge device and server) will not attack each other, because of the extensive punishment mechanism. This non-attacking response brings the game to the horizon of the Nash equilibrium.

In paper [8], a decentralized protocol of mining is proposed where the validator does not consider the Proof of Work (PoW). The validator is chosen from a random set and size to overcome Benzamine 1/3 (one-third) fault tolerance to minimize the attack. Game theory has been used to resolve the problem. The validators were not selected previously. The efficiency of the transaction is enhanced by allowing some of the miners to mining work among the group of selected validators. Most of the emphasis has been given on the selection procedure of the miners to a trade-off between the efficiency and security of the chain.

In paper [9], a bribing aspect of a smart contract using the electronic voting system is analyzed. The incentive (gain) is achieved by the mining nodes by mining the transaction of the smart contract of cryptocurrency. The transfer of bitcoin from one user to another user in a smart contract is considered as bribes. The game theory used here is the "Smart contract bribe game". The type of risks are handled through a proposed election voting model in two ways.

1. The identification of honest and dishonest bribers (mining nodes) function as the miner of transactions of the smart contract.
2. The threshold budget value of bribers to achieve more than 50% vote is only possible if the bribers control more than 20% of the Nash equilibrium.

In paper [10], the incorporation of the evolutionary game has been done. This paper has explored the sharing mechanism to maintain an optimum security level in data mining in smart contract applications. The strategy of handling of sharing of data (data mining) using evolutionary game theory. The proposed model handle three situations.

1. Neither of the player sharing the data or not taking part in mining.
2. Both the player taking part in data sharing.
3. One player taking part in data sharing and the other user is not involving in data sharing.

In paper [11], the Game theory is applied to Smart contract security enhancements. This model proposed to make it decentralized under the strict vigil of its validator to combat the challenger of validation. The paper analyzes and validates "Differentiated Services Code Point (DSCP)" using the tool of smart contract "BITHALO'. The tool has been designed by applying traditional mathematical methods and game theory. The double-spending attack is primarily countered in this paper using game theory. This protocol is used to the vigil at the time of deposit. It verifies the pre-requisite payment amount exceeds the value of the goods to counter the double payment threat.

Authors in paper [12], have proposed to analyze the participation of the miner. It analyses where the incentives are high for participating miners and marginally low incentives for non-participants in the mining process. In a real sense that affects the security measures of the blockchain. The analysis mechanism done here aims to find out the gap in the mining process by incorporating "Gap Game". The game contributes to finding out the average time quantum required for a miner to become active for the honest mining process. The average incentive is assigned to the mining block. It assumes a quasi-static system in which no miner can join or can go out of the respective pool to reach the equilibrium system. The fixed set of miners controls an individual rig (the mechanism used for the mining process, requires electrical power for its function). The start of the rig is determined with a timestamp marking the point of time of conversion of the status of the miner from inactive to active. This paper mainly deals with the mining gap of the blockchain. The gap model considers only the operational expenses. The block size in the blockchain is unbounded; the mining process includes all the pending transactions in the process. When a block is generated, there would not be any pending transactions and unclaimed fees. However, there would not be any incentive due to the mining of the previous block, as there is a gap between the generation and mining between the previous and next block of the blockchain. The findings of papers 3 to paper 12 are illustrated in the tabulated format in Table 1 below.

The Proof of Work (PoW) is a complicated consensus algorithm, used for the mining process of blockchain. It is used for data validation of legitimate transactions to avoid security threats like DDoS and double-spending. In the selfish mining process, the complicacy and energy-consuming amount of PoW is for hash generation. The miners are competing with each other for their incentives. The complicacy and energy consumption of the PoW system is much greater. The minimum time required to generate a block in the PoW system is more than 10 min. That causes security threats as well.

4   Open Research Issues on Blockchain Security for Data Mining

The Blockchain uses the successful PoW consensus algorithm to secure the blockchain network. Several new consensus algorithms have already been proposed and developed meanwhile. Every algorithm has its own merits and demerits. The aspects are important to understand which consensus algorithm is to be chosen for a specific case.

The study finds that each proposed model has merits and demerits. Our objective is to propose such a model where the maximum identified disadvantages can be eliminated. The blockchain still has the following open research issues related to its security and data mining concerned:

4.1. The security threats are regulated by honest and dishonest mining. Therefore there is always a tussle between secure and insecure environments. Game is also a competition of winners and losers. There may be a zero-zero status in between. Hence a suitable game form needs to be proposed for suitable solutions. Therefore we can explore avenues to sort out the maximum security issues of blockchain through suitable game forms.

4.2. The model may be considered without PoW. Alternately, the Proof of Stake (PoS) or Delegated Proof of Stake (DPoS) or Proof of Capacity (PoC) or Proof of Authority (PoA) or Proof of Elapsed Time (PoET) or Proof of Importance (PoI) or some other factor may be considered for future research work.

4.3. The blockchain contains multiple nodes in the network. The game form that will be considered to overcome the security threats needs to be a multiplayer (nodes) game.

Table 1. The findings of the literature review

Ref no.	Observations
[3]	In reality, the miner has to work under security threat and the pay-off is much less in this proposed model. In dynamic systems, past record PoWs are considered. The model is silent about the present state action of the dishonest miner. The difference between Nash equilibrium and Greedy Nash equilibrium in the non-cooperative method is kept silent.
[4]	In this proposed model, a player will use those strategies which are in binary mode. The player either goes for mining or for DDoS attack to reduce the performance. The model does not discuss the case where any player keeps silent without selecting any strategy and hence does not conclude about how the Nash equilibrium will be affected for the silent players. In case if the value of R is large enough the computational pay-offs for both for the big(B) and small(S) miners ($\frac{B}{(B+S+R)}$ and $\frac{S}{(B+S+R)}$ respectively) will be reduced. So another problem is to determine the value of R and how the Nash equilibrium will be maintained in respect to R. In the best response strategies, if S goes for the DDoS attack then B's best strategy also will be the DDoS attack, that contradicts the actual mining interest of the blockchain.
[5]	The introduction of a mining manager is also a good concept for extra vigilance. The introduction of a mining manager will increase mining timing. What strategy will be taken if the mining manager becomes dishonest; how it will affect the Nash equilibrium have not been discussed. The result through any experimental setup or simulation has not been stated for any set of data.
[6]	The concept of the model that the big pool(B) will ways go for mining and the small pool(S) always goes for the attack. This concept contradicts the denial attack of 51% dishonest nodes. Migration from S to B increases the size of the mining pool, B. When the migration happens from B to S the rate of DDoS will increase. In the case of B becomes the dishonest pool then also the security threat will increase. What strategy will be taken in this situation to combat security issues?
[7]	The figures in Theorem-2 and Theorem-4 (fig-a and fig-b) show that the utilities or actions of the server process also diminish along with the diminishing of the performances of the device when the device is punished. In that case, the other read operations of the server for miming will be affected (due to the reduction of performance of the server). How this could be mapped with the security measures of the blockchain? In the case of a multiple payer environment, the Nash equilibrium may be violated.
[8]	The type of risk or the threat that can be combated using the proposed algorithm is also not cleared in the paper. What will be the criteria of a selection of actual miners among the honest mining pools?
[9]	In case of a successful smart contract less than Pj (bribing price), no solution is provided. However, it is not clear how the figure of more than 20% control of the overall budget is reached for a briber to conduct a 51% attack and how Nash equilibrium will be affected.

(*continued*)

Table 1. (*continued*)

Ref no.	Observations
[10]	There may be another case of threat to the system where both the players participate either with one player as honest and the other as dishonest or with both the players as dishonest.
[11]	The mechanism of addressing the double payment issue is silent in this paper.
[12]	The equilibrium point in the quasi-static system cannot be maintained. Joining or leaving cannot be restricted in a real scenario. The inclusion of the time component in the incentives of the miner is a positive contribution to enhancing the security mechanism in mining.

4.4. The introduction of a miner manager or validator leader in a mining process increases the security measures [4, 8]. A suitable alternative also needs to be considered in case of the dishonesty of the miner manager or validity leader.

4.5. Among the honest mining pools, some selected nodes will be allowed for mining work [8] by applying a suitable strategy. This will increase mining efficiency.

4.6. A suitable methodology needs to be adopted so that the honest miners can gain some incentives and the dishonest miner can get the punishment. It also needs to record the silent player who is not taking part in miner voting and consider such a player as a partially dishonest miner.

4.7. To increase the mining efficiency only some miners within the mining pool need to be allowed for mining.

4.8. A strategy needs to be determined that allows threshold limit of the attack and to determine a strategy in case the limit is crossed

4.9. The findings of other mining gaps and the introduction of time constraints can enhance the security features and mining efficiency in blockchain technology. The inclusion of time constraints also strengthens the desired model.

The authors feel that there's a strong need for an efficient security model that addresses, if not all, then most of the issues identified above. In Sect. 5, we have taken two interesting existing models for further study.

5 Analysis of Simulation Result

After a thorough study, we try to analyze the result outputs of the above-mentioned papers with their respective outcomes. In particular, we have considered two models proposed by B. Johnson, A. Laszka and that are described in [4] and [6]. We have analyzed using simulation and tried to present a critical comparison of these two models [4, 6]. A brief definition of these models is included in Annexure 1 for the sake of completeness.

We recapitulate some of the definitions used in the two models [4, 6] for better understanding of the simulation and for proper interpretation of the results. The big and small size mining pools are represented by B and S respectively. R represents the rest of the bitcoin mining market. The rate of increase in computation power is ε. The probability of an attack is σ and γ and λ are two arbitrary constants such that $\lambda < \gamma$. The notations $a_B^{(k)}$, $a_S^{(k)}$ represent the attack pools at any iteration k.

Let, $M \in [0, 1]$ be the rate of migration and $C \in [0, 1]$ is the unit cost of attack. AB and AS are the relative attractiveness of the pool B and S respectively.

Here, A_B, $A_S \in [0, 1] \wedge A_B + A_S \in [0, 1]$. $S_B^{(k)}$ and $S_S^{(k)}$ are the relative size of the pool at any iteration k, where $S_B^{(k)}$, $S_S^{(k)} \in [0, 1]$ and $S_B^{(k)} + S_S^{(k)} \in [0, 1]$.

5.1 Discussion on Simulation Result

The payoff matrix of Table 3 [4] is converted into the corresponding data value for further analysis. Figure 1a and Fig. 1b shows the graphical representation of the corresponding data (Shown in [13]). It can be stated that in the Nash equilibrium strategy both B and S will attack each other. However, the best strategy obtained whenever the ratio of B and S is 80:20,70:30, 60:40 and even 50:50. The mining cost is best either S involved in computing or B involved in computing. The value of mining incentive is much better for B:S is 90:10 when the value of ε changes from 0.1 to 0.2.

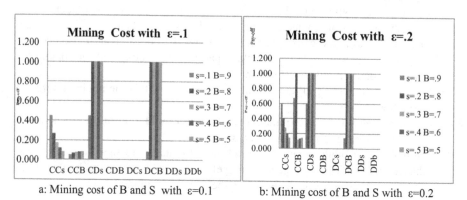

a: Mining cost of B and S with $\varepsilon=0.1$ b: Mining cost of B and S with $\varepsilon=0.2$

Fig. 1. a. Mining cost of B and S with $\varepsilon = 0.1$. **b.** Mining cost of B and S with $\varepsilon = 0.2$

In the enhanced model of [4] as stated in pay-off in Table 4, it is seen that (Fig. 2a, Fig. 2b and Fig. 2c) the highest rate of attack incurred when the S go for computing and B go for the attack. The attack in the enhanced approach is reduced in the CDs component. However, the DCB component of mining of B is get reduced. In general concept, the tendency of attack is increased in the respective areas of DDs and DDB which was nil in the previous case. The computation value of S is decreasing for each size of S with the increasing probability of attack ($\sigma = 0.1, 0.2$, and 0.3) respectively.

In the peaceful equilibrium in the proposed model [6], the unit cost of attack due to migration has been shown in Fig. 3a (where, As = 0.2, AB = 0.3, $a_s = 0$, $a_B = 0$ and using Eq. 3a). The attacking cost is maximum (near about .6) when the migration rate is 0.1. The rate of the cost of attack reduces with the increased rate of migration until the migration rate is 0.7. After this threshold value (0.7) of the migration rate, the attacking cost remains the same.

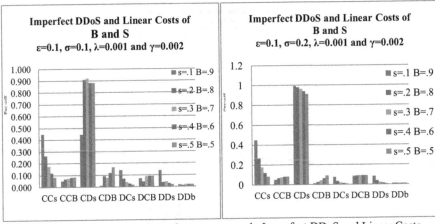

a : Imperfect DDoS and Linear Costs
of B and S, $\varepsilon=0.1$, $\sigma=0.1$, $\lambda=0.001$, $\gamma=0.002$

b: Imperfect DDoS and Linear Costs
of B and S, $\varepsilon=0.1$, $\sigma=0.2$, $\lambda=0.001$

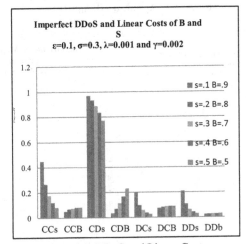

c: Imperfect DDoS and Linear Costs
of B and S $\varepsilon=0.1$, $\sigma=0.3$, $\lambda=0.001$ and $\gamma=0.002$

Fig. 2. a. Imperfect DDoS and Linear Costs of B and S, $\varepsilon = 0.1$, $\sigma = 0.1$, $\lambda = 0.001$, $\gamma = 0.002$.
b. Imperfect DDoS and Linear Costs of B and S, $\varepsilon = 0.1$, $\sigma = 0.2$, $\lambda = 0.001$. **c.** Imperfect DDoS
and Linear Costs of B and S $\varepsilon = 0.1$, $\sigma = 0.3$, $\lambda = 0.001$ and $\gamma = 0.002$.

In the case of one side attack equilibrium, the unit cost of attack slightly increases
with both the cases whether the attacker size $a_S = 1$ (where $A_S = 0.2$, $A_B = 0.3$, $a_B = 0$ and using Eq. 3b) or the attacker size $a_B = 1$ (where $A_S = 0.2$, $A_B = 0.3$, $a_S = 0$ and
using Eq. 3c) shown in Fig. 3b and Fig. 3c respectively.

The value of C is remained equal in Fig. 3a and Fig. 3c after the migration rate is
0.7. The value of C is slightly higher in Fig. 3c ($a_B = 1$) than that of Fig. 3b ($a_S = 1$)
for the same set of values of $A_S = 0.2$, $A_B = 0.3$, and M (i.e., migration rate is same in
both the figure).

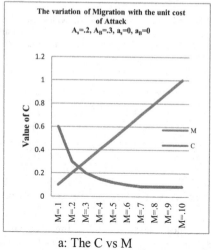

a: The C vs M
(for A_s=.2, A_B=.3, a_s=0, a_B=0)

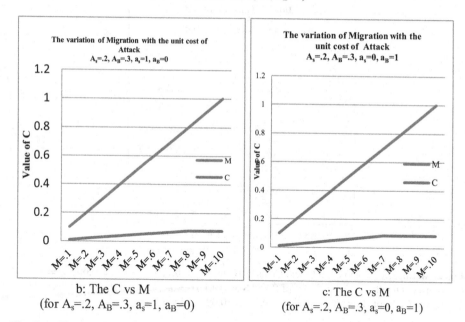

b: The C vs M
(for A_s=.2, A_B=.3, a_s=1, a_B=0)

c: The C vs M
(for A_s=.2, A_B=.3, a_s=0, a_B=1)

Fig. 3. a. The C vs M (for $A_s = .2$, $A_B = .3$, $a_s = 0$, $a_B = 0$). **b.** The C vs M (for $A_s = .2$, $A_B = .3$, $a_s = 1$, $a_B = 0$). **c.** The C vs M (for $A_s = .2$, $A_B = .3$, $a_s = 0$, $a_B = 1$)

5.2 Comparative Analysis of Model

(See Table 2).

Table 2. Critical comparison of models proposed in [4] and [6]

Sl. No	Descriptions	Proposed model [4]	Proposed model [6]
1	Addressing issue(s)	DDoS (by slowing down the performance or motivating the minor to be dishonest).	DDoS attack on the mining pool is addressed.
2	Type of Game Theory incorporated	A non-cooperative game is used.	A sequential Game is used.
3	Mining Strategy	PoW (increases either by cooperating with other miner or investing extra power).	The computation utility value $U_B^{(k)}$ and $U_S^{(k)}$ are used after each round of k by B and S respectively shown in Eqs. 1a and 1b.
4	Pool Size of mines	Arbitrarily chosen Big honest pool (B) and small dishonest pool (S). The variation of size is not reflected in the proposed model.	The relative size of the honest pool ($S_B^{(k)}$) and dishonest pool ($S_S^{(k)}$) is considered after each iteration(k).
5	Cost incurred	It is assumed that the cost to invest or cost to attack is negligible with respect to the revenue of bitcoin. The pay-off cost of B and S is shown in Table 3.	The unit cost of the attack is calculated. The cost of an attack, non-attack and partial attack are also calculated.
6	Migration of B to S or S to B pool	The migration or the attraction of migration is not considered distinctly.	After each round, the miner can migrate from one pool to another pool. At a particular round k, the size of the miner B and S are defined by Eqs. 2a, 2b, 2c, and 2d after migration.
7	Attacking cost or other evaluations	The attack is assumed to be negligible concerning the revenue of bitcoin.	The unit cost of an attack is calculated in terms of fixed and variable costs
8	Nash Equilibrium (NE)	NE is both B and S will attack each other.	NE is expressed through Eq. 3b and 3c.
9	Efficiency	The enhanced proposed model reducing the overall mining efficiency by introducing DDoS attacks in a different stage of mining.	The efficiency can be achieved through a peaceful equilibrium where there is no size of the miner in attacking strategy.

(continued)

Table 2. (*continued*)

Sl. No	Descriptions	Proposed model [4]	Proposed model [6]
10	Comparative issues	1. Assumption of no cost of attack or investment. 2. The theoretical background of the assumption value of R, ε, σ, λ, and γ. 3. The attraction of incentives of migration the miner from one pool to another pool.	1. The basis of the assumption of A_S and A_B. 2. The calculation of the unit cost of incentive and also the threshold value of the incentive to get initiated the mining process. 3. The silent miners are also taken into consideration.

6   Conclusions

In this paper, we have analyzed some of the security solutions for blockchain mining that have used different game theory approaches. We have presented graphical results for simulation. We have also changed the values for the rate of increase in computation power, ε from 0.1 to 0.2 (in case of the model represented in [4]) and the probability of attack σ from 0.1 to 0.2 and 0.3 (in case of the model represented in [6]) to find out the change in the behavioral response of the said models. The results are evident in Sect. 5. With the increase of investment of mining resources, the profit increases up to a certain limit before it saturates In a process of the non-cooperative game theory approach, we have seen that the cost of computation is high when B goes for computing and S go for attack for all combinations of B and S (80:20,70:30, 60:40, 50:50) excepting 90:10. With the introduction of the probability of attack the mining value decreases. The introduction of the pool manager and its invitation to the set of potential miners provide the extra vigil to the mining security. It is shown that the unit cost of an attack decreases with the increasing rate of migration to the attacking pools. In fact, after crossing a threshold value of migration, the cost of attack does not change. In case of increasing the punishment rate to the dishonest miner, the utility rate does not change. In future, we plan to focus on the policy of selection of miners using game theory and also shall put an effort to find out the threshold mining and attacking cost to eliminate the security threat of blockchain mining in an improved way.

Annexure 1

Formalism in the Model Proposed by B. Johnson, A. Laszka et al. [4]

The payoff is defined for B and S of DDoS attack and computation is

Table 3. The pay-off matrix of mining of B and S

		Player B	
		Computation	*DDoS*
Player S	*Computation*	$\frac{B}{B+S+R}, \frac{S}{B+S+R}$	$\frac{B}{B+R(1+\varepsilon)}, 0$
	DDoS	$0, \frac{S}{S+R(1+\varepsilon)}$	$0, 0$

Table 4. Payoff Matrix for B and S with Imperfect DDoS and Linear Costs

		Player B	
		Computation	*DDoS*
Player S	*Computation*	$\frac{B}{B+S+R} - \gamma B,$ $\frac{S}{B+S+R} - \gamma S$	$\frac{B}{B+(\sigma S+R)(1+\varepsilon)} - \lambda S,$ $\frac{\sigma S(1+\varepsilon)}{B+(\sigma S+R)(1+\varepsilon)} - \gamma S$
	DDoS	$\frac{\sigma B(1+\varepsilon)}{S+(\sigma B+R)(1+\varepsilon)} - \gamma B,$ $\frac{S}{S+(\sigma B+R)(1+\varepsilon)} - \lambda B$	$\frac{\sigma B}{\sigma(B+S)+R(1+\varepsilon)} - \lambda S,$ $\frac{\sigma S}{\sigma(B+S)\,R(1+\varepsilon)} - \lambda B$

Formalism in the Model Proposed by B. Johnson, A. Laszka et al. [6]

The **Short term policy** The calculated utility function of B and S are $U_B^{(k)}$ and $U_S^{(k)}$ respectively in kth iteration are given by the equn

$$U_B^{(k)} = \frac{S_B^{(k)} \cdot \left(1 - a_S^{(k)}\right)}{1 - S_B^{(k)} \cdot a_S^{(k)} - S_S^{(k)} \cdot a_B^{(k)}} - C \cdot a_B^{(k)} \tag{1a}$$

$$U_S^{(k)} = \frac{S_S^{(k)} \cdot \left(1 - a_B^{(k)}\right)}{1 - S_S^{(k)} \cdot a_B^{(k)} - S_B^{(k)} \cdot a_S^{(k)}} - C \cdot a_S^{(k)} \tag{1b}$$

The **Long term policy** The calculated size of B and S are $S_B^{(k+1)}$ and $S_S^{(k+1)}$ respectively in k_{th} iteration are given by the equn

a) Migration of miner into B pool

$$S_B^{(k+1)} = S_B^{(k)} + A_B \cdot \left[\left(1 - S_B^{(k)}\right) \cdot M + S_S^{(k)} \cdot a_B^{(k)}(1 - M)\right. \tag{2a}$$

b) Migration of miner out of B pool

$$S_B^{(k+1)} = S_B^{(k)} - S_B^{(k)} \cdot (1 - A_B) \cdot \left[M + \cdot a_S^{(k)}(1 - M)\right] \tag{2b}$$

c) Migration of miner into S pool

$$S_S^{(k+1)} = S_S^{(k)} + A_S \cdot [\left(1 - S_S^{(k)}\right) \cdot \text{M} + S_B^{(k)} \cdot a_S^{(k)}(1-\text{M}) \qquad (2c)$$

d) Migration of miner out of S pool

$$S_S^{(k+1)} = S_S^{(k)} - S_S^{(k)} \cdot (1 - A_S) \cdot \left[\text{M} + \cdot a_B^{(k)}(1-\text{M}) \right] \qquad (2d)$$

In case of peaceful equilibrium where $(a_S, \ a_B) = (0,0)$

$$C \geq \frac{A_B A_S}{\text{Min}(\text{M}, \ 1 - A_S, \ 1 - A_B)}. \qquad (3a)$$

In case of one side attack equilibrium where $(a_S, \ a_B) = (0,1)$

$$C \leq \frac{A_B A_S}{(1 - A_S)^2} \cdot \text{Min}(\text{M}, 1 - A_S) \qquad (3b)$$

$$C \leq \frac{A_B A_S}{(1 - A_B)^2} \cdot \text{Min}(\text{M}, 1 - A_B) \qquad (3c)$$

References

1. Pindyck, R.S., Rubinfeld, D.L.: Microeconomics, 8th edn. The Pearson Series in Economics (2013). ISBN-13: 978-0-13-285712-3
2. Gupta, N.: Security and privacy issues of blockchain technology. In: Kim, S., Deka, G.C. (eds.) Advanced Applications of Blockchain Technology, pp. 207–226. Springer, Singapore (2020). https://doi.org/10.1007/978-981-13-8775-3_10
3. Singh, R., Dwivedi, A., Srivastava, G., et al.: A game theoretic analysis of resource mining in blockchain. Cluster Comput. 23(3), 2035–2046 (2020). https://doi.org/10.1007/s10586-020-03046-w
4. Johnson, B., Laszka, A., Grossklags, J., Vasek, M., Moore, T.: Game-theoretic analysis of DDoS attacks against bitcoin mining pools. In: Böhme, R., Brenner, M., Moore, T., Smith, M. (eds.) FC 2014. LNCS, vol. 8438, pp. 72–86. Springer, Heidelberg (2014). https://doi.org/10.1007/978-3-662-44774-1_6
5. Nojoumian, M., Golchubian, A., Njilla, L., Kwiat, K., Kamhoua, C.: Incentivizing blockchain miners to avoid dishonest mining strategies by a reputation-based paradigm. In: Arai, K., Kapoor, S., Bhatia, R. (eds.) Intelligent Computing: Proceedings of the 2018 Computing Conference, Volume 2, pp. 1118–1134. Springer, Cham (2019). https://doi.org/10.1007/978-3-030-01177-2_81
6. Laszka, A., Johnson, B., Grossklags, J.: When bitcoin mining pools run dry. In: Brenner, M., Christin, N., Johnson, B., Rohloff, K. (eds.) Financial Cryptography and Data Security, pp. 63–77. Springer, Heidelberg (2015). https://doi.org/10.1007/978-3-662-48051-9_5
7. Xu, D., Xiao, L., Sun, L., Lei, M.: Game theoretic study on blockchain based secure edge networks. In: IEEE/CIC International Conference on Communications in China (ICCC), Qingdao, pp. 1–5. IEEE (2017). https://doi.org/10.1109/ICCChina.2017.8330529

8. Alzahrani, N., Bulusu, N.: Towards True decentralization: a blockchain consensus protocol based on game theory and randomness. In: Bushnell, L., Poovendran, R., Başar, T. (eds.) Decision and Game Theory for Security: 9th International Conference, GameSec 2018, Seattle, WA, USA, October 29–31, 2018, Proceedings, pp. 465–485. Springer, Cham (2018). https://doi.org/10.1007/978-3-030-01554-1_27

9. Chen, L., et al.: The game among bribers in a smart contract system. In: Zohar, A., et al. (eds.) FC 2018. LNCS, vol. 10958, pp. 294–307. Springer, Heidelberg (2019). https://doi.org/10.1007/978-3-662-58820-8_20

10. Xuan, S., Zheng, L., Chung, I., Wang, W., Man, D., Du, X., et al.: An incentive mechanism for data sharing based on blockchain with smart contracts. Comput. Electr. Eng. **83**, 106587 (2020). https://doi.org/10.1016/j.compeleceng.2020.106587,Elsevier

11. Bigi, G., Bracciali, A., Meacci, G., Tuosto, E.: Validation of decentralised smart contracts through game theory and formal methods. In: Bodei, C., Ferrari, G., Priami, C. (eds.) Programming Languages with Applications to Biology and Security, pp. 142–161. Springer, Cham (2015). https://doi.org/10.1007/978-3-319-25527-9_11

12. Tsabary, I., Eyal, I.: The gap game. In: 2018 ACM SIGSAC Conference on Computer and Communications Security (CCS). ACM, USA, Canada (2018). https://doi.org/10.1145/3243734.3243737

13. https://drive.google.com/drive/folders/1aLM7MmyEwEmx_NzCfAMIn4trd0Bl62fp?usp=sharing

Color Image Compressed Sensing Using Modified Stagewise Orthogonal Matching Pursuit

Sujit Das[✉] and Jyotsna Kumar Mandal

Department of Computer Science and Engineering, University of Kalyani,
Kalyani, India

Abstract. In compressed sensing a signal is sampled using random non-linear incoherent measurements which is a dense subspace from a sparse vector space. The reconstruction from the measurements is based upon some nonlinear optimization algorithms like l_1 minimization. Such reconstruction can be improvised by tuning the various resource requirements. The color image compressed sensing suffers from requirement of high physical resources as signal size increase for small dimension images due to three color channels. In this paper an efficient methods has been proposed for minimizing resource requirements. An approach for selecting coefficient for three channels in parallel and using partial circulant matrix as sensing matrix. The simulation shows the better performance of the proposed technique over existing method.

Keywords: Compressed sensing · Color image · Stagewise orthogonal matching pursuit

1 Introduction

The conventional signal acquisition employs Nysquist sampling rate. The required sample data is huge even for the moderate size of signals. The signal like images, represents redundant information content in some canonical basis. The redundant property is not exploited in conventional sampling methods. The compressed sensing methods use this redundant information to generate sparse representation of signal which inherently reduces the required number of samples using random sampling with non-adaptive incoherent measurements. The random sampling reduces number of sample at considerable level. The complete random sampling methods has been evolved based upon ground breaking theory of Candes et al. [2] and Donoho [5]. The reconstruction of the original signal is depended on specific models used in signal acquisition. The general compressed sensing model can represented as in Eq. (1):

$$y = \Phi x \tag{1}$$

P. Dutta et al. (Eds.): CICBA 2021, CCIS 1406, pp. 20–28, 2021.
https://doi.org/10.1007/978-3-030-75529-4_2

where $x \in \mathcal{R}^n$, $y \in \mathcal{R}^m$ and $m \ll n$. In this model signal x can reconstructed if it is q-compressible in some canonical basis if it follows power law decay, i.e.

$$|c_i| < C_1 i^{-q} \tag{2}$$

where c_i is sorted coefficients in descending order and q, C_1 are constants.

Definition 11. *Coherence*
Coherence of any sensing matrix is defined as the maximum of correlation between any two columns as

$$\mu = \max_{i \neq j}\{| < a_i, a_j > |\} \tag{3}$$

where a_i is the column of matrix A.

Definition 12. *Reduced Isometry Property*
Any sensing matrix is said to have Reduced Isometry Property (RIP) δ_s of order s if following inequality holds:

$$(1 - \delta_s)||x||_2^2 \leq ||Ax||_2^2 \leq (1 + \delta_s)||x||_2^2 \tag{4}$$

A few random matrices with elements from identically independent Gaussian distribution, Radematcher sequence, Bernoulli distribution are said have such property. The RIP ensures that the energy of the signal varies only in factor of δ_s.

The signal reconstruction using measurements obtained from Eq. (1) is convex optimization problem where the prior knowledge about signal is, it is sparse. This prior information is used all the reconstruction algorithms for example-Basis Pursuit (based on linear programming), Orthogonal Matching Pursuit, Stagewise Orthogonal Matching Pursuit (Greedy techniques) etc.

There are very wide applications of compressed sensing on 1D and 2D signals. Recently 3D signal like color images has been also used in compressed sensing methods. The major problem of 2D as well 3D signals like images is-i) the input data size increases many folds even for moderate size of the data, second ii) the computational burden increases as well. However, there are few solution to these problems like block based processing [6], but it comes with unwanted blocking artifacts issue which has be manages using different filters. There are frequency domain block based processing implementations alleviating use of filters. The color images based compressed sensing has to deal with a massive surge of data handling as it contains three color channel-red, green and blue resulting a three fold increase of data size for a single image. In group sparse based [7] compressed sensing three color channel has been treated separately with same sensing matrix. The problem with such approach is the measurement length becomes high. In tensor based [3] compressed sensing for higher dimension data such as images has been implemented and group of non local similar blocks are treated as tensors, processed using higher order singular value decomposition (HOSVD). The finding of nonlocal similar patches along with HOSVD is hard to compute large size blocks. Even for the small size blocks it becomes too much cluttering for large size input signal. In this paper color images has been used as group sparse data but measurement is not separate for each color channel thus reducing number of measurements. As the input signal length increases the sensing matrix size increases as well. This issue is resolved using partial circulant matrix as it does not require keep full matrix at any instant. Along with that the searching of correct indices is done for three color channel at the same time thus optimizing computational time.

The rest of the paper are arranged as Sect. 2 contains literature review, Sect. 3 contains proposed method. The results and simulation has been discussed in Sect. 4. The comparison has been discussed in Sect. 5 and conclusion is given in Sect. 6.

2   Literature Review

In compressed sensing the general objective is to reconstruction sparse signal represented in some canonical basis from its dense representation i.e. recover x from y as in Eq. (1). The structure of the data is different for 1D, 2D, 3D signals respectively. The major challenge is to manage these different structured data in smooth fashion. The major issue is to manage the sensing matrix as it requires massive physical resources compared to compressed sample and the signal itself. In group sparse signal based [7] compressed sensing for color images, the image is represented as group sparse signal but processed separately for each color channel. There are high order representation [3] of color images as tensors and sparse representation is performed through High Order Singular Value Decomposition (HOSVD) to learn the dictionary followed by group formation using similar non local patches collection. The reconstruction is performed using weighted l_p-norm minimization. The color and near infrared (NIR) images [8] is also managed by separating green from RGB color space and NIR and mosaic image is constructed. In other RGB color based compressed sensing [9], RGB color transformed to YUV color channel. The Y color channel has been divided into blocks and transformed whereas UV is kept intact. In reconstruction phase saliency regions are considered for perfect reconstruction followed by collaboration with UV channels and then reversed back to RGB color channel.

The block based processing [3,9] manage computation time for large size input signal, but involves other processing like finding non local similar patches or saliency regions to avoid the block artifacts. In tensor based approach [3], the blocks size maintains the performance of the method as the large size blocks as well as large number of patches in single element in the group, increases processing time. In this paper these problems have been addressed. The input signal is considered as the collection of three color channels. The sensing or measurement matrix is partial circulant matrix whose first columns is constructed using elements drawn from identically independent Gaussian distribution. The complete physical storage of such matrix is not needed during processing and any required column can be generated at any instant. The indices for the signal coefficients of three color channels is obtained at the same time.

3   Proposed Method

The signal $x = \{x_i\}_{i=1}^{n}$ is represented in some canonical basis $\Psi \in \mathbb{R}^{n \times n}$ with coefficients $c = c_{i\,i=1}^{n}$ which can be formulated as in Eq. (5):

$$c = \Psi x \tag{5}$$

The sparse representation of c is obtained keeping only 10% of largest coefficients as in Eq. (6):

$$\bar{c} = \tau(c) \tag{6}$$

here, τ is hard thresholding operator.

For the RGB color channel the input signal $x_{RGB} = \{x_R, x_G, x_B\}$ is sparsified each channel separately using Eq. (6) before merging into single input signal $c_{RGB} = \{c_R, c_G, c_B\}$. The measurement vector y is obtained according to Eq. (7):

$$y_{RGB} = A x_{RGB} \tag{7}$$

The measurement or sensing matrix A is constructed using partial circulant matrix [4]. The first column of the matrix $a_1 = \{a_{1j}\}_{j=1}^{n}$ is obtained from identically independent Gaussian distribution.

$$\Phi = \{a_{ij}\} \tag{8}$$

where,

$$a_{ij} = \begin{cases} a_{ij} & \text{if } j = 1 \\ a_{((i-1)\%n)j} & \text{otherwise} \end{cases} \tag{9}$$

For the construction of the sensing matrix A, m random rows are selected from Φ. The sensing matrix is completely created for the proposed method, the columns are generated when needed. Due to construction of the sensing matrix the measurement vector is generated as

$$y_{RGB} = \sum_{j=1}^{n} a_j x_j \tag{10}$$

where a_j is obtained from Eq. (9). The operations used to temporary vector $\bar{x}$ in each iteration of StOMP is given in Eq. (11):

$$\bar{x} = \cup_{j=1}^{n} A_j^T y_{RGB} \tag{11}$$

The indices obtained in each iteration using Stagewise Orthogonal Matching Pursuit (StOMP) are calculated for the three color channel at the same time which save computational time considerable level. The algorithm for the proposed methods is as given in Algorithm 1:

Algorithm 1: Color Image StOMP

Input: Color Image $Img_{RGB}, t = 4.2, \epsilon = 1e - 5$
Output: Reconstructed sparse Image

1 Set $x = 0^{n \times 1}, i = 0, r = y_{RGB}, p = n/3, \lambda = \{\}$;
2 **while** $i \leq maxIter$ and $||r||_2 \geq \epsilon$ **do**
3   set $threshold = \frac{1}{\sqrt{m}} ||r||_2 * \alpha$;
4   Set $t_R = \bar{x}_R$ using equation(11);
5   Set $t_G = \bar{x}_G$ using equation(11);
6   Set $t_B = \bar{x}_B$ using equation(11);
7   **for** $j=1$ to p **do**
8   **if** $|t_R[j]| > threshold$ **then**
9           $\lambda = \lambda \cup j$;
10   **end**
11   **if** $|t_G[j]| > threshold$ **then**
12           $\lambda = \lambda \cup (p * j)$;
13   **end**
14   **if** $|t_B| > threshold$ **then**
15           $\lambda = \lambda \cup (2 * p * j)$;
16   **end**
17   **end**
18     $x_\lambda = \min ||y_{RGB} - A\bar{x}_\Lambda||_2$;
19   Set $r = y_{RGB} - Ax_\Lambda$;
20 **end**
21 x is transformed to three color channel image.

3.1 Complexity Analysis

The Eq. (11) takes $O(p)$ where $p = n/3$ to compute the $\bar{x}_C$ where $C = R, G, B$ and total time taken for three color channel is $O(3p)$ ans for state S it is $O(3Sp)$. The searching for indices takes same amount of time for all three channels is $O(p)$ and after S stages it is $O(Sp)$. The least solution after stage S is $O(2mK^2 - \frac{2}{3}K^3)$ where K is the sparsity of the signal. Therefore, the total time complexity of the proposed method is $O(3Sp + p + 2mK^2 - \frac{2}{3}K^3)$.

4 Results and Simulations

The simulations for the proposed methods have been carried out for four images-Couple, Female_belllab, Girl, pepper [1] with dimension 128×128. The images used in proposed technique are given in Fig. 1:

The simulation results for Fig. 1 images is consolidated in Table 1 and for quality assessment Peak Signal to Noise Ratio (PSNR), measure in Decibel (dB), has been used in proposed technique:

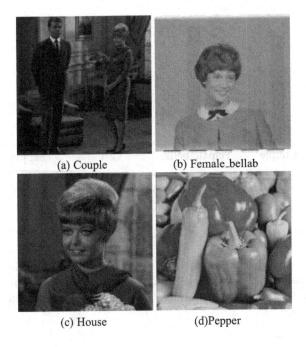

(a) Couple   (b) Female_bellab

(c) House   (d)Pepper

Fig. 1. Images for simulations

Table 1. Simulation data for selected images

Image	PSNR between originad and reconstructed image (dB)	Execution time (sec.)
Couple	30.86	638.623
Female_bellab	33.57	634.371
Girl	31.87	591.936
Pepper	28.09	602.303

In Table 1 the first column represents images name for selected image of Fig. 1. The second column represents PSNR (dB) between original image and reconstructed image. The third column represents the execution time (sec.) for simulation of each selected image. In Table 1 the PSNR for Female_bellab image is 33.57 (dB) which the high PSNR obtained. The minimum PSNR, 28.09 (dB) is obtained for the image Pepper and rest of the image has PSNR around 30 (dB). The graph plot of the simulation result is given in Fig. 2:

In the Fig. 2, x axis represents image names and y axis represents PSNR (dB) between Original Image and reconstructed image. It is prominent from the figure is that the Female_bellab possesses maximum PSNR among the selected images.

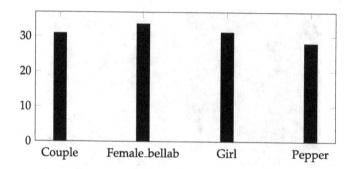

Fig. 2. Graph plot of the simulation for selected images

5 Comparison

The proposed technique has been compared with two existing methods- group compressed sensing based method [7] and tensor based compressed sensing method [3] for the four selected images given in Fig. 1. The comparison data is given in Table 2:

Table 2. Comparision Data for existing methods along with proposed method

Methods	Sl. No.	Image	PSNR
Group CS	1	Couple	–
	2	Female_bellab	–
	3	Girl	30.69
	4	Pepper	26.11
Tensor Based	1	Couple	26.96
	2	Female_bellab	23.18
	3	Girl	31.45
	4	Pepper	27.26
Proposed	1	Couple	**30.86**
	2	Female_bellab	**33.57**
	3	Girl	**31.87**
	4	Pepper	**28.09**

In Table 2, the first column represents existing along with proposed method name, the second column represents serial number for images, third column represents the image name for each methods and the last column represents PSNR (dB) for each method of respective images. The PSNR for proposed methods is observed to see better than all the existing methods even for keeping only 10% of data coefficients. The PSNR for girl image in tensor base CS is close to proposed method but for the rest of the images it is much better than other methods. All the results simulated for selected images has shown a better performance for proposed method over existing method. The comparison data is shown in Fig. 3:

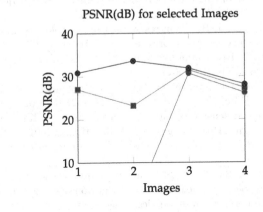

PSNR(dB) for selected Images

Fig. 3. Compared data plot for exiting method along with Proposed method in terms of PSNR (dB)

In Fig. 3, the x axis represents images- Couple, Female_bellab, Girl, Pepper respectively. The y axis represents the the PSNR for different methods of respective image in Fig. 1. The Fig. 3 validates the claims of the proposed method as it can be seen that PSNR for all images is better that rest of existing methods.

6 Conclusion

In this paper an improved color image based compressed sensing technique has been proposed. The stagewise orthogonal matching pursuit has been used for first selection of indices and it has been modified as to obtain indices for three color channels at the same time to speed the computation along circulant matrix to optimally use the physical resource to have better performance which is validated by simulation.

Acknowledgements. The research was funded by PURSE Scheme of the Department of Science and Technology, Govt. of India awarded to the CSE Department, University of Kalyani, WB, India. The authors would like to thank the anonymous reviewers for their helpful comments on the manuscript.

References

1. The USC-SIPI Image Database. http://sipi.usc.edu/database/database.php?volume=misc. Accessed 1 Sept 2020
2. Candes, E., Tao, T.: Near optimal signal recovery from random projections: Universal encoding strategies? Appl. Comput. Math. (2006)
3. Dinh, K.Q., Canh, T.N., Jeon, B.: Compressive sensing of color images using nonlocal higher order dictionary. arXiv preprint arXiv:1711.09375 (2017)
4. Dirksen, S., Mendelson, S.: Robust one-bit compressed sensing with partial circulant matrices. arXiv preprint arXiv:1812.06719 (2018)
5. Donoho, D.L.: Optimally sparse representation from overcomplete dictionaries via Γ 1-norm minimization. Proc. Nat. Acad. Sci. USA **100**, 2197–2002 (2003)
6. Gan, L.: Block compressed sensing of natural images. In: 2007 15th International Conference on Digital Signal Processing, pp. 403–406. IEEE (2007)
7. Majumdar, A., Ward, R.K.: Compressed sensing of color images. Signal Process. **90**(12), 3122–3127 (2010)
8. Sadeghipoor, Z., Lu, Y.M., Süsstrunk, S.: A novel compressive sensing approach to simultaneously acquire color and near-infrared images on a single sensor. In: 2013 IEEE International Conference on Acoustics, Speech and Signal Processing, pp. 1646–1650. IEEE (2013)
9. Zhang, Z., Bi, H., Kong, X., Li, N., Lu, D.: Adaptive compressed sensing of color images based on salient region detection. Multimed. Tools Appl. **79**, 14777–14791 (2019). https://doi.org/10.1007/s11042-018-7062-6

Duplicate Frame Detection in Forged Videos Using Sequence Matching

Sk Mohiuddin[1(✉)] , Samir Malakar[1], and Ram Sarkar[2]

[1] Department of Computer Science, Asutosh College,
Kolkata, India
[2] Department of Computer Science and Engineering, Jadavpur University,
Kolkata, India

Abstract. This paper presents a method that can detect multiple frame duplication in forged videos. In this kind of forgery, a number of frames are copied and placed somewhere in a video for hiding or highlighting some incidents and/or objects. It becomes very challenging to identify the duplicated frames in such digital videos, as it is difficult to detect by the human eyes as well as by computer program. In past works, various methods have been proposed so far to detect the same. Despite that, there are very a few methods which can determine frame duplication in the video with both static and non-static background. To this end, this work proposes a simple yet effective method to detect the frame duplication forgery found in the videos. In this method, the structural similarity index measure (SSIM) is used to assess the resemblance between the consecutive frames. Finally, to detect and localize tampered frames, a searching algorithm is used. For experimental need, we have collected original videos from Urban Tracker, derf's collection and REWIND databases, and then prepared the forged videos using frame duplication. Experimental results on these videos confirm that the present method detects such forgery with an impressive average frame duplication detection accuracy of 98.90%.

Keywords: Frame duplication forgery · Video forgery detection · Sequence matching · LCSC · SSIM

1 Introduction

Digital videos are becoming an integral part in different sectors of our society such as bank, office, home, railway station, airport and many more to ensure security. Ongoing events can be presented live or recorded through a surveillance camera, and such videos can be used to establish security in those sectors. Thus, the demand for surveillance systems is increasing day by day. Besides, surveillance video footage is considered as important evidence in the court to judge criminal activity. However, due to the advancement of technology and freely available tools for video editing, it becomes easier to modify or hide some

© Springer Nature Switzerland AG 2021
P. Dutta et al. (Eds.): CICBA 2021, CCIS 1406, pp. 29–41, 2021.
https://doi.org/10.1007/978-3-030-75529-4_3

activity by frame duplication in the same video. Thus, to ensure the authenticity and integrity of a video, we must need a suitable method.

Existing video forgery detection techniques can be categorized as active and passive video forgery detection techniques. Active video forgery detection techniques require prior information (e.g., fingerprint, digital watermark etc.) that is embedded with the video during its generation which helps to check its authenticity. In contrast, techniques which use passive video forgery detection approach do not require such kind of embedded information to verify the authenticity of a video. As a result, passive approach is proven to be expensive in terms of cost and hardware requirements. In the present work, we propose a passive approach to be used for forged video detection.

Among the different video forgery techniques, copy-move video forgery is the most popular type of video tampering techniques. In this tampering, the viewers' perception of an event in a video is changed by insertion and/or removal of objects and/or frames from the video (see Fig. 1). Creating the copy-move forged videos is relatively easy. Hence, it causes much damage to the trustworthiness of the video footage. However, it is very difficult to detect by the bare human eyes. Thus, a suitable computerized method is required to detect the copy-move forgery which is the main focus of the current work.

Here, we propose a method which can detect frame duplication, which is a type of copy-move video forgery detection technique, in videos with both static and non-static background. The basic difference between the static and non-static background videos is that one is created with non-movable cameras, whereas the other one is created with movable cameras. In our method, at first, we measure the similarity between every two consecutive frames in the video frame sequence. Then, we estimate an automatic threshold value to partition the similarity score sequence of the video frame pairs into multiple parts. In the last step, to detect and localize the copied frames in the query video, we use longest common sequence checker (LCSC) searching algorithm.

The rest parts of this work are organized as follows: in Sect. 2, we summarize the related works that describe several state-of-the-art frame duplication detection methods. Section 3 presents the current frame duplication detection technique. We discuss our experimental results in Sect. 4, and finally, in Sect. 5 conclusion and future research directions have been described.

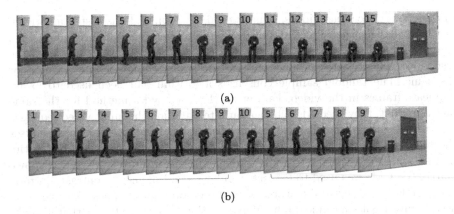

(a)

(b)

Fig. 1. Diagram showing the frame duplication process: (a) shows the original video frame sequence. (b) shows the forged sequence (to hide the sitting posture of the man, duplicate frames are inserted)

2   Related Work

In the past decades, many copy-move video forgery detection methods have been introduced by the researchers to detect different types of copy-move forgery in the surveillance videos. In the proposed method, we deal with frame duplication video forgery which is a kind of copy-move forgery. Hence, in this section, we discuss some of the existing methods used to detect frame duplication forgeries in the digital videos.

Yang et al. [8] calculated features for each frame using singular value decomposition (SVD) to perform detection of duplicate frame in digital video. It measures the distance between each frame and the reference frame using Euclidean distance. They calculated the correlation coefficient of different sub-sequences and compared them with other methods to find out the matching similarity. In another work, Zhao et al. [9], introduced a video shot selection strategy to group the similar looking frames in a single video. For the detection of duplicated frames in a video shot, they first calculated color histograms of every frame in a video shot and then compared the similarity between the histograms of the frames under consideration. In this work they made use of speeded-up robust features (SURF) feature descriptor having a fast library for approximate nearest neighbours (FLANNs) matching. Sing et al. [6] detected frame duplication by calculating nine features like mean, ratio and residue from four sub-block of each frame of the video. Root mean square error (RMSE) is calculated between the feature vectors of adjacent frames to detect suspected frames. They were able to detect frame duplication in videos with static background and non-static background with satisfactorily.

Lin and Chang [4] used a histogram difference method where the red-green-blue (RGB) channel intensities of overlapping clips of consecutive frames were used as a feature vector. Their method is computationally high and also not suitable for static scene videos. Kharat et al. [3] proposed a two-step algorithm in which the suspicious (i.e., duplicated) frames were identified first and then features from these frames were extracted to compare with other frames of the test video. They used scale invariant feature transform key-points features for the same. The random sample consensus algorithm had been used to locate duplicate frames in the video. Fadl et al. [1] developed a method for the same purpose. First, they used edge change ratio to partition the input video sequence into variable length smaller clips instead of using fixed size for clips. It uses the temporal average of each clip as a discriminating frame instead of entire frames, which is invariant to frame order. Afterward, gray level co-occurrence matrix (GLCM) was used to extract angular second moment, contrast, entropy and correlation of textural features of each temporal image. These features were used to investigate in frame duplication detection. The limitation is that it might fail in detecting frame duplication at multiple positions. Singh and Singh [5] proposed a two-step approach for detecting duplicate frame(s). The first step was used to detect different forms of frame duplication. It computed the correlation coefficient between the consecutive frame sequences of the entire video. Whereas, in the second step it detected region duplication which was performed by locating the erroneous position that was decided by a user defined threshold value. This method can detect both the regular and irregular duplicated region(s).

From the literature review, it has been observed that most of the existing methods concentrate in detecting frame duplication only in surveillance video forgery. However, our proposed method has dealt with videos having either static or non-static background to detect the copy-move forgery. Another issue is that the performance of a system can be affected by the external noise found in the video. This is also handled in the present work. In a nutshell, the highlights of the proposed method are as follows.

– Proposed a frame duplication detection method in video having either static or non-static background
– Introduced technique, called LCSC, to detect and locate duplicate frames in a video
– Obtained reasonably satisfactory accuracy on a dataset containing 37 videos
– Method performed well on noisy videos as well.

3   Proposed Methodology

The proposed work is used to detect duplicate frames in a surveillance (static background) and non-surveillance (non-static background) video that is affected by copy-move forgery. In this method, we first calculate a sequence of SSIM values by comparing each successive pair of frames in the input video. After that, the sequence of the similarity indices is broken into multiple sub-sequences using automatically set threshold values. Application of SSIM returns lesser value when the current frame is relatively different from its preceding frame. If this is occurred then we cut the sequence at the points where SSIM values are lesser than the automatically calculated threshold value. We call these parts of the entire video as shot. Initially, we assume these points as starting or ending position of the copied frame set. Later, a LCSC algorithm is applied to all possible pair of shots in order to search the longest common identical frame sequence. The key modules of the present work, as shown in Fig. 2, are presented in the below subsections.

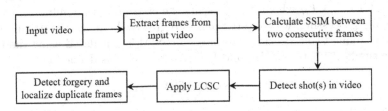

Fig. 2. Key modules of the proposed method used to detect duplicate frames in the forged videos

3.1 Measuring Similarity Between Two Frames

In the proposed work, we use the concept of SSIM index for calculating the similarity between two frames. The SSIM index can be viewed as a similarity measurement of two frames by comparing their luminance, contrast and structure. It can also be said that SSIM index represents the perceptual difference between two similar frames and it cannot judge which of the two is better. SSIM looks for similarities within pixels of two frames i.e., it checks whether the corresponding pixels' intensity values in the two frames are similar or not. When we compare two frames by calculating the SSIM score, its value lies between -1 and 1. A score 1 represents they are very similar and a score -1 denotes that they are very different. Here, we briefly discuss the steps to calculate the SSIM index.

In image analysis to measure the quality of image or to compare between two images, the SSIM [7] is used. Given a reference grey-level image R and a test image T, both of size $M \times N$, the SSIM between R and T is defined by

$$SSIM\,(R,\,T) \;=\; l(R,\,T)\,*\,c(R,\,T)\,*\,s(R,\,T) \tag{1}$$

where

$$l(R,T) = \frac{2\mu_R\mu_T + C_1}{\mu_R^2 + \mu_T^2 + C_1}, \quad c(R,T) = \frac{2\sigma_R\sigma_T + C_2}{\sigma_R^2 + \sigma_T^2 + C_2}, \quad s(R,T) = \frac{\sigma_{RT} + C_3}{\sigma_R\sigma_T + C_3} \tag{2}$$

The first term $l(R,T)$ in Eq. 1 denotes the luminance comparison operation and it calculates the proximity of the two images' mean luminance. The second one i.e., $c(R,T)$ measures the contrast between two images and it is known as the contrast comparison function. The third term $s(R,T)$ measures the correlation coefficient within the two images R and T and is termed as the structure comparison function. C1, C2 and C3 are small constants designed to characterize the saturation effect of the visual system in low brightness and contrast areas. It also ensures numerical stability when the denominator is close to zero.

3.2   Detection of Shots in a Video

A video is composed of a number of frames. Let us denote the frames in a video by $VF_1, VF_2, ..., VF_N$ where N represents the entire frames number in a video. Before any processing, we convert them into gray scale image. To calculate the harmony among two consecutive frames, the SSIM is calculated using the Eq. 1. Let the similarity between VF_i and VF_{i+1} is S_i and it is defined by

$$S_i = SSIM(VF_i, VF_{i+1}) \tag{3}$$

Here, $i = 1, 2, ..., N - 1$.

Now, we break frames in the video into a number of parts whenever S_i index becomes lesser then a threshold value τ. We call each such part as shot. According to Zheng et al. [10] the human eye and brain cannot process less than 10 frames per second having very minor differences. Hence, we put a constraint i.e., minimum length of a shot should be at least of length 10 to avoid false shot detection. If the length of a shot is less than 10, it is added to the previous shot. The threshold value (τ) is calculated by

$$\tau = \mu_S - \sigma_S \tag{4}$$

where μ_S, σ_S represents the mean and standard deviation of all S_i values, and which can be present mathematically as

$$\mu = \frac{1}{N} \sum_{i=1}^{N} s_i \tag{5}$$

$$\sigma = \sqrt{\frac{1}{N} \sum_{i=1}^{N} |s_i - \mu|^2} \tag{6}$$

After partitioning of the frame sequence of a video, we get a number of shots (say, $SHOT_1, SHOT_2, ..., SHOT_P$) of variable lengths (say, $L_1, L_2, ..., L_P$ and $P < N$) where P is the number of shots detected.

3.3   Detection of Frame Duplication

From the previous step, we obtain a number of shots of variable length. In this section, we try to search whether there exists any frame duplication between any two shots, which is done by searching the largest common identical frame sequence between the shots under consideration using the LCSC technique, described in Algorithm 1. The similarity of the frames from two different shots can be determined by calculating the SSIM score using Eq. 3. However, this would increase the computational cost of the searching process since SSIM function will be called L_1*L_2 times if we try to find the largest common identical frames between two shots of length L_1 and L_2. Therefore, to minimize this computational cost, we use the previously calculated SSIM scores of consecutive frames in the entire video as described in Subsect. 3.2. Let, S_{mi} and S_{nj} represent the SSIM scores of ith frame of $SHOT_m$ and j^{th} of frame $SHOT_n$ respectively. Now, we call i^{th} frame of $SHOT_m$ and j^{th} of frame $SHOT_n$ are identical if $|S_{mi} - S_{nj}| < M_C$, where M_C is a threshold value that is decided experimentally. The LCSC method is described in Algorithm 1 returns the indices of the duplicated frames. Multiple common sequences can be detected when we compare any two shots. We ignore a common sequence if its length is less than 10. We summarize our entire method in Algorithm 2.

Algorithm 1. Pseudo code for LCSC search method

1: **procedure** LCSC($SHOT_m[1..p], SHOT_n[1..q]$)
2:     $SHOT_m[x] : x^{th}$ frame of $SHOT_m$
3:     A : array(1..p, 1..q)
4:     L : L is used to hold the length of the longest common sequence found so far
5:     **for** $x \leftarrow 1$ to p **do**
6:         **for** $y \leftarrow 1$ to q **do**
7:             **if** ($SHOT_m[x]$ is identical to $SHOT_n[y]$) **then**
8:                 **if** $x = 1$ or $y = 1$ **then**
9:                     $A[x, y] := 1$
10:                 **else**
11:                     $A[x, y] := A[x - 1, y - 1] + 1$
12:                 **end if**
13:                 **if** $A[x, y] > L$ **then**
14:                     $L := A[x, y]$
15:                     Store start and end indices of the first matched
                        sequence from both SHOTs
16:                 **else if** $A[x, y] = L$ **then**
17:                     Further detected sequence of the same length as first one
                        and stores new indices also with the previous
18:                 **end if**
19:             **else**
20:                 $A[x, y] := 0$
21:             **end if**
22:         **end for**
23:     **end for**
24:     **return** All indices of the matched sequence
25: **end procedure**

Algorithm 2. Algorithm of proposed frame duplication detection method

1: C: minimum numbers of frames a shot must contain and duplicated in a forged video
2: $N :=$ Number of video frames
3: **for** $i \leftarrow 2$ to N **do**
4:     $S_i := \text{SSIM}(VF_{i-1}, VF_i)$
5: **end for**
6: $\tau := \mu_S - \sigma_S$
        //Frame sub-sequence generation
7: $Count := 1$
8: $k := 1$
9: **for** $i \leftarrow 1$ to $N - 1$ **do**
10:     **if** $S_i < \tau$ *and* $Count > C$ **then**
11:         Break at position i
12:         $SUB_k :=$ [Store all the SSIM values from previous break point]
13:         $Count := 1$
14:         $k := k + 1$
15:     **else**
16:         $Count := Count + 1$
17:     **end if**
18: **end for**
        //Matching of sub-sequences
19: **for** $i \leftarrow 1$ to $length(SHOT) - 1$ **do**
20:     **for** $j \leftarrow i + 1$ to $length(SHOT)$ **do**
21:         $matched := \text{LCSC}(SHOT_i, SHOT_j)$
22:         return with index if $length(matched) \geq C$
23:         //Detected copied sequence
24:     **end for**
25: **end for**

4   Experiment Results and Analysis

4.1   Dataset Description

Although a standard dataset is required to assess the performance of an algorithm, however, we could not found any such video dataset. Therefore, we have selected some original videos from derf's collection[1], REWIND[2], Urban Tracker [2] and YouTube, and prepared our dataset. It contains videos with static background (19 videos) as well as non-static background (18 videos) with variation in terms of video format like uncompressed avi and compressed mp4. The highest and lowest resolutions found in these videos are 626×352 and 320×240 pixels respectively. All videos in this dataset are compressed using libx264 and libavcodec libraries of ffmpeg[3]. This dataset contains 10 videos which have no frame duplication, 10 videos with one-time frame duplication, and

---

[1] https://media.xiph.org/video/derf/.
[2] https://sites.google.com/site/rewindpolimi/downloads/datasets.
[3] https://ffmpeg.org/.

3 videos with multiple time frame duplication. Our dataset contains another 14 videos (9 videos have one-time frame duplication and 5 videos have no frame duplication) that has been modified using operations such as change in sharpness, vintage, blurring and noise. These operations have been performed to experiment the result of the proposed method in noisy environment. Therefore, we have a total of 37 videos in the current dataset; each of which approximately is 6–18 s long and frame rate varies between 25 to 30 fps. Table 1 shows summary of the forged videos used in the current experimentation.

Table 1. Details of the forged videos in present the current dataset. Last three videos contain multiple time frame duplication while the first 10 are having single time frame duplication

Video	Original length	Tampered length	Forgery operation
V1_forged.avi	300	335	185:220 copied at 60:95
V2_forged.avi	300	430	0:130 copied at 170:299
V3_forged.avi	235	335	220:320 copied at 0:100
V4_forged.avi	250	350	60:160 copied at 180:280
V5_forged.avi	180	300	170:290 copied at 20:140
V6_forged.avi	360	470	10:120 copied at 320:430
V7_forged.avi	321	447	180:300 copied at 320:440
V8_forged.avi	209	286	10:87 copied at 200:277
V9_forged.avi	317	417	316:416 copied at 80:180
V10_forged.avi	130	250	5:125 copied at 130:250
V1_Multiple_copy.avi	300	350	10:35 copied at 50:75 and 100:125
V2_Multiple_copy.avi	300	350	155:180 copied at 70:95 and 210:235
V4_Multiple_copy.avi	250	320	135:170 copied at 40:75 and 215:250

4.2 Evaluation Metrics

To measure performance of our proposed system, we use three statistical measures: detection accuracy (DA), true positive rate (TPR) and true negative rate (TNR), which are denoted as

$$DA = \frac{TP + TN}{TP + FP + FN + TN}, \quad TPR = \frac{TP}{TP + FN}, \quad TNR = \frac{TN}{TN + FN} \quad (7)$$

TPR and TNR are also called sensitivity and specificity. TPR illustrates how good is the system in detecting the actual forged frames. On the other hand, specificity (or TNR) estimates how likely the real frames can be predicted as real. TP, TN, FP and FN denote true positive (number of correctly predicted forged frames), true negative (number of correctly predicted real frames), false positive (number of incorrectly predicted forged frames), false negative (number of correctly predicted real frames).

4.3   Results and Discussion

In Subsect. 3.3, we have mentioned that to decide whether two frames are same or not, we have relied on a threshold value (i.e., M_C). To decide the value of M_C we have studied the absolute differences in two SSIM scores in a video, and we have found that this absolute difference never goes beyond 0.300 if no frame duplication takes place and hence, we have choose this value as the threshold for the current experimentation. Figure 3 shows three such cases where consecutive SSIM score difference never goes higher than M_C except when frame duplication takes place.

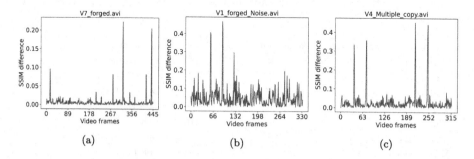

Fig. 3. Illustration of SSIM score difference which is high at copied position, in other cases, it is below M_C (a) 180:300 copied at 320:440, (b) 185:220 copied at 60:95, and (c) 135:170 copied at 40:75 and 215:250

All videos are grouped into four major categories to analyze performance of our system in a better way. The categories are Category 1 (contains only video with no forgery), Category 2 (contains only one-time frame duplication forged videos), Category 3 (containing only videos with post-processing operation (both original and forged)) and Category 4 (containing only videos with multiple time frame duplication forgery). Table 2 shows category-wise average DA, TPR and TNR as well as the overall average performances obtained by the proposed method.

Table 2. Shows category-wise as well as overall performances of proposed frame duplication detection technique

	#videos	DA	TPR	TNR
Category 1	10	0.989	1.0	0.989
Category 2	10	0.985	1.0	0.978
Category 3	14	0.990	1.0	0.988
Category 4	3	1.0	1.0	1.0
Average	37	0.989	1.0	0.987

After analyzing the results shown in Table 2, it is found that for all these categories of videos TPR values are 1.0 which means our system is capable in detecting forged frames correctly. But, while identifying the forged frames, our system identifies few real frames as forged frames and that is why TNR values are low in case of first, second and third categories of videos. However, the videos with multiple time frame duplication operation, our system performs best. Figure 4 shows three examples of detected duplicate frames by the proposed method taking one example from each of the last three categories of the videos. We have also tested the performance of our system while the background of the videos is either static or non-static. In this case also proposed system performs satisfactory (refer to Table 3). Present method detects forged as well as original frames while tested on videos with non-static background with accuracy 100%. However, present method produces some errors in the cases when videos are having static background. After analyzing the errors, we have found that real frames of shots having no object movement are detected as forged.

Table 3. Duplicate frame detection results for the videos with static and non-static background

	#videos	DA	TPR	TNR
Static background videos	19	0.979	1.0	0.974
Non-static background videos	18	1.0	1.0	1.0

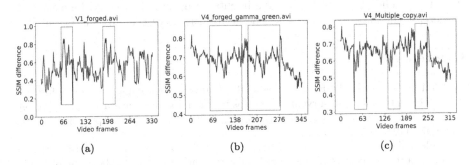

Fig. 4. Localization of frame duplication for (a) Category 2, (b) Category 3, and (c) Category 4 videos

In addition to these, we have also tested the performance of the present method on videos (both original and frame duplication videos) that are affected by some distortion operations as mentioned earlier. In this case also the proposed method performs well. Table 4 shows the detection performance of our method on post-processed videos.

Table 4. Shows the frame duplication detection performances on the videos that are affected by distortion operations like adding noise, vintage and contrast change

	#videos	DA	TPR	TNR
Category 3 (Original videos with post-processing)	5	0.989	1.0	0.989
Category 3 (One time frame duplication videos with post-processing)	9	0.991	1.0	0.987
Average	14	0.990	1.0	0.988

5   Conclusion

This paper presents a method to detect frame duplication forgery in digital videos with static as well as non-static background. Structural similarity between frames and a simple search algorithm are used to perform the task under consideration. Experimental results show that the average TPR and TNR scores regarding frame duplication detection of this method are 100.0% and 98.66% respectively. The average accuracy for the proposed method is found to be 98.90%. In spite of the success of the current method, there are still some rooms for improvement. Although our method detects the duplicate frames with 100% accuracy but it detects few real frames as forged. Therefore, in future more sophisticated features are to be used to overcome this problem. Besides, we have experimented the present method only on 37 videos that include both forged and real videos. Therefore, in future experiments on more videos could be executed to increase the accuracy and establish the robustness of the current system.

References

1. Fadl, S., Megahed, A., Han, Q., Qiong, L.: Frame duplication and shuffling forgery detection technique in surveillance videos based on temporal average and gray level co-occurrence matrix. Multimed. Tools Appl. **79**, 1–25 (2020). https://doi.org/10.1007/s11042-019-08603-z
2. Jodoin, J.P., Bilodeau, G.A. and Saunier, N.: Urban tracker: multiple object tracking in urban mixed traffic. In: IEEE Winter Conference on Applications of Computer Vision, pp. 885–892. IEEE (2014)
3. Kharat, J., Chougule, S.: A passive blind forgery detection technique to identify frame duplication attack. Multimed. Tools Appl. **79**, 1–17 (2020). https://doi.org/10.1007/s11042-019-08272-y
4. Lin, G.-S., Chang, J.-F.: Detection of frame duplication forgery in videos based on spatial and temporal analysis. Int. J. Pattern Recognit. Artif. Intell. **26**(07), 1250017 (2012)
5. Singh, G., Singh, K.: Video frame and region duplication forgery detection based on correlation coefficient and coefficient of variation. Multimed. Tool Appl. **78**(9), 11527–11562 (2019)

6. Singh, V.K., Pant, P., Tripathi, R.C.: Detection of frame duplication type of forgery in digital video using sub-block based features. In: James, J.I., Breitinger, F. (eds.) ICDF2C 2015. LNICST, vol. 157, pp. 29–38. Springer, Cham (2015). https://doi.org/10.1007/978-3-319-25512-5_3

7. Wang, Z., Bovik, A.C., Sheikh, H.R., Simoncelli, E.P.: Image quality assessment: from error visibility to structural similarity. IEEE Trans. Image Process. **13**(4), 600–612 (2004)

8. Yang, J., Huang, T., Lichao, S.: Using similarity analysis to detect frame duplication forgery in videos. Multimed. Tools Appl. **75**(4), 1793–1811 (2016)

9. Zhao, D.-N., Wang, R.-K., Zhe-Ming, L.: Inter-frame passive-blind forgery detection for video shot based on similarity analysis. Multimed. Tools Appl. **77**(19), 25389–25408 (2018)

10. Zheng, L., Sun, T., Shi, Y.-Q.: Inter-frame video forgery detection based on block-wise brightness variance descriptor. In: Shi, Y.-Q., Kim, H.J., Pérez-González, F., Yang, C.-N. (eds.) IWDW 2014. LNCS, vol. 9023, pp. 18–30. Springer, Cham (2015). https://doi.org/10.1007/978-3-319-19321-2_2

An Image Encryption Method Using Chaos and DNA Encoding

Mukul Biswas, Sujit Kumar Das$^{(\boxtimes)}$, and Bibhas Chandra Dhara

Department of Information Technology,
Jadavpur University, Kolkata, India

Abstract. A simple method, for image encryption using 1D discrete chaos and DNA encoding, is proposed in this article. Here, chaotic maps are used to encode the secret image as DNA sequence and also to diffuse the encoded image with DNA operations and finally a cipher image is obtained. Additionally, hash function SHA-256 is employed to plain image and this makes the current method more robust. The result of the present method is studied and analyzed to established the aptness of the proposed method.

Keywords: Image encryption · Cryptography · Tent map · Renyi map · DNA encoding · Security analysis

1 Introduction

Information was always considered as a valuable possession. After the age of the internet dawned upon us, the value of information has surpassed any other material in existence. Information is also susceptible to corruption, theft and illegal exposure and images are no different in this regard. So, it is utmost important that the information should be protected so that an authorized person only has the permission to access that information. With respect to images, the process of making meaningless data out of a plain image is called image encryption. Conventional encryption algorithms like, DES [5] and AES [14] they don't work well in image domain. Usually, an image encryption algorithm has two phases, namely, confusion and diffusion. The position of the pixels is altered in the first phase and intensity value of the pixels is modified in the last phase. Chaotic system is well used for encryption purposes due to its sensitivity, pseudo-randomness, ergodicity and reproduction [15] to initial value of the parameters. In recent years, because of these strengths of chaotic systems, many studies have implemented in image encryption algorithms [3,9,20,22,24]. In [21], S-boxes are formulated using chaotic systems for encryption. A method for encrypting an image is proposed in [12] where a 5D multiwing hyperchaotic system has employed. In [17] hyperchaos-based image encryption technique is implemented that uses a 6-dimensional hyperchaotic structure.

Besides the chaos based image encryption many other techniques are also studied for image encryption. In [7], different sine waves have constructed and

© Springer Nature Switzerland AG 2021
P. Dutta et al. (Eds.): CICBA 2021, CCIS 1406, pp. 42–56, 2021.
https://doi.org/10.1007/978-3-030-75529-4_4

using these random sequences are generated to confusion and diffusion phases. In [4], a polynomial interval bisection method is applied to obtain random sequences and these are used for arranging pixels of rows/columns of the plain image. To change the pixels value, in the diffusion phase, value Substitution and iterative XOR operation are applied. Another non-chaotic cryptosystem is developed using the cyclic group in [11]. Here, the cyclic group is employed to get permutation sequences and pixels and bits of the original image are permuted with the help of these permutation sequences. In [8], to get permutation some points are selected using certain distance on the perimeter of a defined circle with user defined radius depending the image size. In both the phases, the generated permutation is employed to get an encrypted image. In [13], a new technique for image encryption is proposed and for this purpose fibonacci transform is used. The pixels are permuted and also the pixel values are changed using this fibonacci transform.

Due to the some features of DNA encoding like parallelism of coding, consumption of low power and high density of information, it is attracted by various researchers in image encryption domain. For enhancing the security of the encryption method, many researchers have studied hybrid techniques using DNA encoding and computing with chaotic system. A chaotic map with DNA sequence based image encryption method is designed in [19], where bitwise XOR is executed among the pixels of the plain image and then DNA encoding is applied on the confused image and finally row/column are permuted to obtain the encrypted image. Using DNA permutation another scheme is proposed in [18] for color image encryption. In this scheme Lorenz map is also applied for random sequences generation and this step is used to increase the security level. A cryptosystem [23] is developed using 2D Hénon-Sine map (2D-HSM) and the DNA encoding. Here, only DNA XOR operation is defined to diffused image pixels. A hybrid model is designed in [10]. The model is composed of DNA coding and computing, SHA-2 and Lorenz map. Here, the DNA coding and operation and the Lorenz chaotic system improve the security of the model. In [16], a new image encryption system is introduced with permutations at pixel-level and bit-level followed by DNA coding. Here, a hyperchaotic (5D) map is applied for random sequence generation that is used in confusion. Then, DNA coding, XOR operation is employed to diffused the permuted image. Based on chaotic system and DNA coding another encryption technique is suggested in [2]. It is composed of two rounds. In the first round keys are generated and the permutation, substitution and diffusion is carried out in the last round. Additionally, to generate initial parameters for the chaotic map SHA-256 system is used.

In this article, a new method for image encryption, using 1D chaotic map and DNA computing, is proposed. The parameter(s) of these maps are initialized with the hash value of original image. To compute hash value, SHA-256 is used. The present method is a private key crypto-system. The Renyi map is applied for generating a key image (same size as the secret image). In this work, both images are encoded as DNA sequence using Tent map and then these encoded image are diffused to generate a diffused image. The proposed method has the provision to iterate the DNA encoding and diffusion a number of times. From the diffused image, an encrypted image is earned through DNA decoding. The presence of 1D maps makes the present method useable in terms of power consumption and computation aspects. The current method having no confusion step, it has only diffusion process. Now, we describe the structure of the rest part of this article. The basics of tools used in this method are discussed in Sect. 2. In Sect. 3 is dedicated for the proposed image encryption technique. The performance and its analysis of the proposed method are presented in Sect. 4. Section 5 highlights the conclusion of the present work.

2   Preliminaries

In the proposed image encryption algorithm, we have used 1D Tent map, 1D Renyi map and DNA encoding technique to encrypt a plain image.

2.1   Renyi Map and Tent Map

Tent map is applied to choose i) the rule of DNA coding and ii) the DNA operation. On the other hand Renyi map is employed for key image generation. According to [1] the randomness of the 1D Renyi system is very good. The 1D Renyi Map is defined in Eq. (1).

$$F(x_n, a, b) = tan(x_n)(1 + x_n) \times b + (1 - x_n)x_n \times a$$
$$x_{(n+1)} = \text{fraction}(F(x_n, a, b)) \times \alpha \tag{1}$$

where a, $b \in [0, 10]$ and $\alpha \in (0, 12345]$. We use the Renyi map as the randomness of this map is very uniform and it has good bifurcation behavior. The bifurcation diagram of the Renyi map is shown in Fig. 1. The Tent map is simple

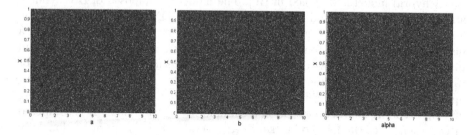

Fig. 1. Bifurcation diagram of 1D Renyi Map.

and extensively applied in image encryption algorithms. The expression of Tent map is offered in Eq. (2).

$$x_{(n+1)} = r \min\{x_n, 1 - x_n\} \tag{2}$$

where x_0 is the initial value, $x_i \in [0, 1]$ and $r \in [0, 2]$. The bifurcation diagram of the Tent map is presented in Fig. 2. From the Fig. 2 it is clear that for $r \in [1.4, 2]$, the randomness is at its highest level.

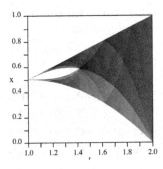

Fig. 2. Bifurcation diagram of 1D Tent map.

2.2 DNA Coding and DNA Operations

DNA is a molecule containing the genetic information of every living organism and various viruses to evolve, create, function, and reproduce. In DNA sequencing, the basic block of genetic code is built upon four bases i.e. Adenine (A), Thymine (T), Guanine (G) and Cytosine (C). According to the Watson–Crick [6] principle, A and T are complement of each other (i.e., A $\overleftrightarrow{complement}$ T), similarly C and G are also complement of each other (i.e., C $\overleftrightarrow{complement}$ G). Generally, these four DNA bases are encoded by 2-bit binary numbers '00', '11', '01', and '10'. So, there are 24 (= 4!) rules to encode these four DNA bases in binary representation.

Suppose, 'A' is represented by '00' and then due to complement relation '11' is the code of 'T'. For 'C', there are two options: i) 'C' ='10' (accordingly 'G'='01') or ii) 'C'='01' (and 'G'='10'). So, for the particular choice of 'A' we have i) 'A' $\sim$ '00', 'T' $\sim$ '11', 'C' $\sim$ '01' and 'G' $\sim$ '10' or ii) 'A' $\sim$ '00', 'T' $\sim$ '11', 'C' $\sim$ '10' and 'G' $\sim$ '01'. Again, 'A' can be represented by any of the four options {'00', '11', '01', '10'}. So, only eight rules out of 24 encoding rules satisfy the complementary relationship within the bases. Inverse of the encoding rules are the DNA decoding rules. The encoding rules for the DNA encoder is described in Table 1. For example, 177 is gray value of a particular pixel of an image and its binary representation is "10110001". With respect to fifth encoding rule, the pixel will be encoded as "ACGT".

Table 1. DNA encoding rules.

Base	Rules							
	1	2	3	4	5	6	7	8
00	A	A	G	C	G	C	T	T
01	G	C	A	A	T	T	G	C
10	C	G	T	T	A	A	C	G
11	T	T	C	G	C	G	A	A

Table 2. DNA Addition using first encoding rule.

+	A (00)	T (11)	C (10)	G (01)
A (00)	A (00)	T (11)	C (10)	G (01)
T (11)	T (11)	C (10)	G (01)	A (00)
C (10)	C (10)	G (01)	A (00)	T (11)
G (01)	G (01)	A (00)	T (11)	C (01)

Table 3. DNA Subtraction using first encoding rule.

−	A (00)	T (11)	C (10)	G (01)
A (00)	A (00)	G (01)	C (10)	T (11)
T (11)	T (11)	A (00)	G (01)	C (10)
C (10)	C (10)	T (11)	A (00)	G (01)
G (01)	G (01)	C (10)	T (11)	A (00)

Table 4. DNA XOR using fourth encoding rule.

⊕	A (01)	T (10)	C (00)	G (11)
A (01)	C (00)	G (11)	A (01)	T (10)
T (10)	G (11)	C (00)	T (10)	A (01)
C (00)	A (01)	T (10)	C (00)	G (10)
G (11)	T (10)	A (01)	G (11)	C (00)

Binary operations like addition, subtraction and XOR are also applied between DNA sequences to obtained an intermediate image. These operations are actually executed on binary strings and here, the operands and result are labeled by bases $\{A, B, C, D\}$. The result of labeling (i.e., binary string $\longleftrightarrow$ DNA sequence) depends on the DNA encoding rule. Hence, the DNA operations are defined with an encoding rule. For example, addition and subtraction operations with the help of first encoding rule are given in the Table 2 and Table 3, respectively. The XOR operation using fourth encoding rule is illustrated in the Table 4.

3   Proposed Image Encryption Method

In this article, we have implemented a new approach for image encryption with the use of DNA encoder and two linear chaotic systems. The encryption algorithm is presented in Fig. 3. In the present method, unlike two conventional

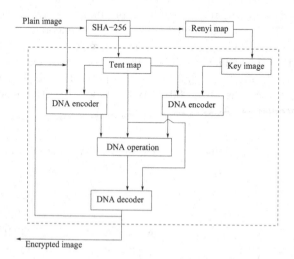

Fig. 3. Proposed model: a schematic diagram.

phases confusion and diffusion, we have implemented only diffusion phase. To carried out the diffusion step, first the plain image and key image are encoded by DNA encoder and then these two images are operated by DNA operations. To perform the proposed technique, we have certain steps which are as follows:

3.1 Generation of DNA Encoded Images

From Fig. 3, it is clear that the current method handles two DNA encoded images: i) one generated from the given plain image and ii) the other one is derived from the key image. Now, we are describing the process of key image generation and then the DNA encoder is presented. To generate the key image Renyi map is used and the DNA encoder is defined with the help of the Tent map. For any chaotic map, initial parameters are required to get the random sequences. The initial parameters can be selected arbitrary, but should be within the domain. In this method, we have generate the initial parameters from the plain image. For this purpose SHA-256 function is applied on the plain image. The reason to use the hash function is discussed later. The initial part of the sequence generated using chaotic map may not be random in nature. For shake of simplicity, we ignore first thousands elements of the sequence and then the rest part is considered as the sequence (which will be used in the experiment) generated by the map. In this implementation it is assumed that when a part of a sequence is used for a particular purpose, then this part will be removed from the sequence and remaining part will be used for future requirement.

Key Image Generation: In this step, we have constructed a key image ($KI_{M \times N}$) using Renyi chaotic map. The size of KI and plain image are same. A sequence $\{S_r\}$ generated using the Renyi map and elements of the sequence is multiplied by a constant '$Fact_1$' which is large enough so that new value is grater than thousand and so. Then, KI computed from new sequence using the following algorithm.

Algorithm 1: Key Image

Input: Sequence $\{S_r\}$, image size M and N
Output: key image $KI_{M \times N}$

Step 1 $x=1$
Step 2 For $p = 1 : M: 1$
Step 2.1　　For $q = 1 : N: 1$
Step 2.1.1　　　$KI_{(p,q)} = int(S_r(x) \times Fact_1, 255)$
Step 2.1.2　　　$x = x + 1$
Step 3 Return KI

---

where '$int\ (u,\ v)$' returns q when $u = q.v + r$.

DNA Encoder: In this section we have converted the plain and key image into DNA encoded images. To convert gray scale value of image into DNA sequence we have to select a rule from the eight DNA encoding rules (which is already illustrated in Sect. 2.2). In this work, each time we have randomly selected a rule using sequences generated by the Ten map. Let, the sequence $\{T_m(r)\}$ is generated using Tent map. Based upon the sequence value $T_m(r)$, i^{th} encoding rule is selected where $i = int(T_m(x) \times Fact_2, 8) + 1$. In the encoding process, we choose pixel-wise encoding rule or row-wise/column-wise encoding rule. For simplicity, in this method, we have fixed the same encoding rule for all pixels of a row. Suppose, the encoding rules (given in Table 1) is stored in the matrix $Rule_{4\times8}$. Also assume that a pixel 'p' is represented by '$p_1p_2p_3p_4p_5p_6p_7p_8$' (binary representation). Respect to t^{th} rule ($1 \leq t \leq 8$), a particular pixel 'p' is encoded as '$X_1X_2X_3X_4$' where $X_i = Rule(dec(p_{(i-1)*2+1}p_{i*2}), t)$, for $1 \leq i \leq 4$ and 'dec()' is decimal to binary converter. The algorithmic flow of the used DNA encoder is as given below:

Algorithm 2: DNA Encoder

Input: $I_{M\times N}$, Tent sequence $\{T_m\}$
Output: Encoded image I_e

Step 1 x=1
Step 1 For $r = 1 : M : 1$ // r^{th} row
Step 1.1 $t = int(T_m(x) \times Fact_2, 8) + 1$ // t^{th} encoding rule
Step 1.2   For $s = 1 : N : 1$
Step 1.2.1 $p = I(r, s)$
Step 1.2.2   For $k = 1 : 4 : 1$ // for $p = (p_1p_2)(p_3p_4)(p_5p_6)(p_7p_8)$
Step 1.2.2.1 $X_k = Rule(dec(p_{(k-1)*2+1}p_{k*2}), t)$
Step 1.2.3 $I_e(r, s) = $ '$X_1X_2X_3X_4$'
Step 1.3 $x = x + 1$
Step 3 Return I_e

3.2 Diffusion Using DNA Operation

From previous step, we have two DNA encoded images in hand and in the present step these two images are diffused (see the Fig. 3). To diffuse the encoded images, we have used base-wise (symbol-wise) addition, subtraction or XOR operations as discussed in Sect. 2.2. In this work, three operations (addition, subtraction or XOR) are defined and result of these operations are also depending on the the encoding rule. Like previous, we can fix the encoding rule as well as the operation pixel-wise, row/column wise (same for all pixels in that row/column). Here, we fix them row-wise, i.e., for each pixel of the row same encoding rule and same operation have used. Henceforth, we use the term 'DNA Operation' to represent the diffusion of DNA encoded images with selection of encoding rule and binary operation. In this step, sequence of the Tent map helps to find the diffused image. Suppose, $Oper_{8 \times 3 \times 4 \times 4}$ is used to store the 'DNA Operation', eight rules, three operations and 4×4 operation table as given in Table 2, 3 and 4. The algorithmic structure of the DNA operation is described as below.

Algorithm 3: DNA Operation

Input: DNA encoded images I_1, I_2 of size $M \times N$, Tent sequence $\{T_m\}$
Output: Diffused image I_d

Step 1 x=1
Step 2 For $i = 1 : M : 1$ // i^{th} row
Step 2.1 $t = int(T_m(x) \times Fact_2, 8) + 1$ // t^{th} encoding rule
Step 2.2 $r = int(T_m(x) \times Fact_2, 3) + 1$ // r^{th} operation
Step 2.2   For $j = 1 : N : 1$
Step 2.2.1 $X = I_1(i,j)$ // $X \leftrightarrow X_1 X_2 X_3 X_4$
Step 2.2.2 $Y = I_2(i,j)$ // $Y \leftrightarrow Y_1 Y_2 Y_3 Y_4$
Step 2.2.3   For $k = 1$ to 4
Step 2.2.3.1 $Z_k = Oper(t, r, X_k, Y_k)$
Step 2.2.4 $I_d(i,j) = \text{`}Z_1 Z_2 Z_3 Z_4\text{'}$
Step 2.3 $x = x + 1$
Step 3 Return I_d

3.3   Generation of Encrypted Image

This is the last step of the proposed algorithm. In this step, diffused image is coded into binary form using DNA decoder. The DNA decoder is the inverse process of DNA encoder and may algorithmically presented as **Algorithm 4: DNA Decoder()**. Due to the space limitation, this algorithm is not presented here. Like DNA encoder, the DNA decoder needs the encoding rule convert the encoded image into binary form. This binary image may be consider as the (final) cipher image or may be consider as an intermediate image and iterated through the DNA encoder, DNA Operation and DNA Decoder as shown as a loop in Fig. 3. The proposed image encryption technique is algorithmically discussed below.

Algorithm 5: Image Encryption

Input: $I_{M \times N}$: plain image, itr: # of iteration
Output: I_{enc}: encrypted image

Step 1 $loop=1$
Step 2 hash=SHA-256(I)
Step 3 $key_1 = f_1(hash)$
Step 4 $key_2 = f_2(hash)$
Step 5 $\{S_r\} \leftarrow Renyi(key_1)$

Step 6 $\{T_m\} \leftarrow Tent(key_2)$
Step 7 $KI \leftarrow$ **Algorithm 1**(S_r, M, N)
Step 8 $KI_e =$ **Algorithm 2**(KI, T_m)
Step 9 $I_e =$ **Algorithm 2**(I, T_m)
Step 10 $I_o =$ **Algorithm 3**(I_e, KI_e, T_m)
Step 11 $I_{enc} =$ **Algorithm 2**(I_o, T_m)
Step 12 If $itr > loop$
Step 12.1 $loop = loop + 1$
Step 12.2 $I = I_{enc}$
Step 12.2   Goto Step 9
step 13 Return I_{enc}

The current method is a private key encryption system and the original image can be retrieved by following the steps in reverse order with inverse operations using same key.

4   Experimental Result and Security Analysis

Here, we have reported the performance of the presented method and also analyze the security of the present method. This method is implemented in MAT-LAB environment.

4.1   Results

To demonstration the performance of this method, we have considered standard grayscale images 'Lena', 'Girlface', 'Barbara' and 'Cameraman'. Size of each image is 512×512. The parameters of the proposed method are set up as: the value of the parameter 'itr' set to 10, '$Fact_1$' set to 2399 (a prime number), '$Fact_2$' is set to 151 (a prime number). To define the keys, we take the hash value of given image and odd positions bit is considered as the key_1 and even positions bit form key_2. The original images are displayed in Fig. 4(a) and the cipher images shown in Fig. 4(b). In Fig. 4(c) and (d), the decrypted images with exact key and different key are illustrated. We have noticed that decryption with incorrect key gives meaningless image and so the achievement of this method is quite good and hence the proposed method can be applied in different applications.

4.2   Security Analysis

Here, the robustness of the proposed method under different different attacks, like differential plaintext attack, statistical attack, brute-force attack etc., have studied.

Histogram Analysis: Histogram analysis measures the defense against statistical attacks. An ideal encryption algorithm will distribute the pixel intensities

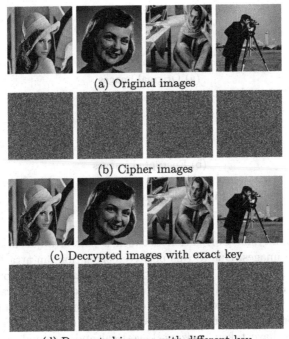

(a) Original images

(b) Cipher images

(c) Decrypted images with exact key

(d) Decrypted images with different key

Fig. 4. Result of the proposed method.

Table 5. Information entropy analysis

Image	Lena	Cameraman	Barbara	Girl face
Original Image	7.4455	7.0753	7.6321	7.0818
Encrypted Image	7.9994	7.9992	7.9993	7.9992

evenly. From an evenly distributed histogram of encrypted images in Fig. 5, we can claim that our proposed algorithm will withstand against statistical attacks.

Information Entropy: The information entropy, which is expressed in bits for given encryption algorithm, is ideally 8 for grayscale images. An encryption algorithm with better information entropy will divulge lesser information to the world. Basically, this is the factor which illustrates the randomness. In case of an 8-bits gray-scale image (I) entropy is calculated with equation $H(I) = -\sum_{p=0}^{255} f(p) log_2 f(p)$ bit, where the $f(p)$ denotes the normalized frequency of occurrences of the intensity p. The comparative analysis of the performance of the proposed method in terms of entropy is reported in Table 5. From this table, it is observed that the present method achieved almost ideal value and hence rate of information disclosure is practically nil. So, any type of entropy attack on encrypted images will get no information.

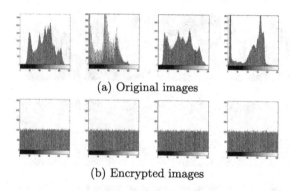

(a) Original images

(b) Encrypted images

Fig. 5. Histogram of images.

Correlation Analysis: Correlation between a pair of adjacent pixels hugely positive in plain images. Due to this positive correlation, an attacker can easily guess the pixel intensity of an adjacent pixel. During encryption, this correlation must be reduced. We are expecting zero (0) correlation value (between two immediate neighbor pixels) for an encrypted image. In Table 6, we have reported the correlation values generated before and after encryption. In case of adjacency, we have taken horizontal, vertical and diagonal adjacent pixels. It is evident from the table that there is very low amount of correlation exists between two adjoined pixels. In implementation, randomly we have chosen 5000 pairs of adjacent pixels and respective distribution diagrams are shown in Fig. 6. From the scattered diagram, we can see that plain image has a huge amount of positive correlation, because of which values generated are alighted at 45°. In contrast to the scattered diagram of original images, it is observed that in case of cipher images points are well distributed all over the area. This implies that two neighboring pixels are not related.

Table 6. Correlation analysis of the images.

Image	Horizontal	Vertical	Diagonal
$Lena_{org}$	0.9851	0.9692	0.9637
$Lena_{enc}$	0.0083	0.0062	−0.0140
$GirlFace_{org}$	0.9868	0.9848	0.9742
$GirlFace_{enc}$	0.0068	0.0190	−0.0199
$Barbara_{org}$	0.9551	0.8934	0.8782
$Barbara_{enc}$	−0.0058	−0.0056	0.0082
$CameraMan_{org}$	0.9900	0.9834	0.9739
$CameraMan_{enc}$	0.0011	0.0138	0.0031

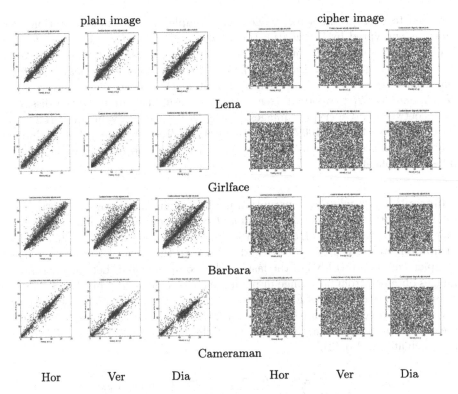

Fig. 6. Scatter diagram of horizontal (= hor), vertical (= ver) and diagonal (= dia) adjacent pixels.

4.3 Key Space Analysis

The proposed method is a symmetric key encryption system and the security of the proposed method depends on the initial parameters of Renyi and Tent maps. Also note that to select the encoding rule or DNA operation, we have used sequence $\{T_m\}$ and parameters '$Fact_1$' and '$Fact_2$'. Someone may consider these two parameters as secret information. In this work, we have taken these as public data. Another important paragenetic is 'itr', which denoted the number iterations the diffusion of the intermediate image will be executed. This can be consider as a private key and it takes some moderate value of size, say, 2^{10}. To initialize the parameters of the chaotic maps, we use SHA-256(I). The space defined by the hash value is 2^{256} and from this value two keys key_1 and key_2 are derived. Therefore, the size of the key space of the present method is (2^{266}), which is notably high and present method can withstand brute-force attacks.

4.4 Key Sensitivity

As per our previous description, the pair $(hash, itr)$ represents the key of the proposed method. To study the robustness, in this experiment, two different keys are used to encrypt the same image. For example, in this implementation, an image is encrypted by $(hash, itr)$, $(hash', itr)$ and $(hash, itr - 1)$. Here, $hash'$ is obtained from $hash$ by complementing the LSB of $hash$. Let these keys give the cipher images Enc_1, Enc_2 and Enc_3. If cipher images are heavily different from other, then it ensures that current method is sensitive to key. The $UACI$ and $NPCR$ parameters (see Eq. (3)) have used to measure the dissimilarity between two encrypted images. Theoretical optimum value of $UACI$ and $NPCR$ are 33.33% and 100%, respectively. From Table 7, it may be concluded that performance of the current method is acceptable and may be applicable to different applications.

Differential Attacks: An encryption method should have power to resist the differential attack, i.e., encryption should return totally dissimilar encrypted image while a very little modification is done in the plain image. In this implementation, we have used two methods: i) where the LSB of the first pixel is complemented and ii) LSB of the last pixel is complemented. Let the encrypted images obtained from no change in plain image, change at first pixel and change at last pixel are denoted as Enc_1, Enc_2 and Enc_3, respectively. Then, the difference in encrypted images are evaluated with UACI and NPCR. These parameters are used to test the strength against the differential attack. UACI and NPCR are calculated in Eq. (3).

$$UACI = \frac{1}{A \times B} \left[\sum_{p,q} \frac{|Enc_1(p,q) - Enc_2(p,q)|}{255} \right] \times 100\%$$

$$NPCR = \frac{\sum_{i,j} Err(i,j)}{A \times B} \times 100\% \tag{3}$$

where $Enc_1(p,q)$ and $Enc_2(p,q)$ are two encrypted images and

$$Err(p,q) = \begin{cases} 1, \text{if } Enc_1(p,q) \neq Enc_2(p,q) \\ 0 \text{ otherwise} \end{cases}$$

The result of the proposed method against the differential attack is presented in Table 8, which shows that UACI and NPCR indexes are very similar to the theoretical values, so it reveals that the encryption algorithm is stable against the differential attack. The keys key_1 and key_2 are obtained from 'hash' of the given image, so for a very small difference in secret image and we have completely different hash value and hence, we have different keys. Different keys means different chaotic sequences. So, different encoding rule, different operation will be selected and as a result we obtained significantly dissimilar encrypted images even if there is a very little modification in the original image.

Table 7. UACI and NCPR values between cipher images, obtained by using different keys.

Image	UACI		NPCR	
	(Enc_1, Enc_2)	(Enc_1, Enc_3)	(Enc_1, Enc_2)	(Enc_1, Enc_3)
Lena	33.4688	33.4990	99.6750	99.6220
Girlface	33.4237	33.4439	99.6201	99.6412
Barbara	33.3982	33.4127	99.6243	99.6184
Camera	33.4537	33.4116	99.6592	99.6313

Table 8. UACI and NCPR values between cipher images, obtained by modifying plain images.

Image	UACI		NPCR	
	(Enc_1, Enc_2)	(Enc_1, Enc_3)	(Enc_1, Enc_2)	(Enc_1, Enc_3)
Lena	33.4473	33.4783	99.6413	99.6137
Girlface	33.4168	33.4228	99.5836	99.6293
Barbara	33.4014	33.4208	99.6073	99.6124
Camera	33.4328	33.4283	99.6346	99.6282

5   Conclusions

Here, a symmetric key image encryption algorithm is proposed. The current method uses Renyi map, Tent map and DNA encoding. Here, the initial parameters are constructed from the secret image itself with the help of SHA-256 hash function for better security. From the performance and analysis of the results it may be noted that the present method is robust against brute force attack, differential attack and statistical attack. Our future target is to modify and extend the current method to make it robust against the plain image attack.

References

1. Alzaidi, A., Ahmad, M., Doja, M., Solami, E., Beg, M.: A new 1D chaotic map and β-hill climbing for generating substitution-boxes. IEEE Access **6**, 55405–55418 (2018)
2. Belazi, A., Talha, M., Kharbech, S., Xiang, W.: Novel medical image encryption scheme based on chaos and DNA encoding. IEEE Access **7**, 36667–36681 (2019)
3. Biswas, P., Kandar, S., Dhara, B.C.: A novel image encryption technique using one dimensional chaotic map and circular shift technique. In: Proceedings of the 6th International Conference on Software and Computer Applications, pp. 112–116 (2017)
4. Biswas, P., Kandar, S., Dhara, B.C.: An image encryption scheme using sequence generated by interval bisection of polynomial function. Multimed. Tools Appl. **79**, 1–24 (2020)

5. Blakley, G., Borosh, I.: Rivest-Shamir-Adleman public key cryptosystems do not always conceal messages. Comput. Math. Appl. **5**(3), 169–178 (1979)
6. Cisse, I.I., Kim, H., Ha, T.: A rule of seven in Watson-Crick base-pairing of mismatched sequences. Nat. Struct. Mol. Biol. **19**(6), 623 (2012)
7. Das, S.K., Dhara, B.C.: An image encryption technique using sine curve. In: 2017 Ninth International Conference on Advances in Pattern Recognition (ICAPR), pp. 1–6. IEEE (2017)
8. Das, S.K., Dhara, B.C.: A new image encryption method using circle. In: 2017 8th International Conference on Computing, Communication and Networking Technologies (ICCCNT), pp. 1–6. IEEE (2017)
9. El Assad, S., Farajallah, M.: A new chaos-based image encryption system. Sig. Process.: Image Commun. **41**, 144–157 (2016)
10. Guesmi, R., Farah, M., Kachouri, A., Samet, M.: A novel chaos-based image encryption using DNA sequence operation and secure hash algorithm SHA-2. Nonlinear Dyn. **83**(3), 1123–1136 (2016). https://doi.org/10.1007/s11071-015-2392-7
11. Kandar, S., Chaudhuri, D., Bhattacharjee, A., Dhara, B.C.: Image encryption using sequence generated by cyclic group. J. Inf. Secur. Appl. **44**, 117–129 (2019)
12. Li, Y., Wang, C., Chen, H.: A hyper-chaos-based image encryption algorithm using pixel-level permutation and bit-level permutation. Opt. Lasers Eng. **90**, 238–246 (2017)
13. Maiti, C., Dhara, B.C.: Image encryption with a new Fibonacci transform. In: 2018 Fifth International Conference on Emerging Applications of Information Technology (EAIT), pp. 1–4. IEEE (2018)
14. NIST FIPS PUB 197: Advanced Encryption Standard (AES) (2001)
15. Ravichandran, D., Praveenkumar, P., Rayappan, J.B.B., Amirtharajan, R.: Chaos based crossover and mutation for securing DICOM image. Comput. Biol. Med. **72**, 170–184 (2016)
16. Sun, S.: A novel hyperchaotic image encryption scheme based on DNA encoding, pixel-level scrambling and bit-level scrambling. IEEE Photon. J. **10**(2), 1–14 (2018)
17. Wang, T., Wang, M.H.: Hyperchaotic image encryption algorithm based on bit-level permutation and DNA encoding. Opt. Laser Technol. **132**, 106355 (2020)
18. Wang, X.Y., Li, P., Zhang, Y.Q., Liu, L.Y., Zhang, H., Wang, X.: A novel color image encryption scheme using DNA permutation based on the Lorenz system. Multimed. Tools Appl. **77**(5), 6243–6265 (2018)
19. Wang, X.Y., Zhang, Y.Q., Bao, X.M.: A novel chaotic image encryption scheme using DNA sequence operations. Opt. Lasers Eng. **73**, 53–61 (2015)
20. Wang, X., Guan, N., Zhao, H., Wang, S., Zhang, Y.: A new image encryption scheme based on coupling map lattices with mixed multi-chaos. Sci. Rep. **10**(1), 1–15 (2020)
21. Wang, X., Wang, Q.: A novel image encryption algorithm based on dynamic s-boxes constructed by chaos. Nonlinear Dyn. **75**(3), 567–576 (2014). https://doi.org/10.1007/s11071-013-1086-2
22. Wang, X., Zhang, H.: A color image encryption with heterogeneous bit-permutation and correlated chaos. Opt. Commun. **342**, 51–60 (2015)
23. Wu, J., Liao, X., Yang, B.: Image encryption using 2D Hénon-Sine map and DNA approach. Sig. Process. **153**, 11–23 (2018)
24. Zhang, Y.: The unified image encryption algorithm based on chaos and cubic S-box. Inf. Sci. **450**, 361–377 (2018)

Computational Intelligence

Modeling and Prediction of COVID-19 in India Using Machine Learning

Arindam Ghosh[1] and Arnab Sadhu[2]([envelope])([ORCID])

[1] Pondicherry University, Pondicherry, India
[2] Vidyasagar University, Medinipur, West Bengal, India
arnabs@mail.vidyasagar.ac.in

Abstract. The inculcation of efficient forecasting and prediction models may assist the government in implementing better design strategies to prevent the spread of the virus. However, most of the machine learning methods along with SEIR models have failed to predict the outcome valid for a longer duration.

In this paper, we propose a simple yet effective method for modeling COVID19 like pandemic based on a non-linear regression curve. With the help of machine learning tools like recurrent neural networks and artificial neural networks, we predict the values of the regression coefficient and regression power. We also evaluate the effectiveness of different measurements taken to combat the pandemic situation in India.

The proposed method outperforms the existing techniques for prediction. This, alongside giving an overview and prediction of the COVID19 in India, would help to model future pandemics.

Keywords: COVID19 · Pandemic progress modeling · Covid19 prediction

1 Introduction

The World Health Organization (WHO) declared novel coronavirus 2019 (COVID-19), an infectious epidemic caused by SARS-CoV-2, as a pandemic in March 2020. As many as 217 countries in the world are halted by the pandemic. The numbers are still increasing as there is no full-proved tested antidote or vaccine available to date. Frequent sanitization, wearing a mask, and social distancing has been ordered as safety measurements across all societies worldwide. In most parts of the world, lock-down has been accepted as a measurement to adjourn the community spread. Almost in all the affected countries, the number of infected and deceased patients has been enhancing at a distressing rate.

The outbreak of every infectious disease parade in certain patterns. Underlying such patterns are the transmission dynamics of such outbreaks. To make a successful prediction of the infection outbreak it is necessary to assess the transmission dynamics. Any outbreak such as COVID-19 in a country or a large geographical area usually occurs at different levels of magnitude concerning time.

© Springer Nature Switzerland AG 2021
P. Dutta et al. (Eds.): CICBA 2021, CCIS 1406, pp. 59–67, 2021.
https://doi.org/10.1007/978-3-030-75529-4_5

There may be various reasons behind that such as seasonal changes, an adaptation of viruses over time, or some external factors like precautional measurements.

In essence, it is now worthy to look back and investigate the success of precautional measurements taken in different communities. This investigation can be useful to make a further prediction to contaminate the spread of the virus. With the kind of large dataset in our hand, the Machine Learning (ML) based intelligent prediction and diagnosis tools come into play [5]. The day-wise COVID19 spread dataset is in nature a time-series dataset. Time series forecasting method Long Short-Term Memory (LSTM) network has been adopted by Azarafza et al. [7] on COVID-19 time series of Iran. Chimmula et al. [8] has applied LSTM on the COVID-19 time series of Canada. Tomar et al. [4] has applied LSTM on COVID-19 time series of India.

The mathematical model of epidemics, Susceptible-Exposed-Infectious-Removed, or popularly known as the SEIR model, has been adopted for current COVID-19 epidemic data. SEIR models are hybridized with an ML-based method. Yang et al. [1] applied SEIR hybridized with LSTM. Tuli et al. [2] and Pinter et al. [6] hybridized it with Artificial Neural Network (ANN). Pandey et al. [3] applied SEIR hybridized with the regression model on COVID-19 data of India.

All these data-driven methods were utilized for forecasting/estimation of the possible number of positive cases and recovered cases of COVID-19. However, as the pandemic progresses and different measurements were taken by the government and authorities, a few changes become inevitable. Firstly, the rate of progress of the epidemic was changing frequently. Essentially, a plain LSTM technique applied to the number of infected or recovered people is not enough for successful prediction. The SEIR model can interpret the dependencies among the suspected, exposed, infected, and removed or deceased cases. But the effects of preventing measures like social isolation and lock-down are yet to be explored.

In the current work, we propose a model that explores the dependencies among the numbers of infected and recovered cases. We also take into consideration the external factors like lock-down, the transmission of population, and the number of tests as well. We use a power growth function to model the cumulative numbers of infected and recovered people throughout time. The function has a coefficient, a variable raised to a fixed real number, and an additive constant. We call these internal parameters. The external parameters are lock-down status, the number of people transmitted, and the number of tests. Objective of our model is to predict number of infection and recovery cases and *plateau* stage of the pandemic. We take a holistic approach by taking all these internal and external parameters to train an ANN. Finally, we predict the internal parameters under a future condition with the help of the trained ANN.

The manuscript is structured as follows: In Sect. 2.1, we discuss the source of data and the representation of the dataset in detail. In Sect. 2.2, we discuss the proposed method in details. In Sect. 3, we apply the method on the dataset and present the result. In Sect. 4, we discuss the obtained result and present a comparative analysis of the result with other methods applied on COVID-19 datasets. In Sect. 5 we present the future work and conclude.

2   Materials and Method

2.1   Dataset Description

COVID-19 related all the data (day-wise cumulative numbers of confirmed (I), active, deceased, and recovered (R) patients) are collected from the bulletin of Govt. of India (https://www.covid19india.org/). We present the numbers graphically in Fig. 1.

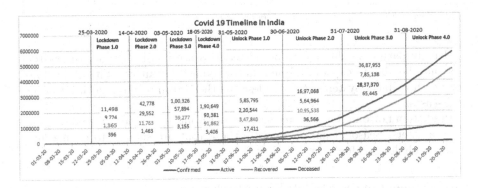

Fig. 1. COVID19 spread in India

The transmission of people has been a huge factor since the beginning of the spread of COVID-19 in India. Here, we concentrate only on the inter-state transmission as it is almost impossible to collect a gross approximation of nationwide local transmissions. Initially, while in the nation-wide complete lockdown merely few people could make such movements. But in the later phases of lock-downs, a few special trains were arranged to run inter-state passengers. The number of such special trains were increased gradually in the unlock phases. Local bus, inter-state bus services, and private vehicles were also allowed to move from the later phases, but they have merely moved across states. We have collected and approximated the data of the passenger transportation from legitimate sources like Times of India and Hindustan times that are pipelined to Indian railways. We present the data in Table 1.

2.2   Method

We have assessed that the accuracy of forecasting is compromised because of the dynamic as well as the temporal nature of the COVID-19 spread. Here we have the following two things to deal with:

Table 1. Data of passenger transportation by Indian railways after lockdown period

Date	No. of trains operated	No. of passenger (Approx.)	Remarks	Reference
12-May-2020	30	30,000	Rajdhani Special Train	Times of India (May 11, 2020)
01-Jun-2020	230	1,85,000	30 Rajdhani Special and 200 Express Special Train	Times of India (May 31, 2020)
12-Sep-2020	310	2,80,000	80 new Special Express along with existing 230 trains	Times of India (Sep 5, 2020)
21-Sep-2020	350	3,15,000	40 new clone train with existing 310 special trains	Hindustan Times (Sep 15, 2020)

Note: Some trains are operated as bi-weekly or tri-weekly

– Usually patterns exhibited in such scenarios are non-linear. So, the system should be able to capture the non-linear dynamic changes. With the help of these non-linear systems, we can describe the transmission of such infectious diseases.
– Prediction not only involves recent past data but also some external seasonal parameters. Seasonal parameters are those that are subject to change in a relatively longer duration.

Establishment of the Model. We use the following nonlinear curve to explain the dynamics of disease spreading

$$I = \alpha D^\beta + \gamma \tag{1}$$

It is a power growth function where I is the number of people infected or recovered whichever is concerned. D is the number of days and α, β, γ are temporal constants. Temporal constants are constants but only for a certain temporary time period. The values of temporal constants will change according to the external parameters. The power here, β, largely controls the growth of the function. A larger value of β, while modeling infected cases, signifies a catastrophic increase in the number. That means the situation is getting worse. Whereas, $\beta < 1$ means the daily number is decreasing. This is often referred to as the *plateau* stage of an epidemic. Mathematically, α and γ are scale factor and offset respectively of the curve in Eq. 1. In the current scenario, these two temporal constants introduce a secondary level of variation in I. This makes the prediction results more robust.

We take into consideration three external seasonal parameters: lockdown status (LD), number of tests (TS), and transmission of the population (PT). For PT, we have relied only upon data shared by the Indian government. Data on other modes of transmission are not available from any reliable source. We had to approximate PT due to the limited availability of data.

We divide the whole time-line (right from the day of the first reported case of COVID-19 in India up to August 31, 2020) into different bins depending upon external seasonal parameters. We then fit the observed data in each of the bins by a nonlinear curve as in Eq. 1. We then assess the values of three dynamic constants α, β, and γ. The cumulative number of confirmed and deceased cases at a certain day depends upon the dynamic constants.

The trend of change in the values of the dynamic constants concerning the seasonal parameters is captured by our proposed model. This is further explained in the Result and Discussions sections.

Prediction. We predict the number of infected and recovered cases in the near future by a two-fold method. First, we employ a Recurrent Neural Network (RNN) to understand the trend in the individual dynamic constants. Then in the second fold, we utilize an ANN. We train a two-layer regression neural network with five inputs for predicting a single dynamic variable at a time. Among the five inputs to the neural network, three are the estimated external constants. Here we transform the lockdown status (LD), which is a categorical variable, into one-hot encoded input. Two other inputs to the neural network are the remaining subset of dynamic constants. For example, while training for α the input vector is $\{LD, TS, PT, \beta, \gamma\}$.

We apply the trained ANN with known values of external seasonal parameters and assess a set of values of the dynamic constants. This time, we use the values of the dynamic constants which are obtained from the RNN previously. For example, while predicting α the input vector is $\{L\acute{D}, T\acute{S}, P\acute{T}, \acute{\beta}, \acute{\gamma}\}$, where are obtained from the RNNs as outputs. To evaluate the final predicted value, we have two outputs: one predicted value from the RNN and the other one from the ANN. We detect the trend of the dynamic constants from the predicted value of RNN and apply a nonlinear function on RNN and ANN to get the final predicted values.

3   Result

We have implemented the method on Python 3.6. To build the model, we divide the whole timespan from 1st March 2020 to 31st August 2020 into eight bins. The partitioning of the bins depends upon the external parameter lock-down phase (LD). Here we convert LD into a hot encoded number. In the initial lock-down phase of 24 days, it was a complete nation wise lockdown, that was further increased to 55 more days in three more phases. In each of the phases, some relaxations were added. We put weightage on the strictness of lockdown phases. So, a higher value of LD means more strictness and a lower value of LD signifies more relaxations. Based upon the decrement in strictness, we encode the phases as $LD = 1.0, 0.9, 0.8$ and 0.7 respectively. The zone-based lockdown was enforced from 19th May 2020 for 13 days. We encode this period as $LD = 0.6$. The unlocking procedure was started on 1st June 2020 and it is continuing to date in different phases gradually adding relaxations. We have worked upon the dataset till 31st August 2020 (unlock phase 3). So, we encode these phases as $LD = 0.4, 0.3$, and 0.2 respectively. A lot of relaxation were added from the initial unlocking phases themselves. So, we deliberately skip $LD = 0.5$ to emphasize the differences between lockdown and unlock phases. Now as the bins are ready for eight different values of LD, we fit the curve formed with the data points (number of infected people) to the 1 and find out the values of α, β, and γ. We repeat the same process for the number of recovered people as well. We present the complete result in Table 2.

Table 2. Formation of the model

Phase	Starting date	No. of days	Infected cases			Recovered cases		
			α	β	γ	α	β	γ
Initial	01-03-2020	24	0.000513	4.363	31.32	0.00348	2.867	2.41
lockdown 1.0	25-03-2020	21	0.000906	4.309	−531.9	3.672e−08	6.398	13.0
lockdown 2.0	25-03-2020	19	0.03119	3.404	−1841	0.001376	3.882	−2482
lockdown 3.0	04-05-2020	15	0.08429	3.231	−1.416e04	8.522e−10	7.173	4567
zone based lockdown	19-05-2020	13	0.009126	3.743	−1.45e04	5.044e−10	7.22	1.419e04
Unlock 1.0	01-06-2020	30	0.000246	4.479	4.078e04	4.045e−07	5.707	2.466e04
Unlock 2.0	01-07-2020	31	6.543e−08	6.113	2.198e05	3.546e−08	6.154	1.119e05
Unlock 3.0	01-08-2020	31	4.145	2.688	−1.403e06	1.773	2.821	−1.492e06

We use the value of α, β, and γ to predict the number of confirmed and recovered cases during the unlock 4.0 phase. For prediction purposes, we use both RNN and ANN. From the LSTM RNN, we get the trend of change of the parameters. Whereas, in the trained ANN we supply the values of external parameters and alternate temporal constants to get the final predicted values of α, β, and γ.

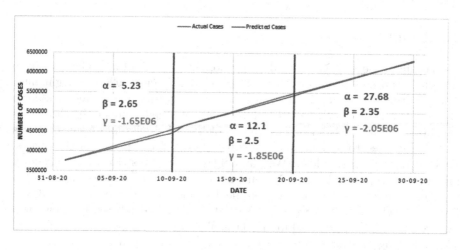

Fig. 2. Prediction of confirmed cases in September, 2020

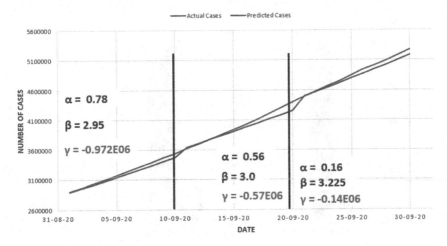

Fig. 3. Prediction of recovery cases in September, 2020

However, to get an accurate day-wise prediction a smoothening function is needed to be applied on the curve. To achieve this, we split our test data i.e. 30 days unlock phase 4.0 into three equal-sized bins. Following the trends from RNN, we gradually change the values of the temporal constants through the three test phases. As a result, each bin has different values of α, β and γ as shown in the Fig. 2 and Fig. 3. This gives almost accurate forecasting of the COVID-19 pandemic all over India. For confirmed cases, the parameter value is following a trend as, α and γ are increasing and β is decreasing. The waning of β signifies a decrease in COVID19 cases from mid-September to October. Whereas in the recovery field, α and γ are decreasing and β is increasing. This indicates an increment in the recovery rate. As a result, the overall infection rate is going to reduce.

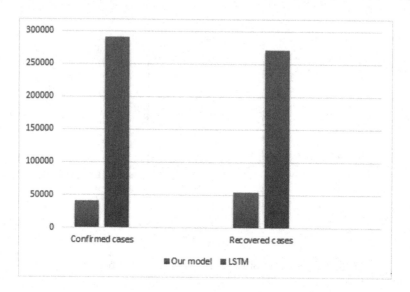

Fig. 4. Comparison of RMSE of prediction between our model and LSTM model

4   Discussion

We present a comparative analysis of predictive results from our model and plain LSTM based approach. We implement an RNN with an LSTM layer in Python 3.6 and train it with five inputs. We compare the prediction of both confirmed and recovered cases with the prediction of our model. Figure 2 and Fig. 3 show the actual cases, LSTM based prediction and Curve fitting with regression-based prediction for confirmed and recovered cases. As shown in the figures, the proposed method of a regression model with LSTM and ANN-based prediction result is closer to actual cases than that of the plain LSTM. Our proposed model produces a comparatively better result than the LSTM model for forecasting the COVID-19 pandemic. We also find the Root Mean Squared Error rate of prediction for both the confirmed and recovered cases done by our model and plain LSTM based approach. As displayed in Fig. 4 RMSE of our model is much lower than that of the simple LSTM model.

5   Conclusion

According to the proposed model, given the similar external conditions, the downward trend of confirmed cases, and the upward trend of recovery cases are likely to continue for the next thirty days as well. Moreover, we find by the prediction analysis that, India has passed the peak of the disease and has achieved the plateau stage. The current research has been conducted with the available reliable data up to September 2020. And as of December 2020, the prediction of the proposed model has been promising. Hence the model has the potentiality to be applied to predict such pandemics in the future.

References

1. Yang, Z., et al.: Modified SEIR and AI prediction of the epidemics trend of COVID-19 in China under public health interventions. J. Thoracic Dis. **12**(3) (2020). https://doi.org/10.21037/jtd.2020.02.64. http://jtd.amegroups.com/article/view/36385
2. Tuli, S., Tuli, S., Tuli, R., Gill, S.S.: Predicting the growth and trend of Covid-19 pandemic using machine learning and cloud computing. Internet Things 1–16 (2020). https://doi.org/10.1016/j.iot.2020.100222
3. Gupta, R., Pandey, G., Chaudhary, P., Pal, S.: SEIR and regression model based covid-19 outbreak predictions in India. medRxiv (2020). https://doi.org/10.1101/2020.04.01.20049825. https://www.medrxiv.org/content/early/2020/04/03/2020.04.01.20049825
4. Tomar, A., Gupta, N.: Prediction for the spread of Covid-19 in India and effectiveness of preventive measures. Sci. Total Environ. **728** (2020). https://doi.org/10.1016/j.scitotenv.2020.138762. http://www.sciencedirect.com/science/article/pii/S0048969720322798
5. Sujath, R., Chatterjee, J.M., Hassanien, A.E.: A machine learning forecasting model for COVID-19 pandemic in India. Stochast. Environ. Res. Risk Assess. **34**(7), 959–972 (2020). https://doi.org/10.1007/s00477-020-01827-8
6. Pinter, G., Felde, I., Mosavi, A., Ghamisi, P., Gloaguen, R.: Covid-19 pandemic prediction for Hungary; a hybrid machine learning approach. Mathematics **8**(6), 890 (2020). https://doi.org/10.3390/math8060890
7. Azarafza, M., Azarafza, M., Tanha, J.: Covid-19 infection forecasting based on deep learning in Iran, pp. 1–7. medRxiv. https://doi.org/10.1101/2020.05.16.20104182
8. Chimmula, V.K.R., Zhang, L.: Time series forecasting of Covid-19 transmission in Canada using LSTM networks. Chaos Solitons Fractals **135**, 1–6 (2020). https://doi.org/10.1016/j.chaos.2020.109864

Exploring Hand-Crafted Features and Transfer Learning for Polyp Segmentation

Shyam Janam Mahato, Debapriya Banik$^{(\boxtimes)}$, and Debotosh Bhattacharjee

Department of Computer Science and Engineering, Jadavpur University,
Kolkata 700032, India
debotosh.bhattacharjee@jadavpuruniversity.in

Abstract. One of the major causes of cancer-related mortality is colorectal cancer (CRC). CRC is the third most frequent cause of cancer world-wide following lung cancer and breast cancer. So, the diagnosis of CRC by localization and removal of colorectal polyp has become a significant public health concern worldwide. The "gold standard" considered for the early diagnosis of CRC is colonoscopy. During colonoscopy examination, clinicians examine the intestinal wall to detect polyps. The methodology is lethargic, expensive and removal of non-cancerous polyps deteriorates the proficiency of the system. In this study, we explored vision-based measurement techniques which include image processing and computational intelligence for automatic segmentation of polyps which acts as a primary step for in-vivo malignancy diagnosis. We explored and extracted various features such as texture features, histogram-based features along with traditional filters from the colonoscopy frames. The extracted features were trained using five unique classifiers to provide adequacy of those features. The segmentation output is further refined using a post-processing step. We have also explored some of the baseline deep learning models for comparative analysis.

Keywords: Colorectal cancer · Polyp · Segmentation · Machine learning · Deep learning

1 Introduction

Colorectal cancer (CRC) is the third most dominant form of cancer found in men and women in western countries and is the second highest cause of mortality from cancer. As per the Globocan 2019 report, the CRC cases in India stands out to be 19,548 deaths out of 27,605 new colon cancer cases and 20,056 deaths out of 24,251 new rectal cancer cases. Moreover, it's expected to cause about 44,020 deaths by 2035 [1]. Recently, the development of various sophisticated medical equipment and sensors has increased the frequency of screening and removal of polyp before they can form into malignant growths. Polyps are

© Springer Nature Switzerland AG 2021
P. Dutta et al. (Eds.): CICBA 2021, CCIS 1406, pp. 68–76, 2021.
https://doi.org/10.1007/978-3-030-75529-4_6

strange tissue developments in the inner lining of the colorectum. The term colorectal malignant growth usually describe colon malignancy, rectum malignancy, or both. Early diagnosis of CRC is highly treatable with a survival rate of more than 90% if it is unlikely to spread through lymph nodes in close proximity. However, the treatment becomes more complex when the disease has spread to the liver, the lungs, or other organs through the lymph nodes. Colonoscopy is recommended as an essential approach to manual colorectal screening. During the examination, a camera is being used to explore the colorectum to detect and remove the polyp accordingly. Some different variations of polyps are shown in Fig. 1.

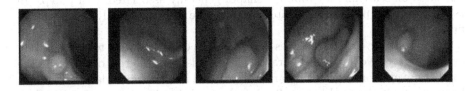

Fig. 1. Different variations of polyps in terms of shapes and sizes.

Automatic diagnosis of polyps using computer-aided techniques is much more challenging due to the immense variability of polyps with respect to shape, size, texture, and color [4]. Furthermore, the polyp frames are prone to several artifacts such as specular highlights, the bending veins dispersed over the polyps, and the inadequate illumination that covers the regions of interest. These artifacts may hinder further processing of the frames and may result in miss-diagnosis of polyps.

This study aims to create a superior, adaptable, and strong automated polyp segmentation system by mitigating such artifacts which may become possible in clinical practice. The normal approach to deal with the diagnosis of CRC is to conduct traditional screening of the colorectum and removal of polyps using colonoscopy, which is the decision-making screening tool. However, the removal of non-cancerous polyps deteriorates the proficiency of the system. Hence, automatic segmentation of polyps acts as a primary step for in-vivo malignancy diagnosis by incorporating an optical biopsy. The polyp segmentation strategy can diminish those downsides by structuring the decision support systems (DSS) to help clinicians to decide the further course of treatment.

The rest of the paper is arranged in the following way. We elaborately discussed a few recent related research works in Sect. 2 . The proposed framework is explained in detail in Sect. 3. The detailed experimental evaluation of the proposed network is in Sect. 4, and the finally concluding remarks are in Sect. 5.

2   Literature Review

During the last decades, automatic segmentation of polyps from colonoscopy frames has been an important research subject, and several methodologies have been proposed. However, the task is still underdeveloped and cannot mitigate error rates. Deep learning approaches have recently become very common in the field of medical image analysis. Traditional methods of machine learning generally uses low-level image processing methods to obtain polyp boundaries. In [9], authors have used Hessian filters whereas, in [6] authors have introduced strength of valleys. In another work, [18] have used Hough transform. In [2] authors have analyzes curvatures of detected boundaries whereas, in [10] concentrated on searching for rounded shapes generally associated with polyps. In [8] authors have proposed a strategy to combine curvature analysis with form-fitting.

Deep learning (DL) techniques generally uses different layers to progressively extract higher-level features to train their models from the raw data. Using the feedback of previous layers, the various layers will learn different data abstraction before they hit the final layer, allowing the final decision for the class. CNN is a DL technique which uses different kernels and pooling strategies to extract complex features from the raw image [14]. In [19] authors have reviewed different CNN architectures and proposed a calibration technique for the segmentation of colonoscopy polyps. In [12], CNN is used as an extractor of components for polyp segmentation in three scales. For each information fix, CNN measures 60 highlights, at which point a completely associated layer with 256 neurons is used to define each data fix. In addition, the Gaussian channel is used to smooth outcomes of the division and rising commotion in the wake of conducting CNN. The suggested strategy in [14] uses a CNN architecture to separate highlights from RGB patches. A new era of CNN uses deconvolution layers to generate likelihood maps in picture division assignments. The current approach is achieved by supplanting with deconvolution a fully related layer and using past layer data to improve division accuracy. FCN [12] and U-Net [15] are two driving strategies currently in use. In some applications, the technique of polyp division is a blend of more than one CNN, called "collection of CNN's", to defeat the assorted variety of forms in polyps and their powers. The suggested technique utilizes three CNNs to coordinate patches for inputs. It makes use of the policy to extricate districts of competitors. It then extricates three patch arrangements around each applicant's locale and fed them to the related CNN organization. These three patch arrangements are split according to shading, surface, fleeting highlights, and shape hints. It also displays the most extreme scores of each of the three CNNs and the fully connected layer for ordering the patches. CNN preparation is a difficult issue in clinical applications due to impediments in the testing of databases.

In this paper, we studied and extracted different hand-crafted features from the polyp frames. The features are fed into various traditional classifiers for the segmentation of the polyp region. We have explored different traditional classifiers to judge the best performing classifier for the polyp segmentation task.

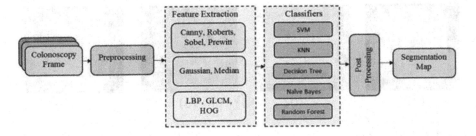

Fig. 2. Flow diagram of our method.

We also compared the ML techniques to some baseline CNN models specifically designed for the segmentation task.

3   Proposed Methodology

This section elaborately describes our polyp segmentation method. The workflow is illustrated in Fig. 2. The steps are elaborately explained in the upcoming subsections.

3.1   Preprocessing

During the clinical examination, the amount of light reflected from the shiny surface of the GI tract generates specular highlights [16]. When a light source falls directly on an object the light is reflected and the camera captures it. This process creates highly saturated areas in the image termed as specular highlights, which contributes to the undesirable outliers, making it difficult to further process the image. Hence, this effect is very much important to be removed before further processing. The removal of specular highlights is a multi-step method as shown in Fig. 3. In the 1st step, the original RGB image as in Fig. 3(a) is converted to greyscale as shown in Fig. 3(b). Next, to detect the specular highlights from the greyscale image, the image median value (μ) is measured on a greyscale, which is then multiplied by a weight (W) that was experimentally chosen as 0.3. The difference between the greyscale image pixels and the median value(μ) will give a binary specular mask, based on the threshold value(U) which is set to 95, showing the locations of the specular highlights as in Fig. 3(c). A structuring element of a morphological structure of size 5*5, 3*3 depending on the thresholded image undergoes multiple iterations. A mask is created, as a result of this operation. After the dilation of the specular highlighting mask, we reconstruct the image regions indicated by the mask via an inpainting algorithm, as shown in Fig. 3(d).

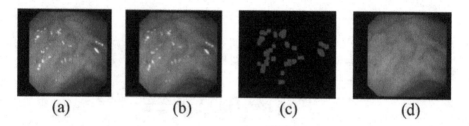

Fig. 3. (a) Original RGB image (b) Greyscale image (c) Detection of specular highlights (d) Reconstructed image without specular highlights.

3.2   Feature Extraction

In the subsection, we have discussed about the significant and meaningful hand-crafted features that were extracted from the pre-processed image. The extracted features significantly contribute in the prediction of the region of interest (polyp). The extracted standard features are essentially texture dependent and gradient dependent. We have eliminated the inessential features to minimize the time and space complexity. The gradient or edged-based features extracted are: Canny with kernel size 5, Sobel with kernel size 7, Prewitt, Roberts, Gaussian with sigma 3, and 7, Median with sigma 3. Such filters were used to get the edge or gradient information to estimate the difference in the area of polyps and non-polyps. Some of the texture features that are considered are Local Binary Patterns (LBP) [13], Gray-Level Co-Occurrence Matrix (GLCM) [17], and Histogram of oriented gradients (HOG) [7].

3.3   Classification

We fed the extracted features on some commonly used classifiers as a part of traditional machine learning(ML) strategy. Although SVM appears to be the most popular classifier and has achieved very good performance in the task of image segmentation, there are no single methods of classification that outperform all others on all datasets. So we decided to test some of the different state-of-the-art classifiers together to assess their output on our dataset. Some of the standard classifiers that are also considered in this study for comparative analysis are: Random forest, Decision tree, KNN, and Naive Bayes classifiers.

3.4   Post Processing

Some of the false-positive regions i.e. non-polyp regions were identified from the segmentation result obtained by different classifiers. To address such drawback, we have ignored the connected regions with less than 10 pixels and then applying hole filling operation [11] to get the final mask.

4   Experimental Results and Discussion

This section evaluates the efficiency of the various traditional ML classifiers mentioned in the previous section. In Subsect. 4.1, we have described the dataset used in this study. In the next subsection, we qualitatively and quantitatively compared the efficiency of the different classifiers along with some baseline pre-trained CNN models generally used in medical image segmentation. The work is implemented using Python 3.5.

4.1   Database Description

In this study, we have considered a benchmark public dataset namely CVC-COLON DB having 300 polyp frames with 574×500 pixels [5,6]. Most of the frames in the dataset are prone to specular highlights. We have divided the dataset into non-intersecting frames where 70% are considered for training, 10% for validation, and rest 20% for testing.

4.2   Qualitative and Quantitative Evaluation

Qualitative Evaluation. This subsection demonstrates the effectiveness of the extracted handcrafted features in the segmentation of the polyps. We have considered polyp frames showing polyps with different shapes, sizes, directions, and shades to legitimize the viability of the various techniques. The first row in Fig. 4 shows the pre-processed images and the ground-truth which are manually outlined by the experts is shown in the next row, while in the following successive rows the segmentation results of the different classifiers are shown. In the 3rd row, we have shown the result of the SVM classifier which outperforms other traditional machine learning classifiers. In the 4th row, 5th row, 6th row, and 7th row we have shown the segmented image by Random Forest, Decision Tree, KNN, and Naive Bayes classifiers. It can be visually perceived that the segmentation output produced by the SVM classifier agrees well with the ground-truth.

Quantitative Evaluation. This subsection demonstrates the quantitative evaluation of the output of different machine learning (ML) classifiers using different metrics such as dice coefficient (DS), precision (Pre), and recall (Rec). The results concerning the comparison of different ML and DL methods are mentioned in Table 1. It can be seen that the SVM classifier exhibits the highest DS amongst the ML classifiers and also Pre and Rec value of SVM is better than the other traditional ML classifiers. However, the pre-trained DL models namely U-net [15] and SegNet [3] exhibit the highest DS and Rec. Since traditional machine learning is very time-consuming to train a model in comparison to the transfer learning approach, so nowadays transfer learning-based approach using pre-trained models is used to precisely segment medical images. A flexible decision boundary in the data space has been provided by using different variety of features which reduces the problem of overfitting and also improves segmentation performance.

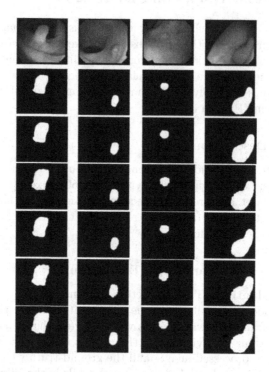

Fig. 4. Qualitative evaluation of segmentation results Row 1. Pre-processed image Row 2. Ground truth Row 3. SVM classifier output Row 4. Random Forest classifier output Row 5. Decision tree classifier output Row 6. KNN classifier output Row 7. Naive Bayes classifier output.

Table 1. Comparative analysis of different ML and DL models on CVC-Colon DB. (Bold for best performing methods)

ML/DL Model	DC↑	Pre↑	Rec↑
SVM	0.67	**0.79**	0.59
Random Forest	0.63	0.63	0.58
Decision Tree	0.61	0.61	0.55
KNN	0.69	0.67	0.45
Naive Bayes	0.59	0.45	0.67
U-net	**0.74**	0.76	**0.69**
SegNet	0.70	0.75	0.66

5 Conclusion

In this paper, we compared both handcrafted and deep learning-based methods for automatic polyp segmentation. We have extracted various hand-crafted features from the polyp frames and evaluated using different traditional ML classifiers for the segmentation of the polyp region. Each of the evaluated classifiers was tested by dividing the images into a non-intersecting train, validate and test set on a publicly accessible dataset. We introduced different classifier characteristics for evaluation purposes, but our goal in designing the classifier was to optimize the performance metric that is most important in finding the exact position of the polyp in the image. As illustrated in Table 1, among various classification techniques, the best classification performance was exhibited by SVM classifier using traditional machine learning techniques although Deep learning based approach by pre-trained models like U-net and SegNet. Therefore, we will aim at reducing the time and complexity of the ML model by enhancing the feature extraction process.

Acknowledgement. The second author is thankful to CSIR for the award of SRF (ACK No. 143416/2K17/1, File No. 09/096(0922)2K18 EMR-I). All the authors are thankful for the Indo-Austrian joint project grant No. INT /AUSTRIA /BMWF /P-25 /2018 funded by the DST, GOI, and the SPARC project (ID: 231) funded by MHRD, GOI.

References

1. Crc fact sheet. http://gco.iarc.fr/today/data/factsheets/populations/356-india-fact-sheets.pdf. Accessed 31 Mar 2020
2. Albregtsen, F., et al.: Statistical texture measures computed from gray level coocurrence matrices. Image processing laboratory, department of informatics, university of oslo 5(5) (2008)
3. Badrinarayanan, V., Kendall, A., Cipolla, R.: Segnet: a deep convolutional encoder-decoder architecture for image segmentation. IEEE Trans. Pattern Anal. Mach. Intell. **39**(12), 2481–2495 (2017)
4. Banik, D., Bhattacharjee, D., Nasipuri, M.: A multi-scale patch-based deep learning system for polyp segmentation. In: Chaki, R., Cortesi, A., Saeed, K., Chaki, N. (eds.) Advanced Computing and Systems for Security, vol. 1136, pp. 109–119. Springer, Heidelberg (2020). https://doi.org/10.1007/978-981-15-2930-6_9
5. Bernal, J., Sánchez, F.J., Fernández-Esparrach, G., Gil, D., Rodríguez, C., Vilariño, F.: Wm-dova maps for accurate polyp highlighting in colonoscopy: validation vs. saliency maps from physicians. Comput. Med. Imaging Graph. **43**, 99–111 (2015)
6. Bernal, J., Sánchez, J., Vilarino, F.: Towards automatic polyp detection with a polyp appearance model. Pattern Recogn. **45**(9), 3166–3182 (2012)
7. Dadi, H.S., Pillutla, G.M.: Improved face recognition rate using hog features and SVM classifier. IOSR J. Electron. Commun. Eng. **11**(4), 34–44 (2016)
8. Hwang, S., Oh, J., Tavanapong, W., Wong, J., De Groen, P.C.: Polyp detection in colonoscopy video using elliptical shape feature. In: 2007 IEEE International Conference on Image Processing, vol. 2, pp. II-465. IEEE (2007)

9. Iwahori, Y., Hattori, A., Adachi, Y., Bhuyan, M.K., Woodham, R.J., Kasugai, K.: Automatic detection of polyp using hessian filter and hog features. Procedia Comput. Sci. **60**, 730–739 (2015)

10. Kang, J., Doraiswami, R.: Real-time image processing system for endoscopic applications. In: CCECE 2003-Canadian Conference on Electrical and Computer Engineering. Toward a Caring and Humane Technology (Cat. No. 03CH37436), vol. 3, pp. 1469–1472. IEEE (2003)

11. Liu, S., Chen, C., Kehtarnavaz, N.: A computationally efficient denoising and hole-filling method for depth image enhancement. In: Real-Time Image and Video Processing 2016. vol. 9897, p. 98970V. International Society for Optics and Photonics (2016)

12. Long, J., Shelhamer, E., Darrell, T.: Fully convolutional networks for semantic segmentation. In: Proceedings of the IEEE Conference on Computer Vision and Pattern Recognition, pp. 3431–3440 (2015)

13. Prakasa, E.: Texture feature extraction by using local binary pattern. INKOM J. **9**(2), 45–48 (2016)

14. Ribeiro, E., Uhl, A., Häfner, M.: Colonic polyp classification with convolutional neural networks. In: 2016 IEEE 29th International Symposium on Computer-Based Medical Systems (CBMS), pp. 253–258. IEEE (2016)

15. Ronneberger, O., Fischer, P., Brox, T.: U-net: convolutional networks for biomedical image segmentation. In: Navab, N., Hornegger, J., Wells, W.M., Frangi, A.F. (eds.) MICCAI 2015. LNCS, vol. 9351, pp. 234–241. Springer, Cham (2015). https://doi.org/10.1007/978-3-319-24574-4_28

16. Sánchez-González, A., Soto, B.G.Z.: Colonoscopy image pre-processing for the development of computer-aided diagnostic tools. In: Surgical Robotics. IntechOpen (2017)

17. Sebastian V, B., Unnikrishnan, A., Balakrishnan, K.: Gray level co-occurrence matrices: generalisation and some new features. arXiv preprint arXiv:1205.4831 (2012)

18. Silva, J., Histace, A., Romain, O., Dray, X., Granado, B.: Toward embedded detection of polyps in WCE images for early diagnosis of colorectal cancer. Int. J. Comput. Assist. Radiol. Surg. **9**(2), 283–293 (2014)

19. Tajbakhsh, N., Gurudu, S.R., Liang, J.: Automatic polyp detection in colonoscopy videos using an ensemble of convolutional neural networks. In: 2015 IEEE 12th International Symposium on Biomedical Imaging (ISBI), pp. 79–83. IEEE (2015)

A Novel Equilibrium Optimization Technique for Band Selection of Hyperspectral Images

Aditi Roy Chowdhury[1]([⊠]), Joydev Hazra[2], Kousik Dasgupta[3], and Paramartha Dutta[4]

[1] Women's Polytechnic, Kolkata, India
[2] Heritage Institute of Technology, Kolkata, India
[3] Kalyani Government Engineering College, Kalyani, Nadia, India
[4] Visvabharati University, Santiniketan, India

Abstract. Band selection of hyperspectral images is a rising research area. Because of the shortage of the labeled information set of hyperspectral imagery, it is additionally challenging task. Band selection problem can be seen as a two-way problem i.e. optimization of the number of chosen bands as well as optimization of the chosen bands itself. In this article, a novel strategy primarily based on Equilibrium Optimization (EO) is proposed. The Equilibrium Law of any object acts as the motivation in favour of this method. This technique suggests a persuasive result in assessment with other popular methods like MI (Mutual Information), WaLuDi (Wards linkage strategy using divergence), TMI (Trivariate MI), ACO (Ant Colony Optimization), and DE (Differential Evolution) for different datasets like Botswana, KSC, etc.

Keywords: Hyperspectral · Band selection · Equilibrium Optimization · Equilibrium pool · Generation rate

1 Introduction

Hyperspectral imagery are described by lots of bands received in adjacent spectral range and slender spectrum interval. A hyperspectral imagery may be considered as a data dice, wherein the primary dimensions x, y denotes the spatial coordinate of the image, whereas z direction depicts the range of bands. So, every pixel in a hyperspectral image represents some spectral information whose size is equal to the band size of that image. However, due to the huge number of band dimensionality computation complexity happens to be a crucial bottleneck for the processing of hyperspectral imagery. Another basic disadvantage present in hyperspectral images is that hyperspectral data usually contains hundreds of bands, that are profoundly corresponded. So the data contains significant information redundancies. Choosing the important bands among a large set of bands while saving precision is necessary for data transmission and storage of hyperspectral images.

© Springer Nature Switzerland AG 2021
P. Dutta et al. (Eds.): CICBA 2021, CCIS 1406, pp. 77–90, 2021.
https://doi.org/10.1007/978-3-030-75529-4_7

Literature survey suggests dimensionality reduction as a popular technique in the field of hyperspectral image processing to scale down associated image data volume. The identification of significant bands acts as one of the major contributors to reduction of dimension. Based on the supply of the dataset, selection of bands are often of three types: supervised, unsupervised and semi-supervised. The Mutual information (MI) technique [4] calculates the mutual information dependence between two independent pixels within the spectral image, that can be further used to determine the utility of each band to facilitate the selection of one band over other. Recently researchers have proposed some extraordinary band determination techniques. Among the various available supervised strategies, in [6] the canonical analysis was been utilized. In maximum variance based principal component analysis (MVPCA), [6] for dimensionality reduction approach the bands are arranged in sorted order based upon the importance of each band and the correlation between the bands. Different stochastic based optimization techniques have also been used in band selection such as Genetic Algorithm (GA) [12,15], Ant Colony Optimization (ACO) [7,21]. Genetic algorithm based techniques are feature-based method using the wrapper method or the filter method as fitness function. ACO based techniques [7] is suitable to find a set of optimized bands. But it prone to be stucked in local minima.

Clonal Selection Algorithm (CSA) has also been utilized as an effective pursuit methodology. Jeffris-Matusita distance metric is used for reduction of dimensionality [14] in CSA approaches. TMI (Trivariate mutual information) and STMI (semisupervised TMI-based) [11] techniques are applied for band selection using CSA as search method. It is based on the trivariate correlation between bands and the ground truth map is calculated. However, all of the above cases required an outsized measure of test information and the method used to rely upon the training data set. The key issues with the supervised method are to optimization of no. of bands and to limit the rate of misclassification. Particle Swarm Optimization (PSO) [9] based technique is a semi-automatic method where a pair of PSO is used, outer PSO and inner PSO. The external PSO manages the ideal number of chosen bands and therefore the internal PSO manages the ideal bands. Yet, the computational expense is amazingly high.

The work done by Liu et al. [23] suggests use of Differential Evolution (DE) for subset generation. The DE method [18] is a simple and efficient method to solve local minima problem since it employs a differential mutation operator. But the problem of this method is that selection of key parameters for any particular problem is little tedious. The Pairwise band determination (PWBS) structure is a semi-directed procedure in band determination [13]. Another semi-supervised band selection procedure on the hybrid paradigm is accounted for in [3]. This hybrid method is a combination of (2D Principal Component Analysis (2DPCA)) and clonal selection.

Because of the inaccessibility of the required prior information, unsupervised strategies are picking up prevalence. Band selection techniques based on clustering methods of hyperspectral images like WaLuDi (Ward's linkage strategy using divergence) [2] or using mutual information (WaLuMI) [2] are unsupervised methodology. WaLuDi technique depends on progressive unsupervised clustering based on mutual information or Kullback-Leibler dissimilarity. Though, some crucial information twisted because of the destruction of band relationship and causing loss of physical importance and interpretation of HSI (hue, saturation, intensity). The multiobjective enhancement method [17] manages the optimization of two fitness functions simultaneously i.e. information entropy and number of selected bands. But, it isn't exceptionally powerful to eliminate redundancies. Unsupervised split and merge [19] procedure split low connected band and consolidation high related bands and sub-bands. However, it relies upon some algorithmic boundaries which again dependent on hyperspectral sensors. In Fuzzy-PSO (Particle Swarm Optimization) method [5] joins fuzzy with PSO to improve the exhibition of band choice. Dominant set extraction is another unsupervised method for band selection prospered in [8]. Different measure metric have been proposed such as CM (consistency measure) [16], IM (information measure) [10], MI (mutual information) [22].

In this article, we proposed a method on Equilibrium Optimization (EO) [1]. It is based on the control volume mass balance model. Particles with their objective functions are considered as search agents. This technique can solve the problems with local minima and also can reduce computational burden. The proposed method is compared with different well known methods. OA (Overall accuracy) and Kappa value for best band combination give convincing results.

This paper is organized as follows: Sect. 1 introduces the domain of hyperspectral images with a critical literature survey of some of the recent approaches in the domain of band selection for the dimensional reduction in hyperspectral images. Section 2 contains a transient description of the relevant concepts used in the proposed work. In Sect. 3, the proposed method is described. The different data sets used for simulation and testing of the proposed methodology is describe in Sect. 4. Different experiments and analysis of results are also presented in this section to highlight the efficacy of the proposed approach. The final conclusion are there in Sect. 5.

2   Prerequisite Methods

This section describes the relevant technique used for the proposed work. It also explains the other prerequisites used in the proposed approach.

2.1   Equilibrium Optimization

Equilibrium Optimization (EO) [1] is a meta-heuristic optimization based on dynamic mass balance model in control volume used to estimate the equilibrium state. In physics, principle of mass conservation states that, for any closed system, the total quantity of mass of that system is always constant over time. The generic mass-balance equation can be represented as a first-order ordinary differential equation as given in Eq. (1)

$$cv\frac{dp}{dt} = v * P_E - v * Cn + m \tag{1}$$

where, cv is the control volume, Cn is the concentration in control volume, $cv\frac{dp}{dt}$ is the amount of change of mass inside the system, v is the flow rate inside and outside the system, m is the amount of mass generation within cv and P_E is the concentration of a particle at an equilibrium state.

But the above mentioned equation is only meaningful in terms of a specific region of space, called the control volume. A steady equilibrium state is reached when $cv\frac{dp}{dt}$ reaches zero. After solving, the Eq. (1) becomes

$$Cn = P_E + (Cn_0 - P_E) * e^{-r(t-t_0)} + \left(\frac{m}{rv}\right) * (1 - e^{-r(t-t_0)}) \tag{2}$$

where t_0 is the initial start time, Cn_0 is the concentration of a solution particle, and $r = \frac{v}{cv}$ is the turn over rate.

In this algorithm, the positions of particles were named as concentrations. Initial populations in the search space with initial positions can be define as

$$P_i^{initial} = P_{min} + rand_i(P_{max} - P_{min}) \tag{3}$$

where $P_i^{initial}$ is the initial population of the ith particle. P_{min} and P_{max} are the minimum and maximum number for the dimension of each particle and n is the number of particles in the population.

Now, each particle can update its position based on combination of the three updation rules:

(a) Equilibrium concentration: Select the best solution particles from the solution set called equilibrium pool. Based on the fitness function, select the four best-so-far particles and create the equilibrium pool. This pool consists of another member which is the average of the above mentioned best-so-far particles as depicted in Eq. (4)

$$P_{eqpool} = (P_{E1-1}, P_{E1-2}, P_{E1-3}, P_{E1-4}, P_{avg}) \tag{4}$$

(b) Direct search mechanism: Each particle in the equilibrium pool acts as explorer and search in the globally search space to reach in an equilibrium state. First four particles help in exploration i.e. to choose best solution set and the average helps in to exploit the best solution among the best solution set.

The exponential term is used to make a balance between exploration and exploitation which can be represented as

$$ET = m_1 sgn(k - 0.5)^{e^{-rT} - 1} \tag{5}$$

where m_1 is the exploration ability, ET is the exponential term, r is the turn over rate and $sgn(k - 0.5)$ selects the direction of exploitation and exploration where k is a random value between 0 and 1.

Time T can be represented as a function of iteration i.e. $maxit$. So, T can be represented by equation

$$T = \left(1 - \frac{i}{maxit}\right)^{m_2 \frac{i}{maxit}} \tag{6}$$

where $maxit$ is the maximum number of iteration and i is the current iteration, m_2 is the constant value for the exploitation ability.

(c) Generation rate: It is exploiter or solution refiner. It is defined as

$$G_F = G_{in} e^{-r(T-T_0)} \tag{7}$$

where G_F is the final generation rate and G_{in} is the initial value.

$$G_{in} = GRCP(P_E - rCn) \tag{8}$$

$$GRCP = \begin{cases} 0.5k_1, k_2 \geq 0.5 \\ 0, k_2 < 0.5 \end{cases} \tag{9}$$

where $GRCP$ is the generation rate control parameter, k_1 and k_2 are random numbers in $[0, 1]$, GP is the generation probability.

Thus the final updating rule used in EO is (combination of three updating rules (a), (b), (c))

$$Cn = P_E + (Cn - P_E) * ET + (\frac{G_F}{rv}) * (1 - ET) \tag{10}$$

which is same as Eq. (2). Here C_n is the is the concentration in control volume, P_E particle chosen randomly, ET is the exponential term, G_F is the final generation rate, r is the turn over rate, v is the flow rate inside and outside the control system.

3 Proposed Work

Here, we represent a novel band selection strategy depend on EO. The proposed technique contains of two stages: subset exploration and best solution exploitation. In the subset exploration stage an equilibrium pool of best solution particles are generated based on the objective function. Here solution particle means the combination of band numbers. In best solution exploitation, a combination of bands with the smallest objective value is chosen from the equilibrium pool.

The detail technique of our proposed technique is described in Algorithm 1. Initially n number of population particles are randomly selected and each consists of d number of bands using Eq. (3) ($d <$ total no. of bands). From empirical study, two constant terms i.e. the exploration ability $m1$ and exploitation ability $m2$ are set to 2 and 1 respectively. Then calculate the objective function value of each population p_i by Eq. (11) and select the four best-so-far particles (in terms of smallest value of objective function). Form the equilibrium pool with these four particles along with their average. As stated in [1], less than four particles degrades the performance of the method and more than four particles will have the negative effect.

Randomly select any particle from the equilibrium pool as given in step 6. To make a balance between exploration term and exploitation term exponential term (ET) is used as shown in step 7. Here time T is a function of $maxit$ i.e.

maximum number of iteration. The GRCP (generation rate control parameter) manages the generation term's commitment in the updating band number of a particle. The most important term is the generation rate i.e. G_F as it is used to identify the most promising particle. Now update the combination of bands in that particular particle using Eq. (10) and cerate a new particle as shown in step 8. Then the fitness value of this new particle are calculated. Particles with smaller objective function are more suited than the higher one. If the fitness value of the new particle is lower than the candidates in the equilibrium pool then a new equilibrium pool is created by selecting the particles with the best fitness value. This technique carry on until stopping criteria is reached. Stopping criterion is any one of these two i.e. either operate the algorithm for some specified no. of iteration or the difference between fitness value of the objective function of two successive iterations for the best subset is very trivial.

Objective Function:

$$D(i,j) = \sqrt{(\sum_i^N v_i - v_j)^2} \tag{11}$$

where $D(i,j)$ is the distance between i and j. $v(i)$ and $v(j)$ are pixel wise intensity values of bands i and j.

Algorithm 1. Proposed Band Selection algorithm

---

1. Initialization:

  - * Set the size of the population n.
  - * Set the size of each population (total number of bands in each population) d.
  - * Set p_i using equation (3) where $i = 1, 2, ..., n$.
  - * Set the exploration ability $m1$ and exploitation ability $m2$.
  - * Set the maximum number of iteration as $maxit$.

2. Calculate objective function of each population by equation (11).
3. Choose P_{eq1-1}, P_{eq1-2}, P_{eq1-3}, P_{eq1-4} among all the populations based on the smallest fitness value.
4. Calculate $P_{av} = ((P_{eq1-1} + P_{eq1-2} + P_{eq1-3} + P_{eq1-4}))/4$
5. Construct the equilibrium pool $P_{eqpool} = (P_{eq1-1}, P_{eq1-2}, P_{eq1-3}, P_{eq1-4}, P_{av})$.
6. Randomly choose a population from the equilibrium pool.
7. Calculate T by equation (6), exponential term ET using equation (5), generation rate control parameter $GRCP$ using equation (9) and final generation rate G_F by equation (7).
8. Update elements of the population by equation (10).
9. Update the equilibrium pool i.e P_{eqpool}.
10. Continue Steps $6 - 10$ until the termination condition is satisfied.

---

4 Experiment and Analysis

In this area, different tests are conducted on distinctive data sets to demonstrate the viability of the proposed method. At First, the data sets used in the experiments is presented. Next, the comparative analysis with few state-of-the-art strategies are appeared and analyzed.

4.1 Illustration of the Different Data Set

To calculate effectiveness of the proposed algorithm, different tests are conveyed out on two notable hypserspectral informational data sets in particular, Botswana and KSC dataset corresponding to the Okavango Delta of Botswana and Kennedy Space Center of Florida. The datasets are portrayed in the following subsections.

Data Set Botswana. Botswana data set contains 145 bands with 1476×256 pixels in each bands. The sensor on EO-1 procured data at 30 m pixel resolution in 242 bands from the 400 nm to 2500 nm portion of the spectrum. Noisy bands were expelled, and the remaining 145 bands were included within the experiment. Fig. 1 represents botswana image of a particular band. Table 1 represents 14 identified classes with sample numbers as represented in ground truth map (GT) used in our experiment.

Table 1. Classes with the corresponding no. of Samples for Botswana Data set.

Class	No. of samples	Land type
CA1	270	Water
CA2	101	Hippo Grass
CA3	251	FloodPlain Grasses 1
CA4	215	FloodPlain Grasses 2
CA5	269	Reeds
CA6	269	Riparian
CA7	259	Firescar
CA8	203	Island Interior
CA9	314	Acacia Woodlands
CA10	248	Acacia Shrublands
CA11	305	Acacia Grasslands
CA12	181	Short Mopane
CA13	268	Mixed Mopane
CA14	95	Exposes Soils

Table 2. Classes with the corresponding no. of Samples for KSC data set.

Class	No. of samples
CLA1	761
CLA2	243
CLA3	256
CLA4	252
CLA5	161
CLA6	229
CLA7	105
CLA8	431
CLA9	520
CLA10	404
CLA11	419
CLA12	503
CLA13	927

Data Set KSC. The KSC data set, obtained over Kennedy Space Center (KSC), by NASA, is of size 512 × 614. It comprises of 224 bands of 10 nm width with frequencies going from 400 nm to 2500 nm. Disposing the bands irritated due to water assimilation or with low SNR value, 176 bands are utilized for experiments. In this data set segregation of different land cover is very troublesome due to the closeness of spectral information for typical vegetation (Fig. 2 and 3). Class names and corresponding no. of samples to each class are represented in Table 2.

Fig. 1. Sample band of Botswana data set.

4.2   Explanation of Results:

The execution of the proposed EO based strategy has been compared with that of MI (Mutual Information) [4], WaLuDi (Wards linkage strategy using divergence) [2], TMI (Trivariate MI) [11], Ant Colony Based (ACO) [7], and Differential Evolution (DE) [23] based methods. In the proposed technique experiments are carried out for suitable values of m_1, m_2 and GP. After several run it is found that $m_1 = 2$, $m_2 = 1$ and $GP = 0.5$ are suitable for different hyperspectral data sets. Execution of the proposed method on the above mentioned data sets are depicted in this paper. In the present experiment, tests are carried out for distinctive band numbers ranging from 5 to 30 with step size 2.

For the suggested strategy, prime solutions are chosen arbitrarily within a specified range i.e., for Botswana data $Pmin$ is 1 and $Pmax$ is 176 and for KSC data the values are 1 and 145 respectively.

Execution of the proposed algorithm is compared with five well known existing techniques in terms of overall accuracy (OA) and Kappa coefficient (Kappa) [20]. The value of Kappa coefficient is within the range of $[-1, +1]$. The value of Kappa close to +1 means better classification.

A comparison of overall classification accuracy with ACO and DE for the varying no. of bands on Botswana data set is depicted in Table 3. From this table, it is clear that the proposed method outperforms the other methods for all the cases and the proposed method gives the best result for band number 19. The confusion matrix and corresponding OA and kappa value of the proposed method for the best result (for band number 19) on Botswana data set are shown in Table 4. From this table it is noticed that classes $C1$–$C3$, $C7$, $C12$ and $C14$ have well classification accuracy than other classes as their classification accuracy is 100%. In this article, bold marks represent the best results.

Fig. 2. Kennedy Space Centre image.

Fig. 3. Sample band of KSC dataset.

A variation of kappa coefficient for varying number of bands is depicted graphically in Fig. 4. From the given Fig. 4 it is cleared that the proposed algorithm is performed well than the other two methods.

Different results of KSC (Kennedy Space Centre) data set are depicted in Table 5. A comparison of OA and Kappa value with ACO and DE for a varying no. of bands is depicted in this table. For all the bands ranging from 5 to 25 proposed strategy performs better than ACO and DE based methodology. From Table 5, it is observed that the proposed technique performs well than the other two methods.

Table 3. Comparison of Overall accuracy between the proposed method, ACO and DE for distinctive no. of chosen bands for Botswana data set.

No. of bands	Proposed	ACO	DE
	OA	*OA*	*OA*
5	**89.15**	88.62	88.58
7	**89.58**	89.28	89.01
9	**90.91**	90.50	90.46
11	**91.96**	91.25	90.98
13	**92.53**	91.49	91.21
15	**93.28**	91.53	91.30
17	**94.96**	91.90	91.66
19	**95.80**	92.25	91.83
21	**95.49**	91.99	91.76
23	**94.32**	91.82	91.56
25	**93.18**	91.79	91.31
27	**92.88**	91.56	91.42
29	**92.61**	91.39	91.21

Table 4. Confusion matrix of proposed algorithm on Botswana Data set with 19 bands.

Class No	CA1	CA2	CA3	CA4	CA5	CA6	CA7	CA8	CA9	CA10	CA11	CA12	CA13	CA14	Classified	Accuracy
CA1	266	0	0	0	0	0	0	0	3	0	0	0	0	0	266	100
CA2	0	101	0	0	0	0	0	0	0	0	0	0	0	0	101	100
CA3	0	2	232	0	0	0	0	6	021	0	0	0	0	0	232	100
CA4	2	0	6	198	0	10	0	0	0	0	0	0	0	0	206	96.11
CA5	2	0	0	17	266	1	0	1	0	0	0	0	0	0	287	92.68
CA6	0	0	13	0	0	265	23	0	0	2	0	0	0	0	303	87.45
CA7	0	0	0	0	0	0	234	0	0	0	0	0	0	0	234	100
CA8	0	0	0	0	3	3	0	201	0	0	1	0	0	0	208	96.63
CA9	0	0	0	0	0	0	0	1	306	0	0	39	1	0	347	88.18
CA10	0	0	0	0	0	0	2	0	6	246	0	0	0	0	254	96.85
CA11	0	0	0	0	0	0	0	0	2	0	303	4	0	1	310	97.74
CA12	0	0	0	0	0	0	0	0	0	0	0	138	0	0	138	100
CA13	0	0	0	0	0	0	0	0	0	0	0	0	267	4	271	98.52
CA14	0	0	0	0	0	0	0	0	0	0	0	0	0	90	90	100
Pixels in Gt	270	101	251	215	269	269	259	203	314	248	304	181	268	95	3315	OA 95.80
P. Accur	98.51	100	92.43	92.09	98.88	98.51	90.34	99.01	97.45	99.19	99.67	76.24	99.62	94.73		Kappa 0.955

A variety of overall classification accuracy for the varying no. of bands is depicted graphically in Fig. 5. Here execution of the proposed method is better than other state-of-the-art strategies namely MI, TMI and WaLuDi for KSC data sets. For the proposed strategy the most excellent execution is obtained when the number of selected bands is 19.

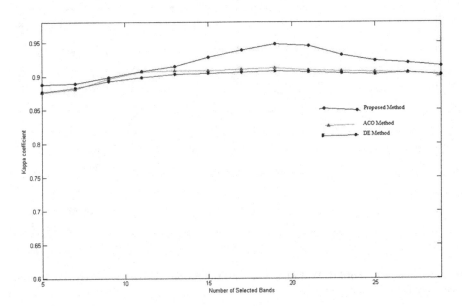

Fig. 4. Comparison of ACO, DE and the proposed method in terms of Kappa Coefficient for Botswana data set.

Table 5. Comparison of OA and Kappa coefficient between proposed method, ACO and DE for different no. of selected bands on KSC data set.

No. of bands	Proposed		ACO		DE	
	OA	*Kappa*	*OA*	*Kappa*	*OA*	*Kappa*
5	**92.98**	**.9217**	89.47	.8836	90.80	.8992
7	**94.18**	**.9351**	91.09	.8988	91.12	.9013
9	**94.96**	**.9218**	91.32	.9021	91.49	.9033
11	**94.66**	**.9406**	91.88	.9083	91.92	.9088
13	**95.11**	**.9455**	92.21	.9166	92.51	.9121
15	**95.21**	**.9461**	92.13	.9133	92.29	.9162
17	**95.46**	**.9473**	92.29	.9151	92.36	.9179
19	**95.72**	**.9490**	92.56	.9169	92.67	.9163
21	**95.36**	**.9461**	92.38	.9144	92.28	.9101
23	**94.98**	**.9426**	92.22	.9136	92.32	.9156
25	**94.61**	**.9391**	92.12	.9128	91.90	.9090

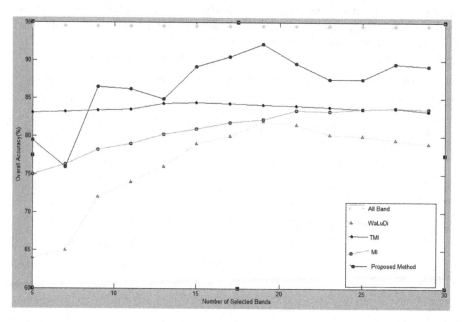

Fig. 5. Comparison of MI, WaLuDi, TMI and the proposed strategy in terms of overall accuracy for KSC data set.

5   Conclusion

In this paper, a novel band selection procedure is proposed based on Equilibrium Optimization in hyperspectral images. Execution of the proposed strategy is compared with few well-known techniques like MI, WaLuDi, TMI, (ACO), and DE based strategies. In terms of overall accuracy (OA) and Kappa coefficient this proposed strategy appear critical advancement improvement over the other strategies for the above mentioned hyperspectral data sets utilized in our experiments.

References

1. Faramarzi, A., Heidarinejad, M., Stephens, B., Mirjalili, S.: Equilibrium optimizer: a novel optimization algorithm. Knowl.-Based Syst. **191** (2020)
2. Martinez-Uso, A., Pla, F., Sotoca, J.M., Garcia-Sevilla, P.: Clustering based hyperspectral band selection using information measures. IEEE Trans. Geosci. Remote Sens. **45**(12), 4158–4171 (2007)
3. Chowdhury, A.R., Hazra, J., Dutta, P.: A hybrid approach for band selection of hyperspectral images. In: Hybrid Intelligence for Image Analysis and Understanding, Chap. 11, pp. 263–282. Wiley (2017)
4. Guo, B., Gunn, S.R., Damper, R.I., Nelson, J.D.: Band selection for hyperspectral image classification using mutual information. IEEE Geosci. Remote Sens. Lett. **3**(4), 522–526 (2006)
5. Chang-I, C., Wu, C.C., Liu, K.H., Chen, H.M., Chen, C.C.C., Wen, C.H.: Progressive band processing of linear spectral unmixing for hyperspectral imagery. IEEE J. Sel. Top. Appl. Earth Observ. Remote Sens. **8**(6), 2583–2597 (2015)
6. Chang, C.I., Du, Q., Sun, T.L., Althouse, M.L.: A joint band prioritization and band decorrelation approach to band selection for hyperspectral image classification. IEEE Trans. Geosci. Remote Sens. **37**(6), 2631–2641 (1999)
7. Samadzadegan, F., Partovi, T.: Feature selection based on ant colony algorithm for hyperspectral remote sensing images. In: 2010 2nd Workshop on Hyperspectral Image and Signal Processing: Evolution in Remote Sensing (WHISPERS), pp. 1–4 (2010)
8. Zhu, G., Huang, Y., Lei, J., Bi, Z., Xu, F.: Unsupervised hyperspectral band selection by dominant set extraction. IEEE Trans. Geosci. Remote Sens. **54**(1), 227–239 (2016)
9. Su, H., Du, Q., Chen, G., Du, P.: Optimized hyperspectral band selection using particle swarm optimization. IEEE J. Sel. Top. Appl. Earth Observ. Remote Sens. **7**(6), 2659–2670 (2014)
10. Huang, R., He, M.: Band selection based on feature weighting for classification of hyperspectral data. IEEE Geosci. Remote Sens. Lett. **2**(2), 156–159 (2005)
11. Feng, J., Jiao, L.C., Zhang, X., Sun, T.: Hyperspectral band selection based on trivariate mutual information and clonal selection. IEEE Trans. Geosci. Remote Sens. **52**(7), 4092–4105 (2014)
12. Ma, J.P., Zheng, Z.B., Tong, Q.X., Zheng, L.F.: An application of genetic algorithms on band selection for hyperspectral image classification. In: Proceedings of the 2nd International Conference on Machine Learning and Cybernetics, pp. 2810–2813 (2003)
13. Bai, J., Xiang, S., Shi, L., Pan, C.: Semisupervised pair-wise band selection for hyperspectral images. IEEE J. Sel. Top. Appl. Earth Observ. Remote Sens. **8**(6), 2798–2813 (2015)
14. Zhang, L., Zhong, Y., Huang, B., Gong, J., Li, P.: Dimensionality reduction based on clonal selection for hyperspectral imagery. IEEE Geosci. Remote Sens. Lett. **45**(12), 4172–4186 (2007)

15. Zhuo, L., Zheng, J., Li, X., Wang, F., Ai, B., Qian, J.: A genetic algorithm based wrapper feature selection methods for classification of hyperspectral images using support vector machine. In: Proceedings of the International Archives of the Photogrammetry, Remote Sensing and Spatial Information Sciences, pp. 397–402 (2008)

16. Lashkia, G., Anthony, L.: Relevant, irredundant feature selection and noisy example elimination. IEEE Trans. Syst. Man Cybern. B Cybern. **34**(2), 888–897 (2004)

17. Gong, M., Zhang, M., Yuan, Y.: Unsupervised band selection based on evolutionary multiobjective optimization for hyperspectral images. IEEE Trans. Geosci. Remote Sens. **54**(1), 544–557 (2016)

18. Storn, R., Price, K.: Differential evolution: a simple and efficient heuristic for global optimization over continuous spaces. J. Glob. Optim. **11**, 341–359 (1997)

19. Rashwan, S., Dobigeon, N.: A split-and-merge approach for hyperspectral band selection. IEEE Geosci. Remote Sens. Lett. **14**(8), 1378–1382 (2017)

20. Congalton, R.G., Green, K.: Assessing the Accuracy of Remotely Sensed Data, 2nd edn, pp. 341–359. CRC Press, Boca Raton (2009)

21. Zhou, S., Zhang, J.P., Su, B.: Feature selection and classification based on ant colony algorithm for hyperspectral remote sensing images. In: 2nd International Congress on Image and Signal Processing, pp. 1–4 (2009)

22. Shannon, E.: A mathematical theory of communication. Bell Syst. Tech. J. **27**(3), 379–423 (1948)

23. Liu, X., Yu, C., Cai, Z.: Differential evolution based band selection in hyperspectral data classification. In: Cai, Z., Hu, C., Kang, Z., Liu, Y. (eds.) ISICA 2010. LNCS, vol. 6382, pp. 86–94. Springer, Heidelberg (2010). https://doi.org/10.1007/978-3-642-16493-4_9

A Fuzzy Logic Approach to Evaluate Discomfort of Body Parts Among Female Sal Leaf Plate Makers in India

Bappaditya Ghosh[1], Subhashis Sahu[2], and Animesh Biswas[1(✉)]

[1] Department of Mathematics, University of Kalyani, Kalyani 741235, India
[2] Department of Physiology, University of Kalyani, Kalyani 741235, India

Abstract. The commonly used ergonomic posture analysis tools are unable to measure exact level of risk associated with human body parts, since these tools exclude several factors, such as uncertainties in the border regions between adjacent ranges of inputs, design of work places, characteristic of works, etc. To capture those uncertainties, a computational methodology is developed for evaluating discomfort level of body parts among the female Sal leaf plate makers using the Mamdani fuzzy inference system. The modified Nordic questionnaire is used, subsequently, to measure consistency in collecting responses from the workers. The body part discomfort (BPD) scale is considered for subjective validation. The scores achieved from BPD scale and rapid entire body assessment worksheet are used to act as the input values of the proposed system. Due to some unavoidable imprecisions associated with the collected data, the membership functions of the input and output variables of the developed fuzzy system are represented by linear type fuzzy numbers. To show feasibility and reliability of the proposed methodology, a comparison is made between the achieved results and the scores obtained through fuzzy decision support system using rapid upper limb assessment.

Keywords: Musculoskeletal problem · Sal leaf plate makers · Fuzzy inference system · Rapid entire body assessment

1 Introduction

In global scenario, musculoskeletal disorders (MSDs) relating to work-cultures are becoming major concerns for occupational health issues. MSDs are mainly caused due to injuries in muscles, nerves, ligaments, body joints, vertebral columns, cartilages, etc. [1]. On the basis of the report of National Institute of Occupational Safety and Health, work related injuries in several unorganized sectors are gradually increasing with significant rate [2]. The epidemiological studies on several job sites confirm that prevalence of occupation-based MSDs among the workers is very high [3]. Working at different strenuous working postures for a prolonged time is one of the main reasons for gradual increase of muscle injuries among the workers in several informal units [1].

Managements of manufacturing units are continuously trying to develop healthy work environments. Modification of the working postures and workplaces can decrease

© Springer Nature Switzerland AG 2021
P. Dutta et al. (Eds.): CICBA 2021, CCIS 1406, pp. 91–104, 2021.
https://doi.org/10.1007/978-3-030-75529-4_8

the rate of such work-related MSDs. Environment sustainable industries are gradually growing up in India. Among them, manufacturing of Sal leaf plates is one of the common occupations of tribals in India [4]. Many female workers are engaged in this occupation. They perform the job in four steps. At first, they collect Sal leaves from nearby Sal forests. Later, these Sal leaves are stitched with one another. Subsequently, those are dried in the Sun light for a few days. Lastly, the final product is made through a semi-automatic machine [4]. But in performing these jobs, the female Sal leaf plate makers have to work in several awkward working postures. Also, they are unaware about several risk factors, such as proper training programs, ergonomically supported working instruments, maintaining proper work-rest cycles, etc. These factors make the whole situation worse. As a result, the female workers suffer from several musculoskeletal problems. But in spite of these problems, the female workers are compelled to continue their works due to their poor economic conditions. Thus the proper analysis of working postures turns out to be an essential process in improving the health of the workers, as these musculoskeletal problems can be reduced significantly by proper analysis of awkward working postures and taking precautionary strategies, well in advance [5].

Several ergonomic techniques are available for analyzing working postures of the workers during their job performances. Among these, rapid entire body assessment (REBA) is one of the most popular methods that rates the risk level of several body parts [6]. It is one kind of observational method containing three steps, viz., recording of working postures, scoring of body parts according to the movements, and identification of risk levels [6]. But in using REBA, sometimes, the users face difficulties in measuring the exact value of inputs, such as body joint angles, force/load, etc. corresponding to several working postures due to computation errors. The visual ambiguity for obtaining those input values very often creates difficulty for observers to achieve the exact value of inputs which results inaccurate outcomes. Also, REBA holds sharp boundaries between two ranges of input parameters and demands exact values of inputs rather than a range of values [7]. As a consequence, discrepancies occur in the boundary area between the ranges of input parameters [7]. Also, identification of most awkward posture correspond-ing to a particular job is a major issue faced by users through the process of REBA as it varies over individuals. Therefore, some sort of discrepancies and uncertainties are unavoidable with the data which are used in REBA.

Thus, the concept of fuzzy logic becomes very much essential to deal with such uncertainties. Fuzzy logic is an effective tool for capturing possibilistic uncertainties and is used to a make proper justifiable decision by resolving the uncertain situations [8]. It is also an efficient tool to deal with collected data having un-sharp boundaries and to categorize them by providing justifiable membership values. In the proposed method-ology, the fuzzy logic approach is introduced to enrich the posture analysis techniques in evaluating the discomfort of several body parts among female Sal leaf plate makers, well in advance. The imprecision associated with the input values and sharp boundaries between the ranges of the input parameters is unified with fuzzy logic for diminishing the human errors for obtaining most acceptable input values.

Fuzzy logic was successfully implemented by Azadeh et al. [9] for assessing perfor-mance of an ergonomic system. Majumder et al. [10] used fuzzy reasoning to analyze risk factors associated with several body parts in construction sites. Later, Rivero et al.

[11] used fuzzy logic in the process of rapid upper limb assessment (RULA) to analyze workers' risk factors. A unified fuzzy system was developed by Golabchi et al. [12] to analyze the awkward working postures using RULA. Further, Debnath et al. [13] generated a fuzzy system in evaluating the occupational risk of different body parts in construction sites. Later, Pavlovic-Veselinovic et al. [14] developed an inference system for evaluating work-related MSDs. A fuzzy decision support system (FDSS) was developed by Kadhim [15] for diagnosing workers' back pain problems. Again, fuzzy inference system was implemented in assessing risk for occupational health and safety by Ilbahar et al. [16]. Samiei et al. [17] introduced fuzzy logic to identify risk factors for low back pain. A fuzzy-based framework was proposed by Gul [18] for assessing occupational risks in the field of health and safety. Later, a fuzzy logic model for checking of quick exposure of work-related musculoskeletal risk was proposed by Kose et al. [19]. Ghosh et al. [7] developed a FDSS using RULA to resolve inexactness relating to the working posture analysis.

In this study, a Mamdani fuzzy inference system (MFIS) [20] is generated to evaluate the level of discomforts associated with different body parts of female Sal leaf plate makers corresponding to several working postures. The modified Nordic questionnaire (MNQ) [21] was used for collecting information towards work-related musculoskeletal risk factors, and subjective perception was noted by body part discomfort (BPD) scale, which are considered as the primary data for the proposed methodology. Due to some inevitable uncertainties and inexactness associated with the collected data, the membership functions (MFs) of the input and output variables are represented by linear type fuzzy numbers. To establish the application potentiality and reliability of the proposed method, Pearson's correlation coefficient (PCC) [22] is evaluated.

2 REBA

REBA [6] is one of the most widely used observation-based methods because of its simplicity, accessibility, and validity. In this process, at first, awkward working postures are selected from freeze photographs or video recordings. Then these postures are analyzed. The stepwise procedure for analyzing a working posture through REBA is summarized as follows:

Step 1. At first, Trunk score, Neck score, Leg score is computed based on body joint angles, and is put into Table A [6, 23] to get Posture score A. Then, Score A is found by adding the score corresponding to Force/load with the Posture score A.

Step 2. In this step, the scores corresponding to Lower arm, Upper arm, Wrist are computed according to their body joint angles, and is put into Table B [6, 23] to get Posture score B. Then, Score B is obtained by adding Coupling score with Posture score B.

Step 3. Further, Score C is achieved by putting Scores A and B in Table C [6, 23]. Finally, REBA score corresponding to that posture is found by adding Activity score with Score C.

The whole process of REBA is summarized in Fig. 1.

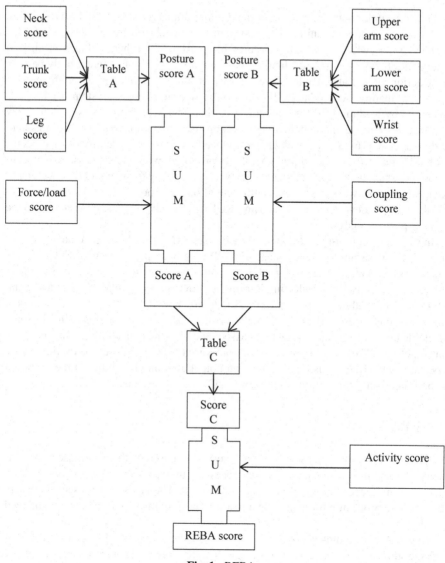

Fig. 1. REBA.

3   Data Collection and Analysis

At first, a team was built to observe the female Sal leaf plate makers from several units during their job performances. The main job of the team was to observe the workers' workloads, duration of works, awkward working postures, etc. After careful observation for a few days, 100 female workers from different units with at least two years of work experiences are taken as subjects. After administrating the notion of MNQ and BPD scale to the workers, the data are collected from them, and are thoroughly analyzed. Finally, the information through MNQ and scores obtained using BPD scale is considered for the proposed methodology. Here, it is to be mentioned that responses to several questions are provided by the workers through MNQ using linguistic terms, which are itself possibilistic in nature. As a result, some sort of uncertainties and imprecisions are inherently included within the collected data. To deal with these types of imprecision corresponding to the linguistic terms, all crisp inputs for the proposed methodology are fuzzified to suitable trapezoidal fuzzy numbers (TFNs) [10].

Here, some photographs of awkward sitting positions of Sal leaf plate makers are presented in Fig. 2.

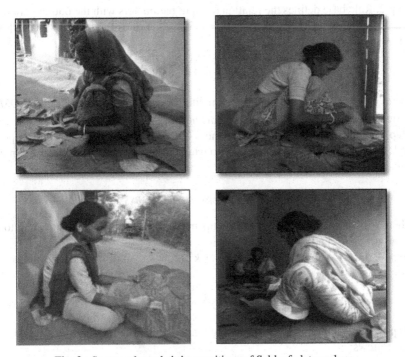

Fig. 2. Some awkward sitting positions of Sal leaf plate makers.

4   Proposed Methodology

In this article, an MFIS [8, 10] is generated to evaluate discomfort scores of body parts of female Sal leaf plate makers. In MFIS, at first, input and output variables are selected on the basis of areas of application. Next, the uncertainties associated with those variables are captured by converting them to suitable fuzzy numbers, which, subsequently, are used in the inference engine to obtain one or more fuzzy sets defined on some relevant universe of discourses. Finally, defuzzifications are performed on the inferred fuzzy sets to find the desired result of the whole inference system.

The step wise procedure of the proposed methodology is presented below.

Step 1. Here, an MFIS is designed with two inputs and one output parameter. *Discomfort Rating* (DR) and *REBA Score* (RS) in the universe of discourses, X, and Y, respectively, as inputs; and *Discomfort Score of Body Part* (DSBP) in the universe of discourse Z, as output are considered to evaluate discomfort associated with different body parts corresponding to several awkward working postures. The input values of DR and RS associated with a discomfort prone body part are the average of the BPD scale score values and average REBA scores corresponding to different awkward working postures, respectively. Due to the uncertainties associated with the collected data, TFNs are considered to express MFs of input and output variables.

Step 2. Rule base defines the relation of input parameters with the output parameter to act as the pillar of an MFIS. The $k^{th} (k = 1, 2, \ldots, r)$ rule of a rule base [10, 24] is of the following form:

$$Rule^k : \text{If } x \text{ is } Q_{DR}^k \text{ and } y \text{ is } Q_{RS}^k \text{ then } = Q_{DSBP}^k, \tag{1}$$

where Q_{DR}^k, Q_{RS}^k, and Q_{DSBP}^k are the qualitative descriptors of DR, RS, and $DSBP$, respectively, for the $k^{th} (k = 1, 2, \ldots, r)$ rule and $x \in X, y \in Y, z \in Z$.

Step 3. The firing strength, γ^k, for the $k^{th} (k = 1, 2, \ldots, r)$ rule of the proposed method [10], which illustrates the degree to which the kth rule satisfies the given inputs, is evaluated using fuzzy intersection as

$$\gamma^k = \min [\max (F_{DR}(x) \wedge Q_{DR}^k(x)), \max (F_{RS}(y) \wedge Q_{RS}^k(y))], \tag{2}$$

where F_{DR}, and F_{RS} are two fuzzy inputs in the form of TFNs corresponding to the input variables DR, and RS, respectively.

Step 4. Fuzzy output, $DSBP^k$, for the $k^{th} (k = 1, 2, \ldots, r)$ rule is evaluated as follows:

$$DSBP^k(z) = \gamma^k \wedge Q_{DSBP}^k(z). \tag{3}$$

Step 5. Fuzzy union is operated to aggregate the outputs through the k number of rules as follows:

$$A_{DSBP}(z) = \vee_{k=1}^r DSBP^k(z). \tag{4}$$

Step 6. The final output, $DSBP$, is evaluated through the defuzzification method, viz., centroid of area as follows:

$$DSBP = \frac{\sum_{i=1}^n A_{DSBP}(z_i).z_i}{\sum_{i=1}^n A_{DSBP}(z_i)}, \tag{5}$$

where $z_i \in Z, i = 1, 2, \ldots, n$ are n quantization of Z.

It is to be mentioned here that the higher value of the output parameter, $DSBP$, corresponding to a body part, signifies more severe condition of that body part and suggests enhanced precautions of that body part.

A flowchart of the proposed methodology is presented in Fig. 3.

5 Evaluation of *DSBP* Among Female Sal Leaf Plate Makers in India

Based on the collected data from workers, seven body parts, viz., neck, trunk, lower back, leg, wrist, lower arm and upper arm are identified as the most discomfort prone body parts. After careful observation of the observation team for a few days, 10 awkward working postures, some of which are shown in Fig. 2, are selected where the female Sal leaf plate makers spent most of their time during job performances. The score through BPD scale and REBA worksheet corresponding to those discomfort prone body parts are presented in Table 1 and Table 2, respectively. The *DSBP* of the female Sal leaf plate makers through MFIS are evaluated below.

The universe of discourse of *DR*, *RS*, and *DSBP* is considered as the closed interval [0, 10]. Since, the maximum score through BPD scale cannot exceed 10, all the input values of *DR* fall in the above universe of discourse. But, the range of score through REBA worksheet corresponding to different body parts is different. Thus, all the score through REBA worksheet corresponding to different body parts are normalized within [0, 10], and hence, the input values of *RS* fall in the above mentioned universe of discourse. For example, according to REBA worksheet, REBA score of neck for Posture-a is 1 as the neck bending angle is found as 14 degrees. Similarly, REBA scores of neck for the remaining postures are evaluated and presented in Table 2. The average REBA score of the neck is found as 1.6, whereas, the maximum REBA score of neck can be 3. Thus, the crisp value *RS* corresponding to the neck is evaluated as 5.3. Similar processes are followed to evaluate the crisp values of *RS* corresponding to remaining body parts. The crisp values of *DR* and *RS* corresponding to the above mentioned discomfort prone body parts are presented in Table 3. Further, each score is fuzzified to a suitable TFN, as shown in the same Table 3, by keeping the score value as the centre point of that TFN. Five linguistic hedges, viz., Very High, High, Medium, Low, and Very Low are defined on the universe of discourse for the input and output variables. The respective TFNs corresponding to the above mentioned linguistic hedges, as shown in Fig. 4, are as follows:

$<7, 8, 10, 10>$, $<5, 6, 7, 8>$, $<3, 4, 5, 6>$, $<1, 2, 3, 4>$, and $<0, 0, 1, 2>$.

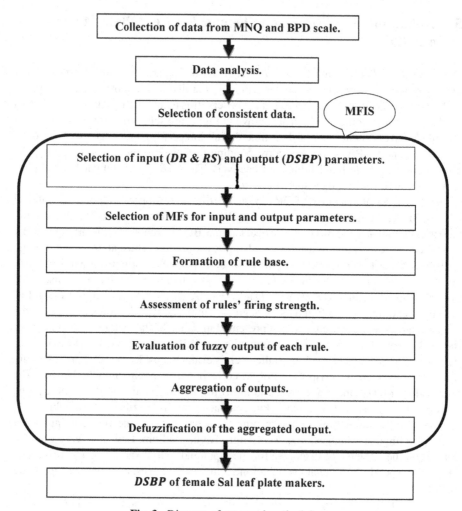

Fig. 3. Diagram of proposed methodology.

In evaluating *DSBP*, the rule base of the proposed MFIS consists of 25 if-then rules, as presented in Table 4.

After generating the rule base, *DSBP* of female Sal leaf plate makers, which is the final output of the proposed methodology, is evaluated by following the processes from Step 3 to Step 6 and is shown in Table 5.

To ensure applicability of the developed methodology, PCC is calculated between the above results and the assessed score values obtained through FDSS using RULA, and are presented in Table 6.

Table 1. Score through BPD scale corresponding to discomfort prone body parts.

Score through BPD scale											
Body part	Posture										Average
	a	b	c	d	e	f	g	h	i	j	
Neck	6	7	7	8	7	7	7	6	7	8	7
Trunk	7	7	8	9	7	9	9	8	8	8	8
Lower back	8	8	9	10	9	9	10	9	8	10	9
Leg	6	7	6	8	7	6	8	7	7	8	7
Upper arm	3	4	3	3	4	2	4	2	2	3	3
Lower arm	2	3	2	2	3	1	3	1	1	2	2
Wrist	4	5	4	4	5	4	4	3	4	3	4

Table 2. REBA score corresponding to discomfort prone body parts.

REBA score											
Body part	Posture										Average
	a	b	c	d	e	f	g	h	i	j	
Neck	1	2	1	2	2	2	2	1	1	2	1.6
Trunk	3	3	3	3	3	3	3	3	3	3	3
Lower back	3	3	3	3	3	3	3	3	3	3	3
Leg	4	1	4	4	4	1	1	1	1	1	2.2
Upper arm	2	2	3	3	2	3	2	2	2	3	2.4
Lower arm	1	1	1	1	1	1	1	1	1	1	1
Wrist	2	2	2	2	2	2	2	2	2	2	2

5.1 Comprehensive Discussions

From the achieved results, it is found that the highest value of *DSBP* is 8.7334, which corresponds to lower back. Without proper ergonomic seating arrangement, the female Sal leaf plate makers are compelled to perform their jobs in several awkward sitting postures for a prolonged time. Thus, lower back is mostly discomfort prone body part of the female Sal leaf plate makers. Trunk stands just below from lower back in Table 5 with *DSBP* of 8.0238. Trunk carries very high risk in making of Sal leaf plates, as this portion of the body part is supposed to be bent at most of the time. Consequently, the female Sal leaf plate makers suffer from several kinds of spinal problems. The high value of *DSBP* corresponding to leg signifies the high risk level of postural discomfort. The female workers have to work in several static positions where the legs are situated in several swatting positions. Also, sometimes, legs do not receive sufficient blood flow due to muscle compression in sitting postures for prolonged time. *DSBP* of neck is found as

Table 3. Input values of the proposed methodology.

Body part	DR		RS	
	Crisp value	Fuzzified value	Crisp value	Fuzzified value
Neck	7	<6, 6.5, 7.5, 8>	5.3	<4.5, 5, 5.5, 6>
Trunk	8	<7, 7.5, 8.5, 9>	6	<5, 6, 6, 7>
Lower back	9	<8, 8.5, 9.5, 10>	6	<5, 6, 6, 7>
Leg	7	<6, 6.5, 7.5, 8>	5.5	<5, 5.3, 5.7, 6>
Upper arm	3	<2, 2.5, 3.5, 4>	4	<3, 4, 4, 5>
Lower arm	2	<1, 1.5, 2.5, 3>	5	<4, 4.5, 5.5, 6>
Wrist	4	<3, 3.5, 4.5, 5>	6.7	<6, 6.5, 7, 7.5>

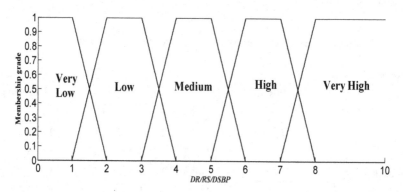

Fig. 4. MFs corresponding to the linguistic hedges representing $DR/RS/DSBP$.

Table 4. Rule base of the developed MFIS.

DSBP					
DR	RS				
	Very High	High	Medium	Low	Very Low
Very High	Very High	Very High	Very High	High	Medium
High	Very High	Very High	High	Medium	Low
Medium	Very High	High	Medium	Low	Low
Low	High	Medium	Low	Very Low	Very Low
Very Low	Medium	Low	Low	Very Low	Very Low

7.5175 which also establishes the higher level of strain in that body part. Due to working in several bending postures, neck muscles may sometimes be strained which causes to several kinds of neck pains, and consequently, the female workers face discomfort in

Table 5. *DSBP* of the female Sal leaf plate makers.

Body part	*DSBP*	Membership grade
Neck	7.5175	High: 0.4825 Very High: 0.5175
Trunk	8.0238	Very High: 1
Lower back	8.7334	Very High: 1
Leg	7.6909	High: 0.0985 Very High: 0.9015
Upper arm	2.931	Low: 1
Lower arm	3.3655	Low: 0.6345 Medium: 0.3655
Wrist	6.2226	High: 1

Table 6. PCC between final results and achieved FDSS scores using RULA.

Body part	*DSBP*	Score through FDSS on RULA	PCC
Neck	7.5175	4.9	0.8878
Trunk	8.0238	4.73	
Lower back	8.7334	4.73	
Leg	7.6909	5	
Upper arm	2.9310	3.3	
Lower arm	3.3655	3.49	
Wrist	6.2226	5.07	

moving their heads frequently. The *DSBP* of the upper arm is obtained as 2.931 which is the least. Thus, upper arm of the female workers carries low postural risk in performing their daily jobs.

PCC between final results and achieved FDSS scores using RULA establishes the reliability of the proposed method. The positive value of PCC also signifies the steadiness and strength of the proposed processes in evaluating the discomfort level of the body parts of female Sal leaf plate makers. It is worth mentioning that the developed method is more reliable than the existing method [7], since this process includes the workers' opinions of together with REBA under fuzzy environment. But FDSS using RULA [7] does not consider the opinions of workers.

6   Conclusions

Through the proposed study, a computational methodology is developed to evaluate the discomfort level of body parts of workers which will be helpful to them in taking extra precautions on postural risk associated with different body parts, well in advance. The outcomes of the proposed research work identify the most affected body parts, viz., lower back, trunk, leg, neck, etc. of female Sal leaf plate makers with their causes of discomfort, which will be helpful in spreading the health awareness in the whole community. Most of the female Sal leaf plate makers are from poor economic backgrounds. Thus, in spite of having pain in different body parts, they are bound to carry out their jobs. Based on the achieved scores through the proposed method, some instructions can be suggested to the workers to reduce discomforts associated with their body parts, viz., sitting on ergonomically supported stools during their works, maintenance of proper workloads and examination of their work-rest cycles, etc. Further, the proposed methodology may also be helpful to authorities in taking proper safety measures of the workers, which will play a major role in the economic growth of those units by developing ergonomic friendly working environments.

It is hoped that the proposed methodology may be applied to assess the discomfort level of body parts among the workers who are involved with some other fields of manually handled jobs in different manufacturing industries. In that case, the input parameters may vary according to the context of the job. Finally, the proposed study provides a computational path between fuzzy logic and the existing methods for evaluating postural risk levels in different body parts, which may explore an extensive range of research scopes in the field of computations, mathematics, and ergonomic studies.

Some of the research scopes for future studies are summarized as follows:

- Here, according to the context of jobs, two input parameters (DR and RS) are considered for generating the MFIS. But, depending on the collected data and contexts, more input parameters can be taken into account in developing MFIS, which may strengthen the rule base of the inference system.
- In this article, the fuzzy inputs are taken in the form of TFNs. But depending on different contexts, triangular fuzzy numbers, Gaussian fuzzy numbers, etc. may be considered to tackle imprecisions related to inputs.
- The proposed method can also be extended in several fields of applications under intuitionistic fuzzy, Pythagorean fuzzy, q-rung orthopair fuzzy, and other variants of fuzzy environments.

Acknowledgements. The authors are grateful to all the female Sal leaf plate makers for participating in the study. The authors appreciate the reviewers' feedback on improving the quality of the manuscript.

References

1. Sahu, S.: Musculoskeletal pain among female labours engaged in manual material handling task in informal sectors of West Bengal, India. Asian-Pac. Newsl. Occup. Health Saf. **17**(3), 58–60 (2010)

2. Bernard, B.P.: Musculoskeletal disorders and workplace factors - a critical review of epidemiological evidence for work-related musculoskeletal disorders of the neck, upper extremity, and low back. Cincinnati (OH): Department of Health and Human Services (DHHS), NIOSH Press, USA (1997)
3. Yasobant, S., Mohanty, S.: Musculoskeletal disorders as a public health concern in India: a call for action. Physiotherapy –J. Indian Assoc. Physiotherapists **12**, 46–47 (2018)
4. Dey, M., Sahu, S.: Ergonomics survey of leaf plate making activity of tribal women. In: Gangopadhyay, S. (ed.) Proceeding of International Ergonomics Conference, HWWE, 2009-Ergonomics for Everyone, pp. 433–440 (2009)
5. Sahu, S., Chattopadhyay, S., Basu, K., Paul, G.: The ergonomic evaluation of work related musculoskeletal disorder among construction labourers working in unorganized sector in West Bengal India. J. Hum. Ergol. **39**(2), 99–109 (2010)
6. Hignett, S., McAtamney, L.: Rapid entire body assessment (REBA). Appl. Ergon. **31**, 201–205 (2000)
7. Ghosh, B., Sahu, S., Biswas, A.: Development of Fuzzy Decision Support System to Deal with Uncertainties in Working Posture Analysis using Rapid Upper Limb Assessment. Deep Learning Techniques for Biomedical and Health Informatics, pp. 119–140. Elsevier (2020)
8. Zadeh, L.A.: The concept of a linguistic variable and its application to approximate reasoning-II. Inf. Sci. **8**(4), 301–357 (1975)
9. Azadeh, A., Fam, I.M., Khoshnoud, M., Nikafrouz, M.: Design and implementation of a fuzzy expert system for performance assessment of an integrated health, safety, environment (HSE) and ergonomics system: the case of a gas refinery. Inf. Sci. **178**, 4280–4300 (2008)
10. Majumder, D., Debnath, J., Biswas, A.: Risk analysis in construction sites using fuzzy reasoning and fuzzy analytic hierarchy process. Procedia Technol. **10**, 604–614 (2013)
11. Rivero, L.C., Rodríguez, G.R., Pérez, M.D.R., Mar, C., Juárez, Z.: Fuzzy logic and RULA method for assessing the risk of working. Procedia Manuf. **3**, 4816–4822 (2015)
12. Golabchi, A., Han, S.U., Fayek, A.R.: A fuzzy logic approach to posture-based ergonomic analysis for field observation and assessment of construction manual operations. Can. J. Civil Eng. **43**(4), 294–303 (2016)
13. Debnath, J., Biswas, A., Sivan, P., Sen, K.N., Sahu, S.: Fuzzy inference model for assessing occupational risks in construction sites. Int. J. Ind. Ergon. **55**, 114–128 (2016)
14. Pavlovic-Veselinovic, S., Hedge, A., Veselinovic, M.: An ergonomic expert system for risk assessment of work-related musculo-skeletal disorders. Int. J. Ind. Ergon. **53**, 130–139 (2016)
15. Kadhim, M.A.: FNDSB: a fuzzy-neuro decision support system for back pain diagnosis. Cogn. Syst. Res. **52**, 691–700 (2018)
16. Ilbahar, E., Karasan, A., Cebi, S., Kahraman, C.: A novel approach to risk assessment for occupational health and safety using Pythagorean fuzzy AHP & fuzzy inference system. Saf. Sci. **103**, 124–136 (2018)
17. Samiei, S., Alefi, M., Alaei, Z., Pourbabaki, R.: Risk factors of low back pain using adaptive neuro-fuzzy system. Arch. Occup. Health **3**(2), 339–345 (2019)
18. Gul, M.: A fuzzy-based occupational health and safety risk assessment framework and a case study in an international port authority. J. Mar. Eng. Technol. **19**, 161–175 (2019). https://doi.org/10.1080/20464177.2019.1670994
19. Kose, Y., Karabayir, A., Cevikcan, E.: The quick exposure check (QEC) model proposal based on fuzzy logic for work-related musculoskeletal risk assessment. In: Kahraman, C., Cebi, S., Cevik Onar, S., Oztaysi, B., Tolga, A.C., Sari, I.U. (eds.) INFUS 2019. AISC, vol. 1029, pp. 82–88. Springer, Cham (2020). https://doi.org/10.1007/978-3-030-23756-1_12
20. Mamdani, E.H., Assilian, S.: An experiment in linguistic synthesis with a fuzzy logic controller. Int. J. Man-Mach. Stud. **7**(1), 1–13 (1975)
21. Kuorinka, I., et al.: Standardised Nordic questionnaires for the analysis of musculoskeletal systems. Appl. Ergon. **18**, 233–237 (1987)

22. Pearson, K.: Notes on regression and inheritance in the case of two parents. Proc. Roy. Soc. Lond. **58**, 240–242 (1895)
23. https://www.ergo.human.cornell.edu/cutools.html
24. Lee, H.K.: First Course on Fuzzy Theory and Applications. Springer, Heidelberg (2005)

Multispectral Object Detection with Deep Learning

Md Osman Gani[1], Somenath Kuiry[2(✉)], Alaka Das[2], Mita Nasipuri[1],
and Nibaran Das[1]

[1] Department of CSE, Jadavpur University, Kolkata 700032, India
`nibaran.das@jadavpuruniversity.in`
[2] Department of Mathematics, Jadavpur University, Kolkata 700032, India
`skuiry.math.rs@jadavpuruniversity.in`

Abstract. Object detection in natural scenes can be a challenging task. In many real-life situations, the visible spectrum is not suitable for traditional computer vision tasks. Moving outside the visible spectrum range, such as the thermal spectrum or the near-infrared (NIR) images, is much more beneficial in low visibility conditions, NIR images are very helpful for understanding the object's material quality. In this work, we have taken images with both the Thermal and NIR spectrum for the object detection task. As multi-spectral data with both Thermal and NIR is not available for the detection task, we needed to collect data ourselves. Data collection is a time-consuming process, and we faced many obstacles that we had to overcome. We train the YOLO v3 network from scratch to detect an object from multi-spectral images. Also, to avoid overfitting, we have done data augmentation and tune hyperparameters.

Keywords: Multispectral images · RGB · NIR · THERMAL · YOLO · Object detection · DCNN · MAP · IoU

1 Introduction

In the last couple of decades, the field of computer vision has grown considerably. In terms of efficiency, pace, and scalability, many complex tasks such as object detection, localization, segmentation, and natural scene understanding have received a significant boost, particularly after implementing deep learning approaches such as convolutional neural networks [1]. However, deep learning approaches rely heavily on the availability of abundant quantities of data of good quality. Although visible light provides information close to what the human eye processes, it is unable to provide useful information in some cases. In a foggy atmosphere or a setting where the lighting is low, RGB systems can not provide adequate details, so there is a need for alternate imaging systems if such conditions have a fair chance of occurring. Thermal infrared imaging is also one such reliable device because since it captures heat signatures, infrared information can be independent of the efficiency of the light source(s). In warm environments, however, thermal infrared imaging can suffer and is based on costly camera hardware.

P. Dutta et al. (Eds.): CICBA 2021, CCIS 1406, pp. 105–117, 2021.
https://doi.org/10.1007/978-3-030-75529-4_9

Near-infrared cameras have been found to perform efficiently in situations that can not be used by RGB cameras due to lighting conditions, such as foggy environments. For night-time conditions, near-infrared (nonvisible) illumination may also be introduced. Therefore, if we can integrate the additional information from Near-infrared and Thermal spectra into different deep learning tasks along with our existing visible spectra, it is expected to work better as the model gets more information on any object than the only visible spectrum. There are many [2] datasets available for classification purposes, but there are very few in the Multi-spectral domain. In Table 1, some of the well-known multi-spectral datasets have been mentioned. However, on these three spectrums, visible, near-infrared, and thermal, there are no datasets available publicly for the object recognition task.

So in this work, we have collected some Multi-spectral (RGB, NIR, and Thermal) natural scenes. The collected dataset not only brings into the learning process three different spectrums, but also other similar variables that work with different sensors, such as different focal lengths, viewpoints, noise sensitivity, resolution of images, sharpness, and so on. The main objectives of this paper are

1. Prepare a dataset of multi-spectral images, which contains RGB, Thermal, and NIR spectrum, of the same scene with annotation of 10 classes in YOLO and Pascal VOC format. The classes are as follows: Car, Motorcycle, Bicycle, Human, Building, Bush, Tree, Sign-board, Road, Window.
2. Prepare an augmented dataset of the dataset mentioned above, which followed the above format and classes.
3. Study of various object detection models where we have mainly focused on three YOLO models.
4. Using the YOLO v3 network, we have trained our dataset in three ways as follows:

   a. Thermal
   b. RGB and Thermal
   c. RGB, NIR, and Thermal

5. Discuss the performances of those models on the mentioned dataset and analyze the overall performances.

Some significant researches, [3–6] has been performed for object detection purposes on Multichannel Convolutional Neural Networks over the past decade. A related philosophy is still used in Multi-spectral imaging; however, the Multi-spectral imaging framework is very diverse. For instance, multi-spectral imaging in medicine [7] helps diagnose retinopathy and macular oedema until it affects the retina. It is used in surveillance for broad scanning areas [8] as well as for facial recognition because face recognition algorithms on Multi-spectral images [9] are found to work better. Multi-spectral data in the agriculture sector helps detect the variety [10] and chemical composition [11] of different plants which are useful for plant health monitoring, nutrient [12], water status, and pesticide requirements [13]. Multi-spectral data is also useful in detecting defects in the food processing industry [14], hazardous compounds in the chemical industry [15], etc.

The rest of the paper is organized as follows. In section "Experiment setup" we have briefly explained the data set collection and annotation process. In the next section, we have discussed the result and analysis performed on the YOLO v3 model performed on the collected data. The conclusion and future work has been discussed in the last section.

Table 1. Some of the Multi-spectral images datasets

Authors	Year	Type	Spectrum
Takumi et al. [16]	2017	Street Images	RGB, NIR, MIR, FIR
Ha et al. [17]	2017	Street Images	RGB, Thermal
Aguilera et al. [18]	2018	Natural Images	RGB, NIR
Alldieck et al. [19]	2016	Street Images	RGB, Thermal
Brown et al. [20]	2011	Natural Images	RGB, NIR
Choe et al. [21]	2018	Natural Images	RGB, NIR
Davis et al. [22]	2007	Natural Images	RGB, Thermal
Hwang et al. [23]	2015	Natural Images	RGB, Thermal
Li et al. [24]	2018	Natural Images	RGB, Thermal

2 Dataset Preparation

2.1 Dataset Collection

Image data within the specific wavelength ranges, captured using instruments which are sensitive to a particular wavelength or with the help of some filters by which the wavelengths may be parted, is called Multispectral Images. Our multi-spectral image dataset includes RGB, NIR (750–900 nm) and Thermal (10410–12510 nm) spectrum images. The difference in reflectivity of some particular objects, combined with decreased distortion and atmospheric haze in the NIR wavelength, helps to get details of the objects and the visibility is often improved [32]. In Thermal images, more heated objects are visualized well against less heated objects in the scene regardless of day-night or haze [33]. The details of the capturing devices are given below:

- Visible Spectrum: Nikkon D3200 DSLR Camera with Nikkon AF-S 3.5–5.6 G standard lens
- Near Infrared Spectrum: Watec WAT-902H2 Camera, 24 mm lens (SV-EGG-BOXH1X), Schnieder 093 IR Pass Filter (830 nm)
- Thermal Spectrum: FLIR A655SC Thermal Camera

The raw image dataset containing multi-spectral images for the same scene is not readily available. No standard dataset is available freely related to the present work. There exist several available datasets either containing RGB, and NIR images [44] or RGB and Thermal images [43] for the same scene and also their annotation format is not uniform. As the required dataset is not available, we are forced to collect our dataset.

The most challenging part of our work is preparing the same scene's dataset having natural images in three spectrums. We have collected 1060 images for each spectrum in the present work and totalling 3180 images of the 1060 scene.

2.2 Data Splitting

We have three spectral image datasets which we had collected on our own for the development of multi-spectral image data sets which are not readily available. We have used this dataset for object detection of 10 classes. The classes are Car, Motorcycle, Bicycle, Human, Building, Bush, Tree, Sign-board, Road, Window. The whole dataset is divided for each spectrum into six-part. One part out of six-part is completely kept separated for testing purposes so that we can understand the performance of our model. Left five parts are divided into 8:1 ratio for training and validation purposes. To increase the amount of data, we use the data augmentation technique, and those data are used only for training purposes. The test set consists of one complete scene which is not included in the training or validation set and 10% data of the training set.

2.3 Augmentation

As the collection of data is highly time-consuming and we need a significantly large amount of data to feed the deep neural network (DCNN) [36–39], we have taken the help of the data augmentation technique [26]. These are the most commonly used method for increasing the volume of the dataset significantly. It helps to reduce overfitting, to bring diversity in data, and to regularize the model. We have used Flip, Rotation, Scale, Crop, Translation, and Gaussian noise-based data augmentation techniques to randomly increase the volume of the dataset. Those augmentation techniques are standard and help to bring diversity in data substantially (Fig. 1).

Fig. 1. Randomly translated NIR image and randomly rotated RGB image from our augmented dataset

2.4   Annotation

The most important thing to be done before feeding the data to a deep neural network (DCNN) is annotation. Among the various annotation methods, we have used the bounding box technique. For completing the annotation, we have taken the help of labelling tools [29]. It is an open-source, free tool used for annotation in the bounding box method. As we have to feed the dataset to the YOLO v3 model, we have saved the annotations in darknet format (Fig. 2).

Fig. 2. Annotation in bounding box method using LabelImg tools

3   Result and Analysis

The natural scene is clicked randomly by three cameras simultaneously for the same scene multi-spectral dataset. All the images are pre-processed and taken together. Annotation is done for all the images, and then we split the dataset into train and test set. After augmentation, all the regular and augmented images and annotation of train part are being fed to the YOLO v3 network for training. The test portion images which are unknown to the model is used for detection. The whole process is presented in Fig. 3.

3.1   Experiment Setup

Among different existing object localization technique, YOLO and its variations are used heavily in the present days. YOLO v1 is a regression-based algorithm which uses the Darknet framework. YOLO v1 has several limitations as a result of the utilization of

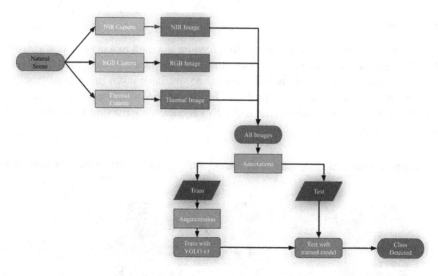

Fig. 3. The proposed work

the YOLO v1 is restricted. It is unable to identify the tiny objects if they have appeared as a cluster. In the interest of improvement of the YOLO v1 network and overcome the limitations of YOLO v1, YOLO v2 [26] is developed. That incremental improvement of YOLO v2 or YOLO 9000 is termed as YOLO v3 [27]. The importance of an object detection algorithm is weighted by how accurate and quickly it can detect objects. YOLO v3 has done a great job and left every object detection algorithm behind in terms of speed and accuracy. It has everything to use for real-time object detection [34, 35]. We have selected the YOLO v3 model architecture for our training purpose. The training was done on a LINUX (Ubuntu 18.04 LTS) Operating system having 4 GB NVIDIA GPU (GeForce GTX 1050 Ti) which helped us to train faster. Also, all the codes have been written and compiled in PyTorch environment. To evaluate the performance of the model, we have used the AP (Average Precision) and mAP (Mean Average Precision) [40] as a metric with IoU = 0.5. As an optimizer, we have used Adams Optimizer and fixed the learning rate into 7*10-4. Firstly, we have trained only the THERMAL dataset, then THERMAL and RGB dataset together and finally we have trained THERMAL, RGB, and NIR together. For each training, we train our network with 380–400 epochs.

3.2 THERMAL Image Dataset Training

To measure the performance of the model, in Thermal dataset, we have kept one scene entirely out of training and validation purpose, which is used for testing the performance of the model. For testing, we have used 212 images. On the Thermal dataset, we get the $mAP_{IoU=0.5} = 53.4\%$, which is comparable to YOLO v3 results on COCO [42] dataset. The results are given in the tabular form, and examples of detection are given below:

Table 2. AP is calculated at the IoU threshold of 0.5 of all classes on the Thermal dataset and mAP@0.5 are given in the table.

Class	AP_{50}
Car	67.1
Motorcycle	43.5
Bicycle	5.5
Human	21.4
Building	61.5
Bush	62.6
Tree	79.3
Sign-board	27.5
Road	73.4
Window	92.5
mAP_{50}	**53.4**

If we closely observe the above table (Table 2), which indicates the result obtained from the test set of Thermal images, we will find that the AP_{50} value of bicycle class too low because the number of samples of that particular class was significantly less. Other classes are giving a moderate AP_{50} value, whereas the window class is giving the highest AP_{50} value. The result depends on the scene's temperature, as the camera automatically normalizes the overall scene temperature if it finds a temperature a considerable variance of temperature (like some burning object, sky scene, etc.). The overall mAP50 is quite satisfactory, and it is comparable to the YOLO v3 mAP for the COCO dataset. The detection of the object on test samples are given below (Fig. 4):

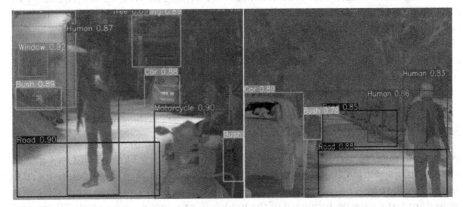

Fig. 4. Object detected on Thermal Images from test set. Non-maximal Suppression = 0.5, Confidence Threshold = 0.75, IoU = 0.5

3.3 RGB and THERMAL Image Dataset Training

As discussed, to measure the model performance of RGB and Thermal dataset, we have kept one scene completely out of training and validation purpose, which is used for testing the performance of the model. For testing, we have used 240 images. No training set data is used for testing. On Thermal dataset we get the $mAP_{IoU=0.5} = 46.4\%$. The results are given in the tabular form, and examples of detection are given below (Table 3):

Table 3. AP is calculated at the IoU threshold of 0.5 of all classes on RGB, and the Thermal dataset and mAP@0.5 are given in the table.

Class	AP_{50}
Car	69.9
Motorcycle	52.6
Bicycle	59.4
Human	78.3
Building	23.4
Bush	35.4
Tree	48.4
Sign-board	14.5
Road	51.4
Window	30.5
mAP_{50}	**46.4**

Adding RGB images with Thermal images for training shows a significant change in the AP_{50} of every class. Here a drastic change is noticeable in AP_{50} for the bicycle class, because of increased visibility due to the visual spectrum. Although AP of some classes, like sign-board, got reduced by a significant margin. This thing happened due to the imbalance in the number of classes. The overall $mAP_{50} = 46.4\%$ is a good achievement for multi-spectral classes. The examples of detection of objects on RGB and Thermal images using this model is presented below (Fig. 5):

3.4 THERMAL, NIR and RGB Dataset Training

We tried to observe and work on improving the performance of the YOLO v3 model on the Multi-spectral dataset. To measure the model performance of the Multi-spectral dataset, we have kept one scene completely out of training and validation purpose, which is used for testing the performance of the model. For testing, we have used 170 images. On Thermal dataset we get the $mAP_{IoU=0.5} = 43.4\%$. The results are given in the tabular form, and examples of detection are given below (Table 4):

Fig. 5. Object detected on RGB and Thermal Images from test set. Non-maximal Suppression = 0.5, Confidence Threshold = 0.4, IoU = 0.5

Table 4. AP is calculated at the IoU threshold of 0.5 of all classes on Thermal, NIR, and RGB dataset, and mAP@0.5 are given in the table.

Class	AP_{50}
Car	30.9
Motorcycle	55.1
Bicycle	61.5
Human	45.8
Building	39.4
Bush	40.7
Tree	31.5
Sign-board	47.1
Road	50.0
Window	31.8
mAP_{50}	**43.4**

After training the model with RGB, NIR, and Thermal images, the performance is slightly reduced. As we started adding more spectral images, the overall performance started to reduce, but each class's AP became stable. The AP50 of all classes is moderate, and no class has got significantly reduced AP50. The class car has got the least AP50 = 30.9%. The overall mAP50 = 43.4%. Using our model, the object detection result is shown below (Fig. 6):

Although the training of only the Thermal image dataset gives a quite good output on the test set the output of the multi-spectral dataset is not that bad. As we started adding different spectral images, the performance started degrading (Table 5).

Mean Average Precision values of only Thermal images are reasonably good. For only Thermal images, mAP50 = 53.4%. The mAP of RGB and Thermal images is 46.4%. When we add one more spectrum (i.e., NIR), the mAP is reduced to 43.4%. The accuracy

Fig. 6. Object detected on NIR, RGB and THERMAL Images respectively from test set. Non-maximal Suppression = 0.5, Confidence Threshold = 0.4, IoU = 0.5

Table 5. Comparison of performance on the different spectral dataset

Input Spectrum	mAP_{50}
Thermal	53.4
RGB and Thermal	46.4
RGB, NIR, and Thermal	43.4

of the models lowers, as we append more spectral image datasets. The performance is reduced due to less visibility and less differentiable pixel values of Thermal and NIR images. More accuracy can be obtained by increasing the volume of the dataset by a large margin.

First of all, we know that thermography depends on the heat emitting from the object. The object emits more heat is more clearly visible. In the case of an RGB image, the object is detected depending on the pattern and the structure. Moreover, for the NIR image, it depends on the reflectivity of certain objects. For some objects, the AP increase but, in some cases, it decreases. Low AP for Bicycle class for only thermal image signifies that the lower temperature of the class Bicycle as the data collected in the winter season, and it started increasing when we add RGB and NIR spectrum respectively. The AP of some objects like Road decreases when we add more spectrum because the model is extracting more complex features from different spectrums. For some objects like Sign-board, it is shown that after adding RGB, it decreases significantly while adding the NIR spectrum it increases. This is because of the class imbalance in our dataset, which will be adjusted before publishing the dataset publicly.

4   Conclusion and Future Work

Firstly, we have collected data on multi-spectral natural images. The spectral bands included Thermal, NIR, and RGB. After collecting and pre-processing the data, we annotate them. To avoid overfitting and increase the amount of data, we perform data augmentation. When the dataset is ready to feed into the network, we prepare the YOLO v3 model to perform training. After training multiple times and tuning hyperparameters, we conclude with the aforementioned results and detection examples.

Our model performance gives a brief outline that the multi-spectrum dataset can be used for object detection. Although the model's performance is not so outstanding, it can be improved by performing better hyperparameter tuning and adding more data into the dataset. The main problems of this dataset are class imbalance and less amount of data. As the dataset has a significantly less amount of data, we had to deal with the model's overfitting. As the instances per class fluctuate very sharply, the model unable to give optimal results. As the number of spectrum increases, the model struggles to perform well. This happens due to a lack of data and class imbalance. In the COCO dataset, we have seen a considerable amount of data with a very large number of instances for a single class, which helps the model perform much more accurately.

In the future, we can increase the amount of data that can handle the class imbalance. We can merge three spectrum images in a single image called image registration. Here we can feed a network with five layers (RGB = 3, NIR = 1, Thermal = 1, totalling = 5) of data at a time, which can help us to improve accuracy. Not only object detection, but we can also use the merged data for object material detection, object temperature detection as well. The model performance can be improved significantly by introducing an ensembling among the different state of the art models [45]. After some processing and adding more images into the dataset, the whole dataset will be made public for research purposes.

Acknowledgement. We want to thank the entire team of people that made the collection of this dataset possible.

– Image Capturing: Priyam Sarkar
– Data Preprocessing: Priyam Sarkar
– Data Annotation: Shubhadeep Bhowmick

This work is supported by the project sponsored by SERB (Government of India, order no. SB/S3/EECE/054/2016) (dated 25/11/2016), and carried out at the Centre for Microprocessor Application for Training Education and Research, CSE Department, Jadavpur University. The second author would like to thank The Department of Science and Technology for their INSPIRE Fellowship program (IF170641) for financial support.

References

1. LeCun, Y., et al.: Gradient-based learning applied to document recognition. Proc. IEEE **86**(11), 2278–2324 (1998)
2. Deng, J., et al.: ImageNet: a large-scale hierarchical image database. In: 2009 IEEE Conference on Computer Vision and Pattern Recognition. IEEE (2009)
3. Wang, L., et al.: Multi-channel convolutional neural network based 3D object detection for indoor robot environmental perception. Sensors **19**(4), 893 (2019)
4. Cheng, Z., Shen, J.: On very large scale test collection for landmark image search benchmarking. Signal Process. **124**, 13–26 (2016)
5. Song, J., et al.: Optimized graph learning using partial tags and multiple features for image and video annotation. IEEE Trans. Image Process. **25**(11), 4999–5011 (2016)
6. Gao, L., et al.: Hierarchical LSTMs with adaptive attention for visual captioning. IEEE Trans. Pattern Anal. Mach. Intell. **42**(5), 1112–1131 (2019)
7. Shahidi, A.M., et al.: Regional variation in human retinal vessel oxygen saturation. Exp. Eye Res. **113**, 143–147 (2013)

8. Ambinder, M.: The secret team that killed Bin Laden. Natl. J. **3** (2011)
9. Di, W., et al.: Studies on hyperspectral face recognition in visible spectrum with feature band selection. IEEE Trans. Syst. Man Cybern.-Part A: Syst. Humans **40**(6), 1354–1361 (2010)
10. Lacar, F.M., Lewis, M.M., Grierson, I.T.: Use of hyperspectral imagery for mapping grape varieties in the Barossa Valley, South Australia. In: IGARSS 2001. Scanning the Present and Resolving the Future. Proceedings. IEEE 2001 International Geoscience and Remote Sensing Symposium (Cat. No. 01CH37217), vol. 6. IEEE (2001)
11. Ferwerda, J.G.: Charting the quality of forage: measuring and mapping the variation of chemical components in foliage with hyperspectral remote sensing. In: ITC (2005)
12. Tilling, A.K., et al.: Remote sensing to detect nitrogen and water stress in wheat. Aust. Soc. Agron. **17** (2006)
13. Flémal, P., et al.: Assessment of pesticide coating on cereal seeds by near infrared hyperspectral imaging. J. Spectral Imaging **6** (2017)
14. Higgins, K.T.: Five new technologies for Inspection. Food Process. **6** (2013)
15. Farley, V., et al.: Chemical agent detection and identification with a hyperspectral imaging infrared sensor. In: Electro-Optical Remote Sensing, Detection, and Photonic Technologies and Their Applications, vol. 6739. International Society for Optics and Photonics (2007)
16. Takumi, K., et al.: Multi-spectral object detection for autonomous vehicles. In: Proceedings of the on Thematic Workshops of ACM Multimedia (2017)
17. Ha, Q., et al.: MFNet: towards real-time semantic segmentation for autonomous vehicles with multi-spectral scenes. In: 2017 IEEE/RSJ International Conference on Intelligent Robots and Systems (IROS). IEEE (2017)
18. Aguilera, C., Soria, X., Sappa, A., Toledo, R.: RGBN multispectral images: a novel color restoration approach. In: De la Prieta, F., et al. (eds.) PAAMS 2017. AISC, vol. 619, pp. 155–163. Springer, Cham (2018). https://doi.org/10.1007/978-3-319-61578-3_15
19. Alldieck, T., Bahnsen, C., Moeslund, T.: Context-aware fusion of RGB and thermal imagery for traffic monitoring. Sensors **16**(11), 1947 (2016)
20. Brown, M., Süsstrunk, S.: Multi-spectral SIFT for scene category recognition. In: CVPR 2011. IEEE (2011)
21. Choe, G., et al.: RANUS: RGB and NIR urban scene dataset for deep scene parsing. IEEE Robot. Autom. Lett. **3**(3), 1808–1815 (2018)
22. Davis, J.W., Keck, M.A.: A two-stage template approach to person detection in thermal imagery. In: 2005 Seventh IEEE Workshops on Applications of Computer Vision (WACV/MOTION'05), vol. 1. IEEE (2005)
23. Redmon, J., Divvala, S., Girshick, R., Farhadi, A.: You only look once: unified, real-time object detection. arXiv preprint arXiv:1506.02640 (2015)
24. Redmon, J., Farhadi, A.: YOLO9000: better, faster, stronger. In: 2017 IEEE Conference on Computer Vision and Pattern Recognition (CVPR), pp. 6517–6525. IEEE (2017)
25. Redmon, J., Farhadi, A.: YOLOv3: an incremental improvement. arXiv preprint arXiv:1804.02767 (2018)
26. Shorten, C., Khoshgoftaar, T.: A survey on Image data augmentation for deep learning. J. Big Data **6**(1), 1–48 (2019). https://doi.org/10.1186/s40537-019-0197-0
27. Arslan, M., Guzel, M., Demirci, M., Ozdemir, S.: SMOTE and Gaussian noise based sensor data augmentation (2019). https://doi.org/10.1109/UBMK.2019.8907003
28. Rusak, E., Schott, L., Zimmermann, R., Bitterwolf, J., Bringmann, O., Bethge, M., Brendel, W.: A simple way to make neural networks robust against diverse image corruptions. In: Vedaldi, Andrea, Bischof, Horst, Brox, Thomas, Frahm, Jan-Michael. (eds.) ECCV 2020. LNCS, vol. 12348, pp. 53–69. Springer, Cham (2020). https://doi.org/10.1007/978-3-030-58580-8_4
29. Tzutalin: LabelImg (2015)

30. Essock, E.A., McCarley, J.S., Sinai, M.J., DeFord, J.K.: Human perception of sensor-fused imagery. In: Hoffman, R.R., Markman, A.B. (eds.) Interpreting Remote Sensing Imagery: Human Factors. Lewis Publishers, Boca Raton (2001)

31. Thermography. https://en.wikipedia.org/wiki/Thermography

32. Zhao, Z.Q., Zheng, P., Xu, S.T., Wu, X.: Object detection with deep learning: a review (2019). https://doi.org/10.1109/TNNLS.2018.2876865

33. Lu, S., Wang, B., Wang, H., Chen, L., Linjian, M., Zhang, X.: A real-time object detection algorithm for video. Comput. Electr. Eng. **77**, 398–408 (2019). https://doi.org/10.1016/j.com peleceng.2019.05.009

34. Liu, L., et al.: Deep learning for generic object detection: a survey. Int. J. Comput. Vis. **128**(2), 261–318 (2019). https://doi.org/10.1007/s11263-019-01247-4

35. Huttenlocher, D.: Computer vision. In: Computer Science Handbook, 2nd Edn. (2004). https://doi.org/10.4324/9780429042522-10

36. Computer vision: algorithms and applications. Choice Rev. Online. (2011). https://doi.org/10.5860/choice.48-5140

37. Du, C.-J., Cheng, Q.: Computer vision. In: O'Donnell, C., Fagan, C., Cullen, P.J. (eds.) Process Analytical Technology for the Food Industry. FES, pp. 157–181. Springer, New York (2014). https://doi.org/10.1007/978-1-4939-0311-5_7

38. Zhang, E., Zhang, Y.: Average precision. In: Liu, L., ÖZSU, M.T. (ed.) Encyclopedia of Database Systems, pp. 192–193. Springer , Boston (2009). https://doi.org/10.1007/978-0-387-39940-9_482

39. Rezatofighi, H., Tsoi, N., Gwak, J., Sadeghian, A., Reid, I., Savarese, S.: Generalized intersection over union: a metric and a loss for bounding box regression. In: Proceedings of the IEEE/CVF Conference on Computer Vision and Pattern Recognition (CVPR), pp. 658–666 (2019)

40. Lin, T.-Y., et al.: Microsoft COCO: common objects in context. In: Fleet, D., Pajdla, T., Schiele, B., Tuytelaars, T. (eds.) ECCV 2014. LNCS, vol. 8693, pp. 740–755. Springer, Cham (2014). https://doi.org/10.1007/978-3-319-10602-1_48

41. FREE FLIR Thermal Dataset for Algorithm Training. https://www.flir.in/oem/adas/adas-dat aset-form/

42. RGB-NIR Scene Dataset. https://ivrlwww.epfl.ch/supplementary_material/cvpr11/index.html

43. Hwang, S., et al.: Multi-spectral pedestrian detection: benchmark dataset and baseline. In: Proceedings of the IEEE Conference on Computer Vision and Pattern Recognition (2015)

44. Li, C., et al.: RGB-T object tracking: benchmark and baseline. Pattern Recognit. **96**, 106977 (2019)

45. Dutta, A., et al.: Using thermal intensities to build conditional random fields for object segmentation at night. In: 2020 4th International Conference on Computational Intelligence and Networks (CINE). IEEE (2020)

Pythagorean Fuzzy *c*-means Clustering Algorithm

Souvik Gayen and Animesh Biswas[✉]

Department of Mathematics, University of Kalyani, Kalyani 741235, India

Abstract. This article presents algorithm for *c*-means clustering under Pythagorean fuzzy environment. In this method Pythagorean fuzzy generator is developed to convert the data points from crisp to Pythagorean fuzzy numbers (PFNs). Subsequently, Euclidean distance is used to measure the distances between data points. From the viewpoint of capturing imprecise information, the proposed method is advantageous in the sense that associated PFNs not only consider membership and non-membership degrees, but also includes several other variants of fuzzy sets for information processing. The proposed algorithm is applied on synthetic, UCI and two moon datasets to verify the validity and efficiency of the developed method. Comparing the results with the fuzzy and intuitionistic fuzzy *c*-means clustering algorithms, the proposed method establishes its higher capability of partitioning data using Pythagorean fuzzy information.

Keywords: Data clustering · Fuzzy *c*-mean clustering · Pythagorean fuzzy sets · Unsupervised learning

1 Introduction

Cluster analysis [1] is an efficient tool to classify data in such a manner that homogeneous data remain in the same cluster and heterogeneous data lie in different clusters. Through cluster analysis the data are classified based on two aspects [2], viz., assigning each element or object to only one cluster, and finding number of clusters.

In unsupervised learning, clustering is a fundamental process. This tool is extensively used in different domains of sciences, like pattern recognition, data mining, machine learning, image processing, banking, web clouding, information retrieval, etc. Clustering analysis is performed through two different techniques, viz., hierarchical and partitional clustering methods.

Hierarchical clustering [3] method generates a hierarchical tree of clusters. It is performed through two approaches, agglomerative and divisive [4]. Partitional clustering method provides *c*-partitions of a set of data points using iterative processes, where *c* is a predefined number of clusters [5].

Fuzzy logic [6] is a powerful tool to deal with imprecision associated with real life data. In crisp clustering one cluster is assigned for an object, but in fuzzy clustering [7] more than one cluster may be assigned with some associate membership degree.

© Springer Nature Switzerland AG 2021
P. Dutta et al. (Eds.): CICBA 2021, CCIS 1406, pp. 118–130, 2021.
https://doi.org/10.1007/978-3-030-75529-4_10

Fuzzy c-means (FCM) clustering (FCMC) [8], introduced by Bezdek (1981), is most commonly used method in partitional clustering. It is a combined method of k-means clustering [9] and fuzzy logic [6]. In FCMC algorithm [8], an objective function consisting of membership value to a cluster of an object and distances from objects to the centroids of respective clusters is minimized.

Intuitionistic fuzzy (IF) set (IFS) [10, 11] is an important generalization of fuzzy sets. Besides membership value, another value, called non-membership value, is added to that set. It attracted many researchers to work in various areas of engineering and science, like edge detection, pattern recognition, data mining, segmentation, etc. In 2010 Xu and Wu introduced intuitionistic FCM (IFCM) [12]. In that method, FCMC process is extended to IFCM clustering (IFCMC) using IF distance measure [13]. Moreover, in FCMC method [8], the p dimensional data point x_k is expressed in the form $\left(x_{k_1}, x_{k_2}, \ldots, x_{k_p}\right)$, but in IFCMC each membership and non-membership degrees associated with each x_{k_i} takes into account. Thus the data points in this case are presented in the form $\left(\left(x_{k_1}, \mu_{k_1}, \nu_{k_1}\right), \left(x_{k_2}, \mu_{k_2}, \nu_{k_2}\right), \ldots, \left(x_{k_p}, \mu_{k_p}, \nu_{k_p}\right)\right)$.

In many cases, the dataset is not given in the form of FS or IFS. So, it becomes difficult to assign exact membership value to each data point. In 2011 T. Charita proposed a new algorithm based on IFS, called 'novel IFCM' clustering algorithm [14] by considering entropy based objective function. Several clustering algorithms based on IFS are performed in the literature [15–18]. In 2018 Lohani [19] pointed out the convergence of the IFCMC method. Bustince et al. [20] developed an IF generator (IFG) by imposing certain conditions on fuzzy complement functions.

Pythagorean fuzzy (PF) set (PFS) [21] is an extension of IFS with simultaneous consideration of membership as well as non-membership values subject to the constraint that the square sum of membership and non-membership values must not exceeds 1. Due to this later condition, PFS becomes more capable and powerful tool to handle uncertain and vague data than IFSs.

Further, it becomes difficult to measure distances for assigning clusters to the data in a precise way, due to the imprecision involved with the available data. From this viewpoint, this article introduces c-means clustering algorithm using PFSs, viz., PF c-means (PyFCM) clustering algorithm. The concept of IFG [20], is extended in PF context to develop PF generator (PFG). Convergence of PyFCM clustering algorithm has been proved. Modified partitional coefficient (MPC) [22] and Xie-Beni (XB) [23] indices for cluster validity [24] are used for validation of PyFCM clustering. With these indices a comparison result between PyFCM method, FCM and IFCM techniques is shown.

2 Preliminaries

In this section some basic concepts which are required in developing the proposed method are discussed.

Definition. [21] Let X be a discrete universal set with $X = \{x_1, x_2, \ldots, x_n\}$. The set A defined on X is said to be a PFS if it can be written as.

$$A = \{(x, \mu_A(x), \nu_A(x)) : x \in X\},$$

where $\mu_A : X \rightarrow [0, 1]$ and $v_A : X \rightarrow [0, 1]$ represent membership and non-membership functions of $x \in A$ with $0 \leq \mu_A^2(x) + v_A^2(x) \leq 1$ for all $x \in X$.

The degree of hesitancy is defined by $\pi_A(x) = \sqrt{1 - \mu_A^2(x) - v_A^2(x)}$.

So, clearly (μ, v, π) satisfies the equation, $\mu^2 + v^2 + \pi^2 = 1$.

2.1 Distance Measure Between Pythagorean Fuzzy Sets (PFS) [25]

Let P_1 and P_2 be two PFSs defined on $X = \{x_1, x_2, \ldots, x_n\}$. Distance between P_1 and P_2, is given by.

$$d(P_1, P_2) = \left(\frac{1}{2n} \sum_{i=1}^{n} \left(\mu_{p_1}^2(x_i) - \mu_{p_2}^2(x_i) \right)^2 + \left(v_{p_1}^2(x_i) - v_{p_2}^2(x_i) \right)^2 + \left(\pi_{p_1}^2(x_i) - \pi_{p_2}^2(x_i) \right)^2 \right)^{\frac{1}{2}}.$$

2.2 FCM Clustering

FCMC [8] is an unsupervised learning process to combine k-means clustering algorithm and fuzzy logic. As like k-means clustering algorithm, FCMC algorithm also follows an iteration process. This process is based on a predefined number of clusters. In this algorithm an object is assigned to clusters with some membership values. FCMC algorithm is based on minimizing an objective function. A mathematical description for FCMC is described below.

$$min \quad J_m(U, V) = \sum_{i=1}^{n} \sum_{j=1}^{c} u_{ij}^m d^2(X_i, V_j)$$

$$\text{such that} \quad \begin{array}{l} \sum_{j=1}^{c} u_{ij} = 1 \; \forall 1 \leq i \leq n \\ u_{ij} \in [0, 1]. \quad \forall 1 \leq i \leq n, 1 \leq j \leq c \\ \sum_{i=1}^{n} u_{ij} > 0 \; \forall 1 \leq j \leq c \end{array}$$

where $= \{X_1, X_2, \ldots, X_n\} \subset \mathbb{R}^p$, p is the dimension of the space, n and c represents the number of samples and clusters, respectively. m is weighting exponent. $V = \{V_1, V_2, \ldots, V_c\}$ represents the set of centroids of c number of clusters; u_{ij} designates the membership value of ith data point, X_i, in j^{th} cluster, V_j; $d(X_i, V_j)$ represents the Euclidean distance between X_i and V_j in $\mathbb{R}^p$.

3 PyFCM Clustering Algorithm

In this section PyFCM clustering technique is introduced by extending FCMC method under PF environment. In the proposed method n data points having p features are considered, which are expressed in the form of PFSs. So, the dataset contains n data points, each of them having p tuples, and each tuple is structured with a triple, (μ, v, π).

Now, the generalized least squared errors functional, $J_m(U, V)$, [8] is used under PF environment to minimize the Euclidean distances between data points as follows:

$$\text{Minimize } J_m(U, V) = \sum_{i=1}^{n} \sum_{j=1}^{c} u_{ij}^m d^2(X_i, V_j)$$

$$\text{such that} \quad \begin{array}{l} \sum_{j=1}^{c} u_{ij} = 1 \; \forall \; 1 \leq i \leq n \\ u_{ij} \in [0, 1]. \quad \forall \; 1 \leq i \leq n, \; 1 \leq j \leq c \\ \sum_{i=1}^{n} u_{ij} > 0 \; \forall \; 1 \leq j \leq c, \end{array} \qquad (1)$$

where $X = \{X_1, X_2, \ldots, X_n\}$, $X_i = (x_{i1}, x_{i2}, \ldots, x_{ip})$ with each x_{ij} having the form of PFN; $V = \{V_1, V_2, \ldots, V_c\}$ represents c number of clusters centroids; u_{ij} designates the membership value of ith data point in j^{th} cluster, V_j; $m(> 1)$ signifies an weight exponent; $d(X_i, V_j)$ represents Euclidean distance between X_i and V_j in PF format.

To minimize the functional J_m, Lagrange multiplier method [26] is applied.

It is worthy to mention here that membership matrix U would be upgraded at every iteration by finding optimal solution of Eq. (1). Let the solution at the tth iteration is found as

$$u_{ij}^t = \frac{1}{\sum_{k=1}^{c} \left(\frac{d^2(X_i, V_j(t))}{d^2(X_i, V_k(t))} \right)^{\frac{1}{m-1}}}; \text{ and cluster centroid, } V_j(t) = \left(\mu_{V_j}^t, \nu_{V_j}^t, \pi_{V_j}^t \right), \text{ where}$$

$$\mu_{V_j}^t(x_l) = \left(\frac{\sum_{i=1}^{n} \left(u_{ij}^t \right)^m \mu_{X_i}^2(x_l)}{\sum_{i=1}^{n} \left(u_{ij}^t \right)^m} \right)^{\frac{1}{2}}, \; \nu_{V_j}^t(x_l) = \left(\frac{\sum_{i=1}^{n} \left(u_{ij}^t \right)^m \nu_{X_i}^2(x_l)}{\sum_{i=1}^{n} \left(u_{ij}^t \right)^m} \right)^{\frac{1}{2}};$$

$$\pi_{V_j}^t(x_l) = \left(\frac{\sum_{i=1}^{n} \left(u_{ij}^t \right)^m \pi_{X_i}^2(x_l)}{\sum_{i=1}^{n} \left(u_{ij}^t \right)^m} \right)^{\frac{1}{2}}$$

$$\forall 1 \leq j \leq c, 1 \leq l \leq p. \qquad (2)$$

The process of updating is terminated when $\sum_{k=1}^{c} \frac{d(V_k(t), V_k(t+1))}{c} < \varepsilon$.

3.1 Convergence of PyFCM Clustering Algorithm

Here the convergence of PyFCM clustering algorithm is verified through the following theorem:

Theorem. Let $\phi : M_{Fc} \rightarrow \mathbb{R}$ is given by $\phi(U) = J_m(U, v)$, where M_{Fc} represents the collection of $n \times c$ order matrices with the elements $u_{ij} \in [0, 1]$, satisfying the condition $\sum_{j=1}^{c} u_{ij} = 1, \forall 1 \leq i \leq n; \sum_{i=1}^{n} u_{ij} > 0, \forall 1 \leq j \leq c$ and $v \in \left(\mathbb{R}^3 \right)^{cp}$, then ϕ attains strict local minimum value at U^* iff U^* is derived from Eq. (2).

Proof: Let $u_{ij} = z_{ij}^2, \forall i, j$ and $Z = \left[z_{ij}^2 \right]_{n \times c}$. So, $\sum_{j=1}^c z_{ij}^2 = 1, \forall 1 \le i \le n$.

Using Lagrange's multipliers $\lambda = (\lambda_1, \lambda_2, \ldots, \lambda_n)$, let

$$\mathcal{L}(Z, \lambda) = \sum_{i=1}^n \sum_{j=1}^c z_{ij}^{2m} d^2(X_i, V_j) - \sum_{i=1}^n \lambda_i \left(\sum_{j=1}^c z_{ij}^2 - 1 \right). \tag{3}$$

Now, if ϕ minimizes at (z^*, λ^*), then $\frac{\partial \mathcal{L}(z^*, \lambda^*)}{\partial \lambda_i} = 0$ and $\frac{\partial \mathcal{L}(z^*, \lambda^*)}{\partial z_{ij}} = 0$.

So, $\sum_{j=1}^c \left(z_{ij}^* \right)^2 = 1$ and $2m \left(z_{ij}^* \right)^{2m-1} d^2(X_i, V_j) - 2\lambda_i^* \left(z_{ij}^* \right) = 0$.

i.e., $\left(z_{ij}^* \right)^2 = \left(\frac{\lambda_i^*}{md^2(X_i, V_j)} \right)^{\frac{1}{m-1}}$.

Consequently, $\left(z_{ij}^* \right)^2 = \sum_{k=1}^c \frac{1}{\left(\frac{d^2(X_i, V_j)}{d^2(X_i, V_k)} \right)^{\frac{1}{m-1}}}$, and so

$$u_{ij}^* = \sum_{k=1}^c \frac{1}{\left(\frac{d^2(X_i, V_j)}{d^2(X_i, V_k)} \right)^{\frac{1}{m-1}}}.$$

Conversely, considering Eq. (3), the Hessian matrix $H_{\mathcal{L}}(U^*)$ of order $nc \times nc$ is constructed as follows:

Taking 2nd order partial derivative of $\mathcal{L}(Z, \lambda)$ w.r.t. z_{st} at (z^*, λ^*), it is obtained that.

$$\frac{\partial}{\partial z_{st}} \left(\frac{\partial \mathcal{L}(z^*, \lambda^*)}{\partial z_{ij}} \right) = \begin{cases} 2m(2m-1)\left(z_{ij}^* \right)^{2m-2} d^2(X_i, V_j) - 2\lambda_i^* & \text{for } s = i, t = j \\ 0 & \text{otherwise} \end{cases}$$

Thus $H_{\mathcal{L}}(U^*)$ becomes a diagonal matrix whose entries are calculated as follows. Let

$$\alpha_j = 2m(2m-1)\left(z_{ij}^* \right)^{2m-2} d^2(X_i, V_j) - 2\lambda_i^*$$

$$= 2m(2m-1)\left(u_{ij}^* \right)^{m-1} d^2(X_i, V_j) - 2\lambda_i^*$$

$$= 2m(2m-1)d^2(X_i, V_j) \left\{ \sum_{k=1}^c \frac{1}{\left(\frac{d^2(X_i, V_j)}{d^2(X_i, V_k)} \right)^{\frac{1}{m-1}}} \right\}^{m-1} - 2m \left\{ \frac{1}{\sum_{k=1}^c \left(\frac{1}{d^2(X_i, V_k)} \right)^{\frac{1}{m-1}}} \right\}^{m-1}$$

$$= 4m(m-1) \left[\sum_{k=1}^c \left(\frac{1}{d^2(X_i, V_k)} \right)^{\frac{1}{m-1}} \right]^{1-m} \quad \forall 1 \le i \le n. \tag{4}$$

Now, from Eq. (4) it is found that there are n distinct eigen values, each of multiplicity c. also $\alpha_j > 0$ implies $H_{\mathcal{L}}(U^*)$ is positive definite.

Hence ϕ attains strictly local minima at U^*.

3.2 Pseudo-Code for PyFCM Clustering Algorithm

Step 1: Fix c, m, ε, X. Define t as an iteration count. Set $t = 0$, and initially choose arbitrary c numbers of cluster centroid, $V(0)$ from the dataset X.

Step 2: Calculate $(t) = (u_{ij}^t)_{n \times c}$, where.

a) $u_{ij}^t = \dfrac{1}{\sum_{k=1}^{c}\left(\dfrac{d^2(X_i,V_j(t))}{d^2(X_i,V_k(t))}\right)^{\frac{1}{m-1}}}$, when $d(X_i, V_k(t)) > 0$ for all i, k with $1 \leq i \leq n$,

$1 \leq j \leq c, 1 \leq k \leq c$.

b) If there exists any i, k such that $d(X_i, V_k(t)) = 0$, then $u_{ik}^t = 1$ and $u_{ij}^t = 0$ for all $j \neq k$.

Step 3: Calculate $V(t+1) = \{V_1(t+1), V_2(t+1), \ldots, V_c(t+1)\}$ using Eq. (2).

Step 4: If $S(t, t+1) = \sum_{k=1}^{c} \dfrac{d(V_k(t), V_k(t+1))}{c} < \varepsilon$, then stop. Else return to step 2 for next iteration $t + 1$.

Note. J_m depends on U and V; and U depends on V, so, if $S(t, t+1) < \varepsilon$, then $|J_m(t) - J_m(t+1)| < \varepsilon$.

A flowchart for describing the proposed algorithm is presented in Fig. 1.

3.3 Cluster Validity Index [24]

Cluster validity index (CVI) is the most important part of clustering techniques. It measures intra cluster similarities and inter cluster dis-similarities. Using CVI, the optimal number of clusters is found. Two well-known processes for calculating validity index are described below.

Modified Partitional Coefficient (MPC) [22]. MPC is calculated using mean value of Euclidean distance between membership values and the centres of the fuzzy *c*-partitions. It is modified from a crisp measure or CVI, viz., partition coefficient (PC), which is used to evaluate competing fuzzy partitions of X. Dave [22] presented MPC to overcome the drawback of tending monotonically increasing trend of PC index for cluster numbers, c, as follows:

$V_{MPC}(c) = 1 - \frac{c}{c-1}(1 - V_{PC}(c))$,

where $V_{PC}(c) = \frac{1}{n}\sum_{i=1}^{n}\sum_{j=1}^{c}(u_{ij})^2$.

The optimal solution is given by $c^* = \arg \max_{2 \leq c \leq n-1} V_{MPC}(c)$.

Xie-Beni Index (XB) [23]. To evaluate quality of clustering, XB index is generally used. Considering geometrical features of clusters, it can validate fuzzy partitions. Separateness and compactness of clusters are calculated by XB index through finding distance between inter clusters and deviations of intra-cluster. It is given as

$V_{XB}(c) = \dfrac{J_m(U,V)}{n.\min_{i,j} d^2(V_i,V_j)} = \dfrac{\frac{J_m(U,V)}{n}}{Sep(V)}$,

where J_m represents compactness measure and $Sep(V)$ designates the separation measure.

The optimal solution is given by $c^* = \arg \min_{2 \leq c \leq n-1} V_{XB}(c)$.

Above two validity indices are used in the context of PyFCM algorithm for finding optimal number of clusters.

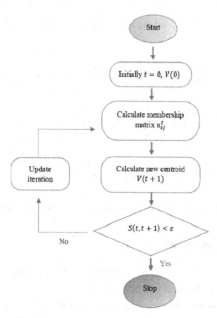

Fig. 1. Flowchart for PyFCM Algorithm

3.4 Data Processing

For clustering a given dataset, if the available data are in the form of PFSs, the proposed method can be applied directly. However, the data available at UCI machine learning repository, synthetic datasets are in the form of crisp numbers. Thus, the conversion of data in PF format is essential to apply the proposed algorithm. To convert real dataset into fuzzy dataset the following method is generally followed:

Let $X = (x_1, x_2, \ldots, x_n)$ be an n un-labeled dataset. The membership values corresponding to the given data points are defined below.

$$\mu_X(x_i) = \frac{x_i - \min x_i}{\max x_i - \min x_i}, \tag{5}$$

Now, to convert fuzzy numbers to PFNs, a technique developed by H. Bustince et al. [20] for IFSs is extended to generate PFNs in the following Subsection.

3.5 Pythagorean Fuzzy Generator

As like IFG [20], fuzzy complementary function is used as a PFG to generate PFNs from fuzzy numbers.

Definition. A function $\psi : [0, 1] \to [0, 1]$ is said to be a PFG if $\psi(x) \leq \sqrt{1 - x^2} \, \forall x \in [0, 1]$. So, $\psi(0) \leq 1$ and $\psi(1) = 0$.

Thus, for a fuzzy set $A = \{\langle x, \mu_A(x)\rangle | x \in X\}$, a PFS can be generated using PFG as. $P = \{\langle x, \mu_A(x), \psi(\mu_A(x))\rangle | x \in X\} = \langle x, \mu_P(x), \nu_P(x)\rangle$, say, where $v_P(x)$ represents non-membership value of $x \in X$ in P.

There are several fuzzy complements which can act as PFG. In this article Yager class of fuzzy complements [27] is used as PFG with the form

$$c_\alpha(x) = \left(1 - x^\alpha\right)^{\frac{1}{\alpha}}, \qquad 0 < \alpha \leq 2. \tag{6}$$

It is to be noted here that in the case of IFG [20], the values of α lies in $0 < \alpha \leq 1$. Whereas, in the case of PFG the range of α is extended to $(0, 2]$. Since, the construction of v and π largely depend on the value of α, it becomes more convenient for PFNs than IFNs to find best results through clustering technique by tuning α within the range $(0,2]$.

4   Experimental Results

The developed methodology for PyFCM clustering is applied on synthetic datasets, UCI datasets and two moon dataset. All the experiments are worked out using the *software* MATLAB 2018a. The default value of weighting exponent m is taken as 2 in all the computational cases [24].

4.1   Synthetic Datasets

Six types of synthetic datasets [19], viz., Two spirals, Cluster in Cluster, Corner, Half-Kernel, Crescent & Full moon and outliers, which are generated using the *software* MATLAB 2018a are taken into consideration to illustrate the developed algorithm. The descriptions about datasets are presented graphically through Fig. 2.

All the datasets are now converted into PFSs using PFG as described in Eq. (6) by varying the value of $\alpha \in (0, 2]$. The developed PyFCM clustering algorithm is then executed on the newly generated PFNs. The cluster validity indices are calculated. Achieved results together with the results achieved by performing FCMC [8] and IFCMC [12] algorithms are presented in Table 1.

4.2   UCI Datasets

Two types of UCI datasets, viz., Iris, Haberman's survival datasets are considered from machine learning repository of UCI (available at: https://archive.ics.uci.edu/ml/index.php). As synthetic datasets, UCI datasets both are given in the form of crisp values, so those numbers are converted into PFSs using PFG as described in Eq. (6) by varying the value of $\alpha \in (0, 2]$. The developed PyFCM clustering algorithm is then executed on the newly generated PFNs. The cluster validity indices are calculated and the achieved results along with the results achieved through FCMC [8] and IFCMC [12] algorithms are presented in Table 2. In addition, the achieved results obtained from Iris dataset through the above mentioned methods are categorically presented in Fig. 3.

4.3   Two Moon Dataset

The proposed method is further applied on two moon dataset. This dataset is a two-dimensional dataset of 300 points which are generated through MATLAB 2018a. The pictorial presentations of the original dataset, results achieved through FCMC, IFCMC and PyFCM clustering are provided, successively in Fig. 4.

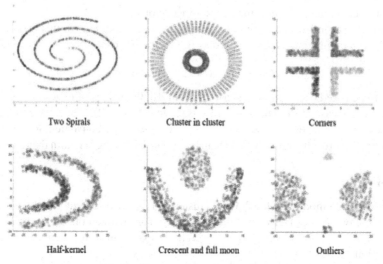

Fig. 2. Six type of Synthetic Datasets

Table 1. Results of Synthetic datasets

Dataset	Method	Parameter	XB	MPC
Two spirals	FCM	$c = 2$	**0.2666**	0.4098
	IFCM	$c = 2, \alpha = 1$	**0.2666**	0.4098
	PyFCM	$c = 2, \alpha = 2$	0.2675	**0.4242**
Cluster in clusters	FCM	$c = 2$	0.6404	0.3206
	IFCM	$c = 2, \alpha = .05$	0.6543	0.3218
	PyFCM	$c = 2, \alpha = 2$	**0.2544**	**0.5019**
Corners	FCM	$c = 4$	0.1421	0.4742
	IFCM	$c = 4, \alpha = .1$	**0.1149**	0.4172
	PyFCM	$c = 4, \alpha = 1.7$	0.1755	**0.4844**
Half-Kernel	FCM	$c = 2$	0.3258	0.4115
	IFCM	$c = 2, \alpha = .25$	0.3290	0.4115
	PyFCM	$c = 2, \alpha = 2$	**0.3027**	**0.4502**
Crescent and Full moon	FCM	$c = 2$	0.2781	0.4344
	IFCM	$c = 2, \alpha = .85$	0.2730	0.4374
	PyFCM	$c = 2, \alpha = 2$	**0.2145**	**0.4707**
Outliers	FCM	$c = 4$	**0.1994**	0.5648
	IFCM	$c = 4, \alpha = .95$	0.2000	0.5652
	PyFCM	$c = 4, \alpha = .1$	0.2698	**0.5801**

Table 2. Results of UCI datasets

Dataset	Method	Parameter	XB	MPC
Iris	FCM	$c = 3$	0.1751	0.6137
	IFCM	$c = 3,$ $\alpha = .95$	0.1797	**0.6138**
	PyFCM	$c = 3,$ $\alpha = 1.4$	**0.1574**	0.5977
Haberman's	FCM	$c = 2$	0.2464	0.4362
	IFCM	$c =$ $2, \alpha = .1$	0.2000	0.5657
	PyFCM	$c =$ $2, \alpha = .1$	**0.1782**	**0.6137**

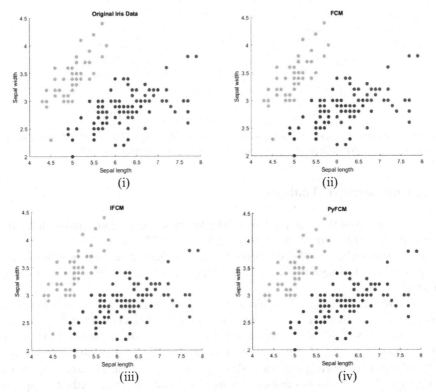

Fig. 3. Results on Iris dataset: (i) original image (ii) clustered using FCMC method (iii) clustered using IFCMC method (iv) clustered using PyFCM clustering method.

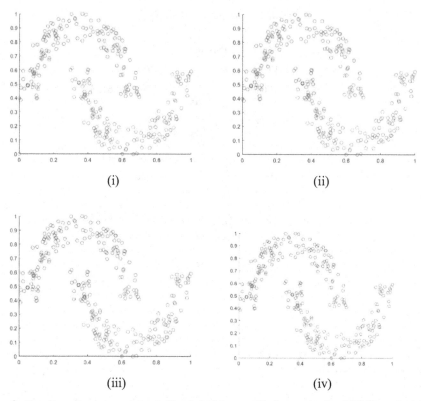

Fig. 4. Results on two moon dataset; (i) original image (ii) clustered using FCMC method (iii) clustered using IFCMC method (iv) clustered using PyFCM clustering method.

5 A Comparative Analysis

The results achieved through developed PyFCM clustering are compared with FCMC [8] and IFCMC [12] methods using MPC [22] and XB [23] indices.

It is to be noted here that FCMC method is applied after normalizing the given dataset using Eq. (5). Subsequently, XB index and MPC values are evaluated for comparison purpose.

For Synthetic datasets, it is observed from Table 1 that the XB value is lower for Cluster in cluster, Half-kernel, Crescent and Full moon datasets in PyFCM clustering method than FCMC, IFCMC methods. For Two spirals, Corners, Outlier datasets, XB value is higher in PyFCM clustering method than IFCMC and FCMC methods. But MPC value of PyFCM clustering method is higher than IFCMC and FCMC methods for all datasets. This fact justifies that the developed PyFCM clustering method is superior to IFCMC and FCMC methods for clustering Synthetic datasets.

Regarding UCI Datasets, it is evidenced from Table 2 that the MPC value is higher for Haberman's dataset and slightly lower for Iris dataset in PyFCM clustering method in compere to IFCMC and FCMC methods. But XB value is lower for both the datasets in PyFCM clustering method than IFCMC and FCMC methods, which justifies the superiority of the proposed PyFCM clustering method than IFCMC and FCMC methods.

Also, better clustering is found when the proposed PyFCM clustering method is applied on two moon datasets. From Fig. 4 it is easily understood that best clustering is performed through the proposed method than both IFCMC and FCMC methods.

6 Conclusions

The newly developed PyFCM clustering algorithm possesses the capability of clustering real datasets through the newly developed PFG. The advantage of using PyFCM clustering algorithm is that the associated PFSs consider membership as well as non-membership degrees, so that uncertainties associated with the datasets are captured efficiently. To assess the effectiveness of the developed algorithm, six types of synthetic datasets, two types of UCI datasets and two moon datasets are used. Comparisons with existing methods reflect superiority of the developed method. In future, the developed clustering algorithm may be applied for data mining, image processing, pattern recognition, etc. Further this method may also be extended to hesitant PF, q-rung orthopair fuzzy and other advanced domain of fuzzy variants for performing proper clustering of datasets.

Acknowledgments. One author, Souvik Gayen, is grateful to UGC, Govt. of India, for providing financial support to execute the research work vide UGC Reference No. 1184/(SC). The suggestions and comments on the reviewers on this article are thankfully acknowledged by the authors.

References

1. Anderberg, M.R.: Cluster Analysis for Applications, 1st edn. Academic Press, New York (1972)
2. Mangiameli, P., Chen, S.K., West, D.: A comparison of SOM neural network and hierarchical clustering methods. Eur. J. Oper. Res. **93**(2), 402–417 (1996)
3. Everitt, B.S., Landau, S., Leese, M.: Cluster Analysis, 5th edn. Oxford University Press, New York (2001)
4. Jain, A.K., Murty, M.N., Flynn, P.J.: Data clustering: a review. ACM Comput. Surv. **31**(3), 264–323 (1999)
5. Beliakov, G., King, M.: Density based fuzzy C-means clustering of non-convex patterns. Eur. J. Oper. Res. **173**(3), 717–728 (2006)
6. Klir, G.J., Yuan, B.: Fuzzy Sets and Fuzzy Logic: Theory and Applications. Prentice-Hall, New York (1994)
7. Bezdek, J.C.: Pattern Recognition with Fuzzy Objective Function Algorithms. Plenum, New York (1981)
8. Bezdek, J.C., Ehrlich, R., Full, W.: FCM: the fuzzy C-means clustering algorithm. Comput. Geosci. **10**, 191–203 (1984)
9. Forgey, E.: Cluster analysis of multivariate data: efficiency vs Interpretability of Classification. Biometrics **21**, 768–769 (1965)
10. Atanassov, K.T.: Intuitionistic fuzzy sets. Fuzzy Sets Syst. **20**(1), 87–96 (1986)

11. Atanassov, K.T.: Intuitionistic Fuzzy Sets: Theory and Applications. Physica-Verlag, Heidelberg (1999)
12. Xu, Z., Wu, J.: Intuitionistic fuzzy c-mean clustering algorithms . J. Syst. Eng. Electron. **21**(4), 580–590 (2010)
13. Szmidt, E., Kacprzyk, J.: Distances between intuitionistic fuzzy sets. Fuzzy Sets Syst. **114**(3), 505–518 (2000)
14. Chaira, T.: A novel intuitionistic fuzzy C means clustering algorithm and its application to medical images. Appl. Soft Comput. **11**(2), 1711–1717 (2011)
15. Kumar, S.A., Harish, B.S.: A Modified intuitionistic fuzzy clustering algorithm for medical image segmentation. J. Intell. Syst. **27**(4), 1–15 (2017)
16. Wu, C., Zhang, X.: Total Bregman divergence-based fuzzy local information C-means clustering for robust image segmentation. Appl. Soft Comput. **94**, 1–31 (2020)
17. Zeng, S., Wang, Z., Huang, R., Chen, L., Feng, D.: A study on multi-kernel intuitionistic fuzzy C-means clustering with multiple attributes. Neurocomputing **335**, 59–71 (2019)
18. Verman, H., Gupta, A., Kumar, D.: A modified intuitionistic fuzzy c-mean algorithm incorporating hesitation degree. Pattern Recognit. Lett. **122**, 45–52 (2019)
19. Lohani, Q.M.D., Solanki, R., Muhuri, P.K.: A Convergence theorem and an experimental study of intuitionistic fuzzy C-mean algorithm over machine learning dataset. Appl. Soft Comput. **71**, 1176–1188 (2018)
20. Bustince, H., Kacprzyk, J., Mohedano, V.: Intuitionistic fuzzy generators: application to intuitionistic fuzzy complementation. Fuzzy Sets Syst. **114**(3), 485–504 (2000)
21. Yager, R.R., Abbasov, A.M.: Pythagorean membership grades, complex numbers, and decision making. Int. J. Intell. Syst. **28**, 436–452 (2013)
22. Dave, R.N.: Validating fuzzy partition obtained through c-shells clustering. Pattern Recognit. Lett. **17**(6), 613–623 (1996)
23. Xie, X.L., Beni, G.: A validity measure for fuzzy clustering. IEEE Trans. Pattern Anal. Mach. Intell. **13**(8), 841–847 (1991)
24. Pal, N.R., Bezdek, J.C.: On cluster validity for the fuzzy c-means model. IEEE Trans. Fuzzy Syst. **3**(3), 370–379 (1995)
25. Li, D., Zeng, W.: Distance measure of pythagorean fuzzy sets. Int. J. Intell. Syst. **33**, 338–361 (2017)
26. Ito, K., Kunisch, K.: Lagrange multiplier approach to variational problems and applications. Advances in Design and Control, Philadelphia (2008)
27. Higashi, M., Klir, G.J.: On measures of fuzzyness and fuzzy complements. Int. J. Gen. Syst. **8**(3), 169–180 (1982)
28. Wu, K.-L.: An analysis of robustness of partition coefficient index. In: 2008 IEEE International Conference on Fuzzy Systems (IEEE World Congress on Computational Intelligence), Hong Kong, pp. 372–376 (2008)

Data Science and Advanced Data Analytics

Application of a New Hybrid MCDM Technique Combining Grey Relational Analysis with AHP-TOPSIS in Ranking of Stocks in the Indian IT Sector

Swagata Ghosh[✉]

Indian Institute of Management Shillong, Shillong, India

Abstract. Ranking of stocks based on an ever-increasing number of financial and technical indicators with varying success rates in predicting the future performance of the stocks both in the short and in the long run, is a major decision problem for financial analysts and it involves applying certain weightage or degree of importance to some of the criteria i.e. stock performance indicators relative to others. The multi-criteria decision problem of ranking of stocks for portfolio construction have been approached by several trading analysts and researchers in the past, using different Multi-Criteria Decision Making (MCDM) techniques. The present paper proposes a novel and hybrid MCDM techniques that combines three of the most popularly used techniques: the Grey Relational Analysis (GRA), Analytic Hierarchy Process (AHP) and Technique of Order of Performance by Similarity to Ideal Solution (TOPSIS) and this new hybrid MCDM method has been applied to the problem of ranking 8 stocks from the Indian IT sector in order of preference of inclusion in a portfolio based on the stock performance indicated by Price-to-Book Value Ratio, Price-to-Earnings Ratio, Return on Equity (ROE), Momentum (%), MACD(12,26,9) and 125-day Rate of Change (ROC) metric. The novelty of the proposed hybrid model lies in the unique step-by-step approach to combining the three existing MCDM methods. Application of the GRA compares the alternatives based on actual quantitative parameters. Thus, the relative weights of the decision matrices are not formulated based on any individual's assumption or opinion.

Keywords: MCDM methods · Grey Relational Analysis · Analytic Hierarchy Process (AHP) · TOPSIS · Portfolio construction · Ranking of stocks

1 Introduction

Ranking of stocks for portfolio construction is a very important aspect for financial analysis and there are several financial ratios and technical indicators which are used by analysts to rank the stocks in order of their future potential. Many of these stocks financial and technical indicators have become popular over the years due to their relatively higher success rates in predicting the returns from the stocks both in the short and in the long run. Over the years, the number of financial and technical indicators, as well as the number of financial instruments has exponentially increased, because any combination

P. Dutta et al. (Eds.): CICBA 2021, CCIS 1406, pp. 133–149, 2021.
https://doi.org/10.1007/978-3-030-75529-4_11

or variation of the existing financial and technical indicators can be used by analysts and researchers to come up with newer ones. This has led the analysts to stumble upon the confounding question: which financial and technical indicators must be used to measure the performance of the stocks, that is, based on which financial and technical indicators, stocks must be compared and good performing stocks must be selected for the portfolio. This brings us to formulate this question of selection of stocks based on multiple performance metrics into a multi-criteria decision problem. There are several Multi-Criteria Decision Making (MCDM) methods which have been used by trading analysts and researchers in the past to decide on such problems of selection of alternatives based on multiple criteria with different weights or degrees of importance. The present paper discusses a novel hybrid technique that combines three of the most famous MCDM methods – the Grey Relational Analysis (GRA), Analytic Hierarchy Process (AHP) and Technique of Order of Performance by Similarity to Ideal Solution (TOPSIS). These three existing MCDM techniques have been combined together in a novel way to get a hybrid MCDM technique that has been applied to the decision problem of ranking 8 stocks from the Indian IT sector based on multiple financial and technical performance indicators.

India has emerged as one of the fastest growing economies in the world and the emergence of this trend which is estimated to continue in the future, is largely credited to the rapid development of the IT industry of the country. According to the figures estimated by World Bank, India's GDP grew by 6.8% in the fiscal year 2018–19 due to various initiatives taken by the government. The IT sector of India has remained and still remains one of the major sectors contributing greatly to the robust growth curve of the Indian Economy. Almost half of India's GDP of nearly 3 trillion dollars is generated by the services sectors that include IT, software and telecommunications. The main reason for this boom in IT is massive outsourcing from foreign companies, especially companies in the US and in the UK.

Based on the market capitalization and the stock performance over the last few years, 8 stocks have been selected for the scope of this study. The problem at hand is to rank 8 stocks from the Indian IT sector based on the performance metrics as indicated by the most popular financial indicators like Price-to-Book Value ratio, Price-to-Earnings (P/E) ratio and Return on Equity or ROE (%), and the most commonly used technical indicators like the Momentum (%), 125-day Rate-of-Change (ROC) or ROC (125) and Moving Average Convergence/Divergence or MACD (12,26,9) indicator which takes the difference between 12-day EMA (Exponential Moving Average) and 26-day EMA (Exponential Moving Average) and also takes 9-day EMA as the MACD Signal line. The objective is to rank the 8 IT stocks – TCS, Infosys, Wipro, HCL Technologies, L&T Technologies, Mphasis, Sasken Technologies and Hexaware Technologies – which have been selected from the top 10 Indian IT stocks taken from the NSE (National Stock Exchange) list based on market capitalization.

The novelty of the proposed hybrid model lies in the unique step-by-step approach to combining the three existing MCDM methods have been combined. Application of the GRA compares the alternatives based on actual quantitative parameters. Thus, the relative weights of the decision matrices are not formulated based on any individual's assumption or opinion. The decision matrices are thus extremely accurate.

2   Related Works

Hasan Dincer and *ÜmitHacioğlu* from Beykent University, Turkey, have previously come up with a comparative hybrid method in technical analysis for selection of stocks from Turkish banking sector using Fuzzy AHP-TOPSIS and Vikor methods [1]. E.O. Oyatoye, G. U. Okpokpo and G.A. Adekoya all from Lagos, Nigeria presented an application of the AHP (Analytic Hierarchy Process) technique for portfolio selection using stocks of banking sector from the capital market of Nigeria [2].

In other areas of research work, Ran Li and Tao Sun published an article in March 2020 on assessment of the different factors behind designing a successful B2C e-commerce website using Fuzzy AHP and TOPSIS-Grey methods [3]. Anastasia Cherry Sulu, David P.E. Saerang, James D.D. Massie from the University of Sam Ratulangi Manado have previously researched on the analysis of Consumer Purchase Intention regarding cosmetic products based on the country of origin using AHP technique [4].

Daekook Kang, Wooseok Jang and Yongtae Park (2015) from Seoul National University have researched on evaluating the e-commerce websites using fuzzy hierarchical TOPSIS based on E-S-Qual [5]. Mochammad Sobandi Dwi Putra, Septi Adryana, Fauziah and Aris Gunaryati have researched on the application of Fuzzy AHP method in determining the quality of gemstone. [6] In 2019, Shivani Guru and DK Mahalik from Sambalpur University have comparatively evaluated AHP-TOPSIS and AHP-Grey Relational Analysis to find the efficiency of Indian public sector banks [7].

3   Theory of Operation

The present section presents a brief overview for all the financial trading indicators discussed in the context of this research work, and also the details of the novel hybrid MCDM technique used for ranking of the selected 8 Indian IT stocks.

3.1   Brief Overview of the Financial and Technical Indicators of Stocks

Momentum (%). Momentum is a simple technical indicator used by trading analysts and it is given by the absolute difference between the current day's closing price of the stock and the closing price of the stock N number of periods/days ago. For the present study, the Normalized Momentum score %) evaluated by Trendlyne trading analyst website has been used, and Trendlyne recalculates stock momentum everyday between 5 pm–7 pm.

Rate of Change ROC (125). Rate of Change is similar to momentum but this indicator represents the difference in stock price as a percent change of the old price. In the present study, 125-day ROC which is the rate of change calculated over 125 periods or days has been used, as what has been calculated by Trendlyne.

MACD (12,26,9). Moving Average Convergence/Divergence or MACD $(12, 26, 9)$ indicator takes the difference between 12-day EMA (Exponential Moving Average) and 26-day EMA and also takes 9-day EMA as the MACD Signal line. EMA or Exponential Moving Average is used to measure the direction of trend over time.

Price to Book Value. The price-to-book value (P/B) is the ratio of the market value of a company's shares over the book value of equity which is the total value of the company's assets given in the balance sheet. Ideally, any P/B value less than 1 is good. Value investors consider stocks with P/B less than 3 for investment.

Price to Earnings Ratio. The price-to-earnings (P/E) ratio is the ratio of the current market price per share (MPS) and the earnings per share (EPS) of the company.

Annualized Return on Equity (ROE). This is computed by dividing the annualized net earnings of the company by the average monthly shareholders' equity.

3.2 Detailed Overview of the Proposed Hybrid MCDM Technique

The first input for the proposed hybrid MCDM model is the 8×6 matrix containing 8 rows for the 8 selected stocks and 6 columns for the 6 criteria parameters i.e. the 6 trading indicators which have been discussed in the preceding section. Here, the 8 rows represent the 8 variables which are the Alternatives (IT Stocks) henceforth denoted by S1, S2, S3, S4, S5, S6, S7 and S8, and the 6 columns represent the 6 trading indicators or metrics which are henceforth called the Criteria denoted by C1, C2, C3, C4, C5 and C6. This 8×6 matrix contains the scores of the 6 trading parameters for each of the 8 stocks as obtained from the Trading Analyst websites.

Determination of the Grey Relation Coefficient Matrix Using GRA
The first step in this hybrid technique is to determine the Normalized Weight Matrix from the input matrix containing the performance scores and metrics of the 8 stocks under each of the 6 criteria indicators. This is obtained by the following steps:

Step-1: The minimum and the maximum of the scores/values under each criterion Ci is obtained from the input matrix and these are denoted by $\min_i$ and $\max_i$ respectively.

Step-2: The next step is Normalization and in this step, it needs to be determined what the ideal or best score/value for each criterion is – whether higher values are better, or lower values are better.

If the criterion C_x is such that the alternatives S_a with higher values of C_x, are better than the alternatives S_b with lower values of C_x, then this criterion C_x falls in the category-1 which is "the higher is better".

For such cases, we calculate the normalized coefficient A_{ij} corresponding to the score of the ith alternative under the jth criterion as: $A_{ij} = \frac{a_{ij} - \min_i}{\max_i - \min_i}$ If the target value of the original sequence is infinite, it is the case of "the higher is better".

If the criterion C_x is such that the alternatives S_a with lower values of C_x, are better than the alternatives S_b with higher values of C_x, then criterion C_x falls in the category-2 which is "the lower is better".

For such cases, we calculate the normalized coefficient A_{ij} corresponding to the score of the ith alternative under the jth criterion as: $A_{ij} = \frac{\max_i - a_{ij}}{\max_i - \min_i}$.

If the target value of the original sequence is zero or the lowest possible, it is "lower is better".

After this process, the Normalized Score Matrix is obtained where for every criterion the minimum value for any alternative is 0 and the maximum value can only be 1.

Step-3: In this step, the matrix of Deviation Sequences is obtained. The minimum and maximum values under each criterion obtained from the Normalization step which are only 0 and 1 respectively, are denoted by min_i and max_i respectively. The values of the Deviation Sequences matrix are obtained by the formula: $A_{ij} = max_{ij} - a_{ij}$.

Step-4: The maximum and minimum of the deviation sequences under each criterion C_k are denoted by Δ^k_{max} and Δ^k_{min} respectively.

In this final step, the Grey Relation Coefficient is calculated using the following formula:

$$X_{ij} = \left(\Delta^j_{min} + \epsilon * \Delta^j_{max}\right) / \left(A'_{ij} + \epsilon * \Delta^j_{max}\right)$$

The smaller is the value of ϵ, the larger is the distinguishing ability. Generally $\epsilon = 0.5$ is used.

Determination of the Criterion-wise Weighted Decision Matrix of the Stocks Using Method Similar to Analytic Hierarchy Process (AHP)

After obtaining the Grey Relation Coefficient Matrix in the previous step, the weighted decision matrices for the stocks corresponding to each of the 6 criteria are determined.

Step-1. Using each of the 6 columns of the Grey Relation Coefficient (GRC) matrix, one decision matrix corresponding to one criterion is determined. Using column j of the GRC matrix, the 8×8 decision matrix corresponding to criterion C_j is obtained. There are thus 6 decision matrices of dimension 8×8 obtained – the values in every matrix compare the alternatives with each other based on one criterion. Therefore, for every criterion there is a one-on-one comparison between every pair of alternatives and the average of each row is computed to find the overall weight or score of the corresponding alternatives under each criterion.

Step-2: The weights for the 6 criteria are assumed on the basis of the opinions of several trading analysts and expert financial researchers, and also on the basis of success rates as obtained from different sources across the World Wide Web. The Criteria Weight Matrix is a 6×6 matrix where every element a_{ij} correspond to the comparative importance of criterion "i" over criterion "j", which means the weightage of criterion C_i is a_{ij} times the weightage of criterion C_j. The average weight of each criterion is obtained by computing the average of each row of this matrix.

Step-3: The final Criteria-wise Weighted Decision Matrix is obtained by multiplying the average normalized weight of a criterion with the overall average weight of each alternative (obtained in Step-1). This final 6×8 Criteria-wise Weighted Decision Matrix is the input to the next and final stage of this hybrid MCDM process and the weights of this matrix are used to compute the Performance Score based on the TOPSIS method.

Ranking of the Stocks in order of Performance Score Using TOPSIS Method

The Criteria-wise Weighted Decision Matrix is the input to this last set of steps of the proposed hybrid MCDM model. Here the transpose of the 6×8 criteria-wise weighted decision matrix is taken in order to get an 8×6 matrix where the 8 rows represent the

8 stocks or alternatives, and the 6 columns represent the 6 criteria or parameters for ranking the alternatives.

Step-1.

First and foremost, the values of Ideal Best V_k^+ and Ideal Worst V_k^- are computed for each criterion k as the maximum and minimum weight for any alternative respectively under that criterion k. Using these values, one must calculate the Euclidean distances in the next step.

Step-2.

The Euclidean Distance of every alternative S_i from the Ideal Best value is calculated using the following formula:

$$S_i^+ = \sqrt{\sum_{j=1}^{6} \left(\omega_{ij} - V_j^+\right)^2}$$

Step-3.

The Euclidean Distance of every alternative S_i from the Ideal Worst value is calculated using the following formula:

$$S_i^- = \sqrt{\sum_{j=1}^{6} \left(\omega_{ij} - V_j^-\right)^2}$$

Step-4.

The Performance Score of every alternative P_i is calculated using the formula:

$$P_i = \frac{S_i^-}{S_i^+ + S_i^-}$$

Step-5.

The ranking of the alternatives is determined on arranging the Performance Score values for assigning the rank accordingly from the highest to the lowest P_i value scoring alternatives.

4   Experimental Results

4.1   Input Data

The data of the top 8 stocks from the Indian IT sector are taken from the Trendlyne website and the selected stocks are: TCS, Infosys, Wipro, HCL Technologies, L&T Technologies, Mphasis, Sasken Technologies and Hexaware Technologies, which are denoted as S1, S2, S3, S4, S5, S6, S7 and S8 respectively. The 6 criteria for ranking the alternatives (stocks) are the following 3 financial ratios, namely Price-to-Book Value ratio, Price-to-Earnings (P/E) ratio and Return on Equity or ROE (%), and the three technical indicators namely Momentum (%), 125-day Rate-of-Change (ROC) or ROC (125) and Moving Average Convergence/Divergence or MACD (12,26,9). The data is collected latest till the 20th October 2020 [8] (Table 1).

Table 1. Data on indian IT stocks used as input for the MCDM technique

		Momentum (%)	MACD (12,26,9)	ROC (125)	Price to Book Value	P/E Ratio	ROE (%)
S1	TCS	73.6	78.1	45.4	11.81	−6.23	38.44
S2	INFOSYS	86.4	41.7	69.9	7.28	1.73	25.35
S3	WIPRO	37.7	−0.7	−14.6	3.55	−6.6	17.57
S4	HCL TECH	78.1	26	79.3	4.58	0.93	21.56
S5	L&T TECH	80.7	42	48.6	6.61	−2.25	29.56
S6	MPHASIS	79.7	18.5	93.3	4.32	1.97	20.32
S7	SASKEN	74.5	24.6	54.5	2.18	−1.6	16.57
S8	HEXAWARE	71.7	8.1	62.5	5.1	2.13	23.19

The weights for the 6 criteria are assumed on the basis of the opinions of several trading analysts and expert financial researchers, and also on the basis of success rates as obtained from different sources across the World Wide Web [9, 10]. The Criteria Weight Matrix is a 6 × 6 matrix where every element a_{ij} correspond to the comparative importance of criterion "i" over criterion "j", which means the weightage of criterion C_i is a_{ij} times the weightage of criterion C_j. Pair-wise comparison of criteria has been done based on opinion of a few financial trading experts and trading analyst websites.

Table 2. Criteria Weight Matrix

	C1	C2	C3	C4	C5	C6	
C1	1	0.75	7.5	0.6	0.5	1.875	Momentum%
C2	1.33333	1	10	0.8	0.66667	2.5	MACD (12,26,9)
C3	0.13333	0.1	1	0.08	0.06667	0.25	ROC (125)
C4	1.66667	1.25	12.5	1	0.83333	3.125	Price/Book Value
C5	2	1.5	15	1.2	1	3.75	Price/Earning
C6	0.53333	0.4	4	0.32	0.26667	1	ROE (%)

4.2   Results of the Data Analysis

Determination of the Grey Relation Coefficient Matrix using Grey Relational Analysis (GRA)

The Normalized Weight Matrix is computed from the input matrix containing the performance scores and metrics of the 8 stocks under each of the 6 criteria indicators (Table 3).

Step-1.

Table 3. Minimum and Maximum under each Criterion

	C1	C2	C3	C4	C5	C6
Minimum	37.7	−0.7	−14.6	2.18	−6.6	16.57
Maximum	86.4	78.1	93.3	11.81	2.13	38.44

Step-2:

Normalized Sequences A'_{ij}. are obtained as follows (Table 4):

Table 4. Normalized Matrix

	C1	C2	C3	C4	C5	C6
S1	0.73716	1	0.55607	0	0.957617	1
S2	1	0.53807	0.78313	0.4704	0.045819	0.4015
S3	0	0	0	0.857736	1	0.0457
S4	0.82957	0.33883	0.87025	0.750779	0.137457	0.2282
S5	0.88296	0.54188	0.58572	0.539979	0.501718	0.5939
S6	0.86242	0.24365	1	0.777778	0.018328	0.1715
S7	0.75565	0.32107	0.6404	1	0.427262	0
S8	0.69815	0.11167	0.71455	0.696781	0	0.3027
Min	0	0	0	0	0	0
Max	1	1	1	1	1	1

Step-3.

The maximum and minimum deviation sequences under each criterion C_k are Δ_{max}^k and Δ_{min}^k respectively. It should be noted that $\Delta_{max}^k = 1$ and $\Delta_{min}^k = 0$ (Table 5).

Table 5. Deviation Sequences for Grey Relational Analysis

	C1	C2	C3	C4	C5	C6
S1	0.26283	0	0.4439	1	0.04238	0
S2	0	0.46193	0.216867	0.5296	0.95418	0.5985
S3	1	1	1	0.142264	0	0.9543
S4	0.17043	0.66117	0.12975	0.24922	0.86254	0.7718
S5	0.11704	0.45812	0.414272	0.460021	0.49828	0.4060
S6	0.13758	0.75634	0	0.22222	0.98167	0.8285
S7	0.24435	0.67893	0.359592	0	0.57274	1
S8	0.30184	0.88832	0.285449	0.30322	1	0.6973

Step-4.

For this, the smaller is the value of ϵ, the better. In the present study, $\epsilon = 0.5$ is used (Table 6).

Table 6. Grey Relational Coefficient Matrix (GRC Matrix)

	C1	C2	C3	C4	C5	C6
S1	0.65545	1	0.52970	0.33333	0.92186	1
S2	1	0.51979	0.69748	0.48563	0.34384	0.45515
S3	0.33333	0.33333	0.33333	0.7785	1	0.3438
S4	0.74579	0.4306	0.79396	0.66736	0.36696	0.39313
S5	0.8103	0.52185	0.54688	0.52082	0.50086	0.55185
S6	0.78422	0.39798	1	0.6923	0.33746	0.37635
S7	0.67172	0.42411	0.58167	1	0.466097	0.33333
S8	0.62355	0.36015	0.63658	0.6225	0.33333	0.4176

Determination of the Criterion-wise Weighted Decision Matrix of the Stocks Using Method Similar to AHP

After obtaining the Grey Relation Coefficient Matrix in the previous step, the weighted decision matrices for the stocks corresponding to each of the 6 criteria are determined. There are 6 decision matrices obtained – the dimension of each matrix is 8×8 and the values in every matrix compare the alternatives with each other based on one criterion. The final Criteria-wise Weighted Decision Matrix is obtained by multiplying the average weight of every criterion with the overall average weight of each alternative. The weights of the 6 criteria are obtained from Table 2 using each of the 6 columns of the GRC matrix to compute 1 output matrix based on relative score ratios (Tables 7, 8, 9, 10, 11 and 12).

Table 7. Pairwise Comparison Matrix for Criterion C1

	S1	S2	S3	S4	S5	S6	S7	S8
S1	1	0.6554	1.9663	0.8789	0.8088	0.8358	0.9758	1.05114
S2	1.5257	1	3	1.3409	1.2341	1.2751	1.4887	1.6037
S3	0.5086	0.3333	1	0.4469	0.4113	0.4250	0.4962	0.5346
S4	1.1378	0.7458	2.2374	1	0.9204	0.9509	1.1103	1.1960
S5	1.2363	0.8103	2.4309	1.0865	1	1.0333	1.2063	1.2995
S6	1.1965	0.7842	2.3527	1.0515	0.9678	1	1.1675	1.2576
S7	1.0248	0.6717	2.0152	0.9007	0.8289	0.8565	1	1.0772
S8	0.9513	0.6235	1.8707	0.836	0.7695	0.7951	0.9283	1

Table 8. Pairwise Comparison Matrix for Criterion C2

	S1	S2	S3	S4	S5	S6	S7	S8
S1	1	1.9238	3	2.3223	1.9162	2.5127	2.3579	2.7766
S2	0.5198	1	1.5594	1.057	0.8722	1.1436	1.0732	1.2638
S3	0.3333	0.6413	1	0.7985	0.6588	0.8639	0.8107	0.9546
S4	0.4306	0.9461	1.2524	1	0.7533	0.9878	0.927	1.0916
S5	0.5218	1.1465	1.5178	1.3274	1	1.3866	1.3012	1.5323
S6	0.3979	0.8744	1.1575	1.0123	0.7212	1	0.8874	1.0450
S7	0.4241	0.9318	1.2335	1.0788	0.7685	1.1269	1	1.1776
S8	0.3601	0.7913	1.0475	0.9161	0.6526	0.9569	0.8492	1

Table 9. Pairwise Comparison Matrix for Criterion C3

	S1	S2	S3	S4	S5	S6	S7	S8
S1	1	0.7594	1.5891	0.6672	0.9686	0.5297	0.9106	0.8321
S2	1.3167	1	2.0924	0.8785	1.2754	0.6975	1.1991	1.0957
S3	0.6293	0.4779	1	0.4198	0.6095	0.3333	0.5731	0.5236
S4	1.4989	1.1383	2.3819	1	1.4518	0.7939	1.365	1.2472
S5	1.0324	0.7841	1.6406	0.6888	1	0.5468	0.9402	0.8591
S6	1.8879	1.4337	3	1.2595	1.8285	1	1.7192	1.5709
S7	1.0981	0.8339	1.7450	0.7326	1.0636	0.5816	1	0.9137
S8	1.2017	0.9127	1.9097	0.8018	1.1640	0.6366	1.0944	1

Table 10. Pairwise Comparison Matrix for Criterion C4

	S1	S2	S3	S4	S5	S6	S7	S8
S1	1	0.6864	0.4282	0.4995	0.64	0.4815	0.3333	0.5355
S2	1.457	1	0.6238	0.7277	0.9324	0.7015	0.4856	0.7801
S3	2.3355	1.6031	1	1.1665	1.4947	1.1245	0.7785	1.25
S4	2.0021	1.3742	0.8572	1	1.2814	0.964	0.6674	1.072
S5	1.5625	1.0725	0.669	0.7804	1	0.7522	0.5208	0.8367
S6	2.077	1.4256	0.8893	1.0373	1.3293	1	0.6923	1.112
S7	3	2.059	1.2845	1.4984	1.92	1.4444	1	1.6064
S8	1.8675	1.2818	0.7996	0.9328	1.195217	0.8992	0.6225	1

Table 11. Pairwise Comparison Matrix for Criterion C5

	S1	S2	S3	S4	S5	S6	S7	S8
S1	1	2.6811	0.9218	2.5121	1.8405	2.7318	1.978	2.7656
S2	0.373	1	0.3438	0.9369	0.6865	1.0189	0.7377	1.0315
S3	1.0847	2.9084	1	2.7251	1.996	2.963	2.1455	3
S4	0.398	1.0672	0.3669	1	0.7326	1.0874	0.7873	1.1009
S5	0.5433	1.457	0.5008	1.365	1	1.4842	1.0746	1.5026
S6	0.366	0.9814	0.3375	0.9196	0.6737	1	0.724	1.0124
S7	0.5056	1.3556	0.4661	1.2701	0.9306	1.3812	1	1.398
S8	0.3616	0.9694	0.3333	0.9084	0.6655	0.9878	0.715	1

Table 12. Pairwise Comparison Matrix for Criterion C6

	S1	S2	S3	S4	S5	S6	S7	S8
S1	1	2.1971	2.9085	2.5437	1.812	2.657	3	2.3946
S2	0.455	1	1.3238	1.1577	0.8247	1.2094	1.365	1.0899
S3	0.344	0.7554	1	0.8745	0.623	0.9135	1.0314	0.8233
S4	0.3931	0.8637	1.1434	1	0.7124	1.0446	1.1794	0.9414
S5	0.5518	1.2125	1.605	1.4037	1	1.4663	1.655	1.3215
S6	0.3763	0.8269	1.0946	0.9573	0.682	1	1.129	0.9012
S7	0.3333	0.7323	0.9695	0.8478	0.604	0.8857	1	0.7982
S8	0.4176	0.9175	1.2146	1.0622	0.7567	1.1096	1.2528	1

Table 13. Criteria-wise Decision Matrix & Average Normalized Criteria Weights

	weights	S1	S2	S3	S4	S5	S6	S7	S8
C1	0.15	0.1165	0.178	0.059	0.1326	0.1441	0.139	0.1194	0.111
C2	0.2	0.251	0.1202	0.0853	0.1046	0.137	0.1002	0.109	0.0926
C3	0.02	0.1035	0.1362	0.065	0.1551	0.1068	0.1953	0.1136	0.1243
C4	0.25	0.0653	0.0952	0.1526	0.1308	0.1021	0.1357	0.1961	0.122
C5	0.3	0.216	0.0805	0.234	0.086	0.1173	0.079	0.1091	0.078
C6	0.08	0.258	0.1175	0.0888	0.1015	0.1425	0.097	0.0861	0.1078

The average normalized criteria weights (highlighted in Table 13) have been multiplied with the coefficients to obtain the criteria-wise weighted decision matrix. Further steps of ranking the alternatives was done using TOPSIS method. The final 6 × 8 Criteria-wise Weighted Decision Matrix is the input to the final stage of this hybrid MCDM process. The weights are used to compute the Performance Score based on the TOPSIS method.

Table 14. Criteria-Wise Weighted Decision Matrix

	S1	S2	S3	S4	S5	S6	S7	S8
C1	0.0175	0.02667	0.0089	0.0199	0.0216	0.02093	0.0179	0.0166
C2	0.0502	0.024	0.0170	0.0209	0.0274	0.02004	0.0218	0.0185
C3	0.002	0.0027	0.0013	0.0031	0.0021	0.00391	0.0023	0.0025
C4	0.0163	0.0238	0.0382	0.0327	0.0255	0.03388	0.0490	0.0305
C5	0.0647	0.0241	0.0702	0.0258	0.0352	0.02369	0.0327	0.0234
C6	0.0206	0.0094	0.0071	0.0081	0.0114	0.00778	0.0069	0.0086

Ranking of the Stocks in Order of Performance Score Using TOPSIS Method

Here is the transpose of the 6 × 8 criteria-wise weighted decision matrix (Tables 14 and 15).

Table 15. Transpose of Criteria-wise Weighted Decision Matrix

	C1	C2	C3	C4	C5	C6
S1	0.0175	0.0502	0.002	0.0163	0.0647	0.0206
S2	0.0266	0.024	0.0027	0.0238	0.0241	0.0094
S3	0.0088	0.017	0.0013	0.0381	0.0702	0.0071
S4	0.0198	0.0209	0.0031	0.0327	0.0257	0.0081
S5	0.0216	0.0274	0.0021	0.0255	0.0351	0.0114
S6	0.0209	0.02004	0.0039	0.0339	0.0237	0.0077
S7	0.0179	0.0218	0.0022	0.049	0.0327	0.0068
S8	0.0166	0.0185	0.002487	0.0305	0.0234	0.0086

Step-1.

Values of Positive Ideal Solution (PIS or Ideal Best) V_k^+ and Negative Ideal Solution (NIS or Ideal Worst) V_k^- are computed for each criterion k as the maximum and minimum weight for any alternative respectively under that criterion k (Table 16).

Table 16. Determination of Ideal Best and Ideal Worst under each Criterion

	C1	C2	C3	C4	C5	C6
Ideal Best (V+)	0.02667	0.0501967	0.0039	0.016338	0.023417	0.0207
Ideal Worst (V−)	0.00889	0.0170647	0.0013	0.049015	0.070251	0.0069

Steps-2.

The Euclidean Distance of every alternative S_i from the Ideal Best value is calculated using the following formula: $S_i^+ = \sqrt{\sum_{j=1}^{6} \left(\omega_{ij} - V_j^+ \right)^2}$.

Step-3.

The Euclidean Distance of every alternative S_i from the Ideal Worst value is calculated using the following formula: $S_i^- = \sqrt{\sum_{j=1}^{6} \left(\omega_{ij} - V_j^- \right)^2}$ (Table 17).

Steps-4.

The Performance Score of every alternative P_i is calculated using (Table 18):

$$P_i = \frac{S_i^-}{S_i^+ + S_i^-}$$

Step-5.

The Performance Score values are arranged in descending order. Ranks are assigned to the corresponding alternatives accordingly to get the final ranking of the 8 stocks (Table 19).

Table 17. Euclidean Distances

	S_i^+	S_i^-
S1	0.042393	0.049596661
S2	0.029471	0.055979024
S3	0.065376	0.01085924
S4	0.036527	0.048828732
S5	0.029275	0.045507967
S6	0.037658	0.050545726
S7	0.047221	0.038880171
S8	0.038106	0.051012375

Table 18. Performance Scores

	P_i
S1	0.539153953
S2	0.655104779
S3	0.142443695
S4	0.572061206
S5	0.608532679
S6	0.573054191
S7	0.451562217
S8	0.572411473

Table 19. Ranking of Stocks based on P_i Score

Rank	Stocks	Alternative ID	P_i Score
1	INFOSYS	S2	0.655104779
2	L&T TECH	S5	0.608532679
3	MPHASIS	S6	0.573054191
4	HEXAWARE	S8	0.572411473
5	HCL TECH	S4	0.572061206
6	TCS	S1	0.539153953
7	SASKEN	S7	0.451562217
8	WIPRO	S3	0.142443695

4.3   Discussion of the Results of the Data Analysis

The criteria weights obtained from expert opinion of several trading analysts can be trusted and are perfectly consistent because the consistency index (CI) and subsequently the consistency ratio (CR) is 0.000143254584 (<0.1), very close to true CR = 0.

The hybrid MCDM technique yields results similar to the ranking of these IT stocks done using Capital Asset Pricing Model (CAPM) where the annual risk-free rate is taken as 4.4% (based on RBI repo rate data) and so, the daily risk-free rate is 0.012%.

The following table lists the 8 selected IT stocks in descending order of their alpha value (α) because α-value represents the returns from the stock (Table 20).

Table 20. Ranking of Stocks based on Highest Alpha (α)

1	L&T TECH	0.001284657
2	MPHASIS	0.000876493
3	HEXAWARE	0.000716508
4	SASKEN	0.00064277
5	HCL TECH	0.000546425
6	INFOSYS	0.000529809
7	TCS	0.000427592
8	WIPRO	0.000150457

There are certain deviations of the results of the proposed hybrid MCDM technique from the results of ranking the same stocks using the existing CAPM model based on historical data taken over a period of more than 4 years from 1st August 2016 to 20th October 2020. Except for the ranking of S2 (Infosys), the other stocks are ranked more or less similarly by both the proposed and the existing scheme. Since the existing technique is based only on historical stock returns, the ranking yielded by the proposed MCDM model that considers 6 major financial trading indicators, is more intuitive and much more effective. Even technical analysis results in different ranking of stocks for portfolio construction and multi-criteria decision-making is required to effectively rank and select stocks for the portfolio. The existing techniques focus only on growth stocks or on technical analysis. However, MCDM techniques can help improve the results of stock selection. The proposed MCDM technique is thus useful.

5   Conclusion

The results of the experiments are quite close to the current market predictions and reflects closely the opinions of the financial experts and trading analysts based on the technical analysis of the current stock movements.

The novelty and uniqueness of this new hybrid MCDM technique lies in the unique way in which the three existing methods Grey Relational Analysis, AHP and TOPSIS have been combined. The proposed model serves the purpose of ranking the alternatives in order of preference while taking quantitative values in the decision matrix. The unique application of the GRA ensures that the alternatives are compared based on the actual quantitative parameters and the relative weights of the decision matrices are not formulated based on anybody's assumption or opinion.

The proposed methodology applied in this context of ranking of stocks of portfolio construction can be extended to other areas of management science such as supplier selection, factory/plant location planning, evaluation of the usability of products and/or applications and so on, and the applicability of this new hybrid model is not limited to only financial analysis. The proposed model is quite accurate and precise as it combines the best and most robust techniques of the three most popular and widely used MCDM methods, - Grey Relational Analysis (GRA), Analytic Hierarchy Process (AHP) and Technique of Order of Performance by Similarity to Ideal Solution (TOPSIS).

The proposed hybrid MCDM technique is more effective than existing stock ranking techniques based on CAPM model or technical analysis, and the combination of three most popular MCDM methods is always better than each of the individual methods.

The proposed model does not take into consideration the uncertainty in the assumed or assigned weightage of importance criteria and alternatives under each criterion. However, this limitation of the model can be mitigated once it is extended to be applied in the fuzzy environment. Thus the future scope of the proposed hybrid MCDM method can be extended to include Fuzzy AHP-TOPSIS and Grey Relational Analysis.

References

1. Hacıoğlu, Ü., Dincer, H.: A Comparative Hybrid Method in Technical Analysis for Stock Selection Process in Banking Sector by Fuzzy AHP-Topsis and Vikor Method. Global Strategies in Banking and Finance. Advances in Finance, Accounting and Economics Book series Volume. Business Science Reference, USA (2013). https://doi.org/10.4018/978-1-4666-4635-3
2. Oyatoye, E.O., Okpokpo, G.U., Adekoya, G.A.: An Application of AHP Investment Portfolio Selection in the Banking Sector of the Nigerian Capital Market (2011)
3. Li, R., Sun, T.: Assessing Factors for Designing a Successful B2C E-Commerce Website using Fuzzy AHP and TOPSIS-Grey Methodology. MDPI Symmetry, China (2020)
4. Sulu, A.C., Saerang, D.P.E., Massie, J.D.D.: The analysis of consumer purchase intention towards cosmetic products based on product origin. Jurnal EMBA 4(2) (2016)
5. Kang, D., Jang, W., Park, Y.: Evaluation of e-commerce websites using fuzzy hierarchical TOPSIS based on E-S-Qual. Appl. Soft Comput. 42 (2016). https://doi.org/10.1016/j.asoc.2016.01.017
6. Putra, M., Andryana, S., Kasyfi, F., Gunaryati, A.: Fuzzy analytical hierarchy process method to determine the quality of gemstones. Adv. Fuzzy Syst. 2018, 1–6 (2018). https://doi.org/10.1155/2018/9094380
7. Guru, S., Mahalik, D.K.: A comparative study on performance measurement of Indian public sector banks using AHP-TOPSIS and AHP-grey relational analysis. OPSEARCH 56(4), 1213–1239 (2019). https://doi.org/10.1007/s12597-019-00411-1

8. Trendlyne (Trading Analyst Website). https://trendlyne.com
9. Mishra, D.: 5 Financial Ratios Every Stock Investor Should Know. Groww, April 2020. https://groww.in/blog/financial-ratios-every-investor-should-know
10. IG Markets Limited: 10 Trading Indicators Every Trader Should Know, 4 June 2019. https://www.ig.com/en/trading-strategies/10-trading-indicators-every-trader-should-know-190604

Exploring Knowledge Distillation of a Deep Neural Network for Multi-script Identification

Shuvayan Ghosh Dastidar, Kalpita Dutta[(⊠)], Nibaran Das,
Mahantapas Kundu, and Mita Nasipuri

Jadavpur University, Kolkata, India
kalpitadutta.cse.rs@jadavpuruniversity.in

Abstract. Multi-lingual script identification is a difficult task consisting of different language with complex backgrounds in scene text images. According to the current research scenario, deep neural networks are employed as teacher models to train a smaller student network by utilizing the teacher model's predictions. This process is known as dark knowledge transfer. It has been quite successful in many domains where the final result obtained is unachievable through directly training the student network with a simple architecture. In this paper, we explore dark knowledge transfer approach using long short-term memory (LSTM) and CNN based assistant model and various deep neural networks as the teacher model, with a simple CNN based student network, in this domain of multi-script identification from natural scene text images. We explore the performance of different teacher models and their ability to transfer knowledge to a student network. Although the small student network's limited size, our approach obtains satisfactory results on a well-known script identification dataset CVSI-2015.

Keywords: Natural scene text · Script identification · Dark knowledge · Transfer learning · LSTM

1 Introduction

Multi-lingual script identification is a crucial task in case of scene text recognition. Scene text in the wild consists of multiple languages and therefore, accurate script identification has become an indispensable part of the scene text OCR systems. Text recognition from natural scene images is relatively complicated, which consists of different textures, contrasts, random brightness and saturation. Owing to the difficulties in this domain, it has sought the attention of many researchers with pattern recognition and computer vision expertise.

Deep Neural Networks usually have a vast number of parameters and memory overhead which makes them unsuitable for mobile uses. Distilling the knowledge from the deep neural network and transferring the latter in a smaller student

© Springer Nature Switzerland AG 2021
P. Dutta et al. (Eds.): CICBA 2021, CCIS 1406, pp. 150–162, 2021.
https://doi.org/10.1007/978-3-030-75529-4_12

network with much fewer parameters can make it suitable for mobile uses without much loss in the information of the deep or teacher neural network.

1.1 Motivation

We have applied a new methodology to classify multilingual scripts from natural scene images.

In this paper, we have used the concept of knowledge transfer [7] from deep neural networks to a smaller network, where the learnt features are transferred to the small model with much less parameters. The main advantage of this concept is less memory overhead for the task of multi-lingual script identification leading to much less inference times which facilitates the incorporation of the models in small mobile devices where computation power is limited. Along with this, we also experiment with various neural networks of different architectures as the teacher network and study the effect of knowledge transfer of learnt features in the student network. With increasing distance between the parameters of the teacher network and the student network, proper distillation of knowledge cannot be obtained. So an auxiliary intermediate assistant model is employed to increase the efficiency of knowledge transfer. Through series of experiments and ablation studies, we prove that introduction of the assistant model improves the knowledge transfer from the deep teacher network. The parameters of the intermediate assistant network are less than the teacher model but more than the student network. The key contributions of the paper are:

- Distilling a state of the art deep neural network in the field of multi-script identification from natural scene text images using three steps of training comprising of the teacher, assistant and the student model. We believe this concept of knowledge distillation for multi-lingual script identification from natural scene images has not been introduced before and this is the first work.
- Using an assistant model to distill the knowledge learnt by the teacher network and the transfer the same in a smaller student network. The assistant network consists of conv-nets and a bidirectional stacked LSTM [2] for knowledge transfer between the teacher and the student network, both being convolutional neural networks. It has been inferred that the assistant model helps in boosting the student model's accuracy by bridging the gap between the teacher and the student network and thus diminishing the distance between the parameters of the same.
- Exploring different deep neural networks employed as the teacher model and comparing their performance based on the transfer of knowledge in the student network. Inception-Net V3, Efficient-Net B4 and Vgg19 have been used as a teacher model with one assistant convolutional-LSTM based model and the final inference is done on a 4 layer convolutional student network. All of the teacher networks mentioned above have varying number of parameters, much more than the assistant and the student models.

The remaining paper is written as - Sect. 2 is concerned with some previous works and Sect. 3 briefly presents the proposed method. Section 4 describes some experimental results, and Sect. 5 ends the paper with the conclusion and future works.

2   Related Study

Earlier papers used ensemble methods for model compression [8,9]. Distillation of knowledge from a teacher network and transferring it to a student network to mimic the teacher network is a basic fundamental concept of knowledge distillation. The first proposed concept of knowledge distillation [7] introduces the concept of compressing the knowledge of a more in-depth or larger model to a single computational efficient neural network. It has introduced the concept of dark knowledge transfer from a deep teacher network to a smaller student network by taking the softmax of the results of the teacher network with a specific temperature value and calculating loss between it and the predicted outputs of the student network. They validated their findings by running on MNIST dataset and, JFT dataset by google and other speech recognition tasks. Since then, knowledge distillation has progressed a lot, and adversarial methods [17,18] also have utilized for modelling knowledge transfer between teacher and student. After this study, extensive research has conducted on knowledge distillation. In the paper [11] has introduced the transfer of a hidden activation output and other has proposed transferring attention information as knowledge [20].

Article [19] has briefly described the advantages and efficiency of the knowledge distillation. It has described importance of knowledge transfer from teacher to student model using distilled knowledge. They have compared two student deep neural networks trained with teacher network and without teacher model with same size. They have proposed a method of transferring the distilled knowledge between two layers to shows three important points. The student model is more efficient than the original model and it also outperform the original model which is trained from scratch. The student network understand the flow of solving the problem and it start learning with good initial weights. It can learnt and optimized faster than original or normal deep neural network. This paper proves that, the student model reports better efficiency than a normal network without a teacher model. They have compared various knowledge transfer techniques with a normal network without any teacher model for knowledge transfer. They have learned their model with two main condition. First, the teacher model must pretrained with some different dataset and second condition is the teacher model is shallower or deeper than the student model. Their approach contains two step training.

Article [3] has portrayed an architecture to learn multi class object detection models using knowledge distillation. They have proposed a weighted cross entropy loss for classification task to accounts for the imbalanced in the misclassification for the background class as opposed to object classes. A teacher has bounded regression loss for knowledge transfer and it also adapt layers for hint learning. It allows a student to learn better from the distribution of neurons in the intermediate teacher layers. Using multiple large-scale public benchmarks they have made an empirical evaluation. They have presented the behavior of their framework by relating it to the generalization and under-fitting problems. They have adopted Faster-RCNN to detect object. They have learnt hint based learning to the similar feature representation of a student model with a teacher model. General knowledge transfer models have a large pre-trained teacher model to train a smaller student model. But article [10] has proper knowledge transfer is not obtained with increase in gap of the parameters of student and teacher model. A teacher can successfully transfer its knowledge to the students up to a certain size, not too small, they have proposed a multi-step knowledge distillation method, which employs an intermediate-sized teacher assistant network to minimize the gap of the two models - teacher and student. They have studied the effect of teacher assistant model size and has extended the structure to multi-step distillation. First, the TA network has distilled the knowledge from the teacher model. Then, the TA acts as a teacher model to trains the student model via knowledge distillation. Also some other paper [6] has focused on assistant network. There are some conflicting views regrading whether a good teacher always teaches a student well. Some times if the student model capacity is too low, then knowledge distillation cannot succeed to mimic the teacher model [4]. They have presented an approach to mitigate this issue by early stopping teacher training to improve a solution more amenable for the student model.

In [14] have used densely guided knowledge distillation technique using multiple teacher assistant network. Which progressively decrease the model size to bridge the gap efficiently between teacher and student networks. To stimulate more efficient student learning, each teacher assistant has guided to every other smaller teacher assistant. The existing larger teacher assistants have used to teach a smaller teacher assistant at the next step to increase the learning efficiency. For each mini-batch during training this paper has designed stochastic teaching where a teacher assistant has randomly dropped. The student can always learn rich distilled knowledge from multiple sources ranging from the teacher to multiple teacher assistants.

In paper [11] introduced the concept of FitNets for compressing knowledge from thin and deep neural networks to wide networks with more parameters. They have used the advantage of depth in the network compression problem. A part of the teacher's hidden layer is used in the training of the student model, enabling to learn more efficiently. The part from the teacher network is called hints.

3   Proposed Model

3.1   Model Architecture

With increasing complexity of scene text images, state of the art script identification models [1,6,13] tend to incorporate more convolutional filters and thereby make a more in-depth and broader network. However, for deploying such models in the practical scenario, it needs to be pruned or distilled for coping up with available resources. Thus we try to distill the knowledge in various deep neural networks. For the transfer of knowledge, the training is done in three subsequent phases involving an assistant [14] and a student network. Figure 1 shows the overall model architecture and pipeline to be followed for the knowledge transfer process. This section further describes the details of the three networks mentioned.

Teacher Model. In this literature, we have performed three different experiments involving three various teacher networks. As the teacher network in knowledge distillation theory, is usually taken to be a deep CNN, we have considered three states of the art neural networks pre-trained on the ImageNet dataset [5] InceptionV3 [15], VGG19 and EfficientNet-B4 [16]. Among these networks, EfficientNet-B4 and InceptionNetv3 have the relatively same amount of parameters which are 17 million and 27 million respectively whereas VGG19 has a vast number of parameters due to more fully connected layers amounting to 143 million. However VGG has a very simple architecture consisting mainly of linear layers while Efficient Net-B4 and Inception Net V3 have hybrid convolutions in their architectures due to which they have comparatively quite less parameters. Table 1 shows the total parameters in the three models discussed. The outputs from the teacher network are divide by a certain temperature value τ, and then softmax is taken to generate soft labels which are used to train the assistant model, as shown in Eq. 1.

Table 1. Total number of parameters of three different deep neural networks.

Model	Parameters (in millions)
InceptionV3	~27
EfficientNet-B4	~17
VGG 19	~143

$$\sum_i \frac{\exp(\frac{x_i}{\tau})}{\sum_j \exp(\frac{x_j}{\tau})} \tag{1}$$

Assistant Model is used as a medium to transfer intermediate features from the teacher to the student network and thus helps in diminishing the feature gap between them. We take the assistant network as a combination of conv-nets and a two-layer bi-directional stacked LSTM [1]. Since scene text images contain text instances which are sequential data, recurrent neural networks are the best suited for this purpose. LSTM has gained significant success in the NLU domain and other tasks involving sequential data, and keeping in mind these works, we have incorporated LSTM in our network. There are four convolution layers with 3×3 filters and of depth 64, 128, 256, 300 respectively. A max pooling layer follows each of the convolution layers. The result from the conv-net is directed to a two-layer stacked bi-directional LSTM with 256 hidden layers. The results from the LSTM are subjected to two linear layers to give the classified outputs. The assistant network has 14 million parameters which is less than either of the three teacher networks.

Student Model is a small network with fewer parameters than the teacher model. The student network learns directly from the trained assistant network. It has undergone training using the soft labels from the teacher network. The student model is a basic conv-net comprising of four convolutional filters and four maxpool layers with 32, 64, 128 and 128 channels respectively. All of them have three kernel size. The final logits are generated through two fully connected linear layers and are used to classify the script in the input images. Owing to the small number of convolutional layers, it has a size of 1 million training parameters, where it is almost 27 times lesser than Inception Network and 143 times lesser than VGG teacher network.

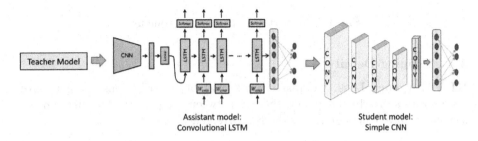

Fig. 1. Flowchart of our proposed work

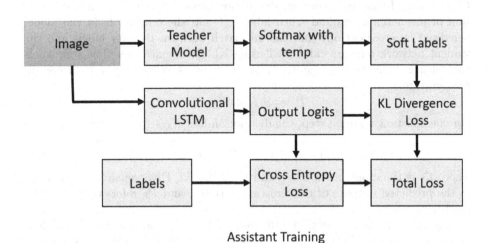

Fig. 2. Flowchart of assistant model training

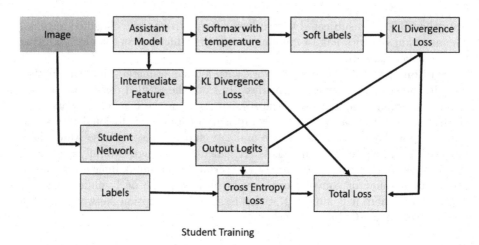

Student Training

Fig. 3. Flowchart of student model training

3.2   Training Detail

KL Divergence Loss. Compares two probability distributions and generates a similarity score. In this paper, the loss between the predicted results and the soft labels have calculated with the KL Divergence loss.

$$D_{KL}(p||q) = \sum_{i=1}^{N} p(x_i) log(\frac{p(x_i)}{q(x_i)}) \tag{2}$$

Distillation Loss. In knowledge distillation theory, the distillation is taken as sum of mismatch of ground truth label y^{cls} and the outputs from the model penalized by cross-entropy and the mismatch between the soft labels and the student network outputs calculated using KL Divergence loss. The soft labels are calculated by taking a softmax of the network outputs ψ with a certain temperature τ.

$$P^\tau = softmax(\psi/\tau) \tag{3}$$

For the assistant training step, the distillation loss K_{DA} is given by

$$K_{DA} = (1 - \alpha)\mathcal{L}_1(P_A, y^{cls}) + \alpha\tau^2\mathcal{L}_2(P_A^\tau, P_T^\tau) \tag{4}$$

where $\mathcal{L}_1$ is the cross-entropy loss and $\mathcal{L}_2$ is the KL Divergence loss. P_A refers to the predicted outputs of the assistant network, and P_T refers to that of the teacher network.

For the student network, the distillation loss K_{DS} also considers the loss between two similar features vectors between the student and the assistant networks. The first two terms are similar to the cross-entropy loss and the loss between the soft labels and the model outputs in case of the assistant training.

$$K_{DS} = (1 - \alpha)\mathcal{L}_1(P_S, y^{cls}) + \alpha\tau^2\mathcal{L}_2(P_S^\tau, P_A^\tau) + \lambda * \mathcal{L}_2(P_{Sf}, P_{Af}) \tag{5}$$

where P_S denotes the predicted results of the student model and P_A refers to the assistant network. P_{Sf} refers to the feature vector from the student network and P_{Af} refers to the feature vector from the assistant network. $\mathcal{L}_1$ and $\mathcal{L}_2$ have the same meanings as in case of the loss of the assistant network.

We have taken λ and α to be equal to 0.4 for all experiments.

Implementation Details. We have used the Pytorch framework for implementation. For training purposes, images were resized to the size of 299 and were transformed to ones with a mean of 0.5 and a standard deviation of 0.5. Augmentations such as random brightness and random contrast were also added to the images during training. We further used the Stochastic Gradient Descent optimizer with nesterov momentum of 0.95 and a learning rate of 0.001 for 150 epochs. We have also used weight decay of 0.001 for training purposes.

Training. The training is done on the CVSI [12] dataset consisting of scene text images. It contains ten classes which are scripts in different languages. The training is a three step process. The first step consists of training of the teacher network. We have studied the performance of three deep neural networks with different architectures - Inceptionet V3, VGG19 and Efficient Net- B4. All three networks have pre-trained on the ImageNet dataset having 1000 classes having a nearly same domain to that of scene text images. The networks are so trained to reduce the loss between the outputs and the ground-truth labels.

The second step consists of assistant model to be trained with the distilled knowledge from the trained teacher network. A detailed representation of this step can be found in Fig. 2. The assistant network is trained subject to minimizing the summation of the loss due to predicted outputs with the hard labels and loss between the soft labels generated from the teacher network after taking softmax with temperature and the predicted outputs. To make the training faster, the soft labels were generated before the training and used in the loss function.

In the third step, the student network is trained from the knowledge imbibed in the assistant network. The visual representation of this step can be found in Fig. 3. The training of the student model is very similar to that of the assistant network with an additional factor. The loss between the feature vector from the assistant network after passing through the lstm module and the feature vector after four convolutional layers in the student network is calculated and added to the distillation loss which is calculated in the same way as in the assistant network.

4   Experimental Results

We have done several experiments to analyse the performance of our models on the CVSI dataset. CVSI comprises of natural scene text images with different scripts, such as Bengali, English, Hindi, Tamil, Kannada, and other Indian languages. Table 2 shows the final accuracy based on the three teacher networks

Fig. 4. Some images of correct prediction

Fig. 5. Some images of wrong prediction

Table 2. Accuracy chart of teacher, assistant and student model using CVSI-2015 dataset

Networks	Teacher model	Assistant model	Student model
Inception Net V3	98.19	88.58	**89.19**
Efficient Net B4	97.19	88.52	87.74
VGG 19	97.28	**89.71**	88.30

Table 3. Multi-script identification results of student model using Inception net v3

Scripts	Precision	Recall	F-Score
Arabic	0.97	0.93	0.95
Bengali	0.81	0.91	0.86
English	0.92	0.82	0.87
Gujrathi	0.94	0.95	0.94
Hindi	0.95	0.88	0.91
Kannada	0.95	0.68	0.79
Oriya	0.85	0.96	0.90
Punjabi	0.95	0.93	0.94
Tamil	0.84	0.95	0.89
Telegu	0.79	0.90	0.84

Table 4. Multi-script identification results of student model using Efficient net b4

Scripts	Precision	Recall	F-Score
Arabic	0.98	0.92	0.95
Bengali	0.77	0.91	0.83
English	0.89	0.82	0.85
Gujrathi	0.97	0.93	0.95
Hindi	0.95	0.86	0.90
Kannada	0.97	0.58	0.72
Oriya	0.89	0.95	0.92
Punjabi	0.93	0.94	0.93
Tamil	0.84	0.94	0.89
Telegu	0.73	0.93	0.82

Table 5. Multi-script identification results of student model using VGG 19

Scripts	Precision	Recall	F-Score
Arabic	0.98	0.95	0.96
Bengali	0.74	0.85	0.79
English	0.91	0.84	0.88
Gujrathi	0.93	0.96	0.94
Hindi	0.87	0.88	0.87
Kannada	0.97	0.65	0.78
Oriya	0.80	0.99	0.88
Punjabi	0.97	0.93	0.95
Tamil	0.88	0.85	0.87
Telegu	0.87	0.92	0.89

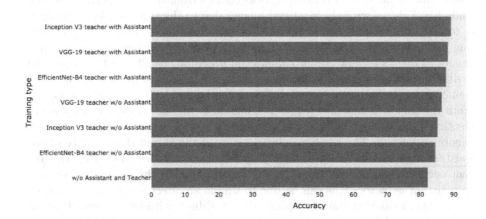

Fig. 6. A visual representation of the accuracies obtained by the student model trained by different methods of knowledge distillation.

Table 6. Comparison of accuracy of the student network trained by different methods

Teacher	Assistant	Accuracy
~	~	82.24
InceptionV3	~	85.18
InceptionV3	Conv-LSTM	89.19
EfficientNet-B4	~	84.51
EfficientNet-B4	Conv-LSTM	87.74
VGG-19	~	86.45
VGG-19	Conv-LSTM	88.30

Table 7. A comparative study of the performance of different methods due to different researchers and our student models trained on three different teacher networks based on script-wise accuracies of the CVSI test dataset.

Methods	English	Hindi	Bengali	Oriya	Gujrati	Punjabi	Kannada	Tamil	Telugu	Arabic	Final accuracy
CUK	65.69	61.66	68.71	79.14	73.39	92.09	**71.66**	82.55	57.89	89.44	74.06
C-DAC	68.33	71.47	**91.61**	88.04	88.99	90.51	68.47	91.90	91.33	**97.69**	84.66
InceptionV3	82.11	**87.73**	91.29	96.01	95.11	93.35	68.15	**94.70**	89.16	89.78	**89.19**
Efficient-B4	81.52	86.19	91.29	95.09	93.27	**94.30**	57.64	93.76	**92.57**	91.75	87.74
VGG-19	**84.16**	**87.73**	84.84	**99.38**	**96.02**	93.35	64.97	85.36	92.26	94.72	88.30

and the assistant and student networks, trained with knowledge transfer, on the test dataset of CVSI. The teacher network with the highest accuracy enables the highest degree of knowledge transfer in the student network, which is the Inception Net V3 network. For the VGG-19 network, the assistant model has the highest accuracy among the three. Figure 4 shows some correctly identified images due to the three student networks trained from their respective teachers, while Fig. 5 shows wrongly identified images due to the three student networks. It can be inferred that the Inception Net fails for difficult images due to blurring and colour contrasts whereas in case of VGG it even fails on some simple images. Table 3, Table 4, Table 5 shows the precision, recall and f-score related to different scripts in the CVSI dataset of the predictions of the student network trained from the InceptionNet v3, Efficient Net b4 and VGG 19 teacher network. From the tables, it has inferred that Kannada is the most difficult language to identify. Table 6 shows accuracy of the student models based on different experiments performed. The teacher networks were changed and the presence of the assistant network was analysed during the experiments. We can see that the student network learnt better from the VGG as the teacher than inception without an assistant network. This can be due to simple architecture of VGG favouring knowledge distillation than Inception V3. In Table 6 without the knowledge of the teacher model, the student network alone has the accuracy of 82.24% on the test dataset. When the student network is trained just on the presence of the teacher network, without the influence of the assistant network, it achieves an accuracy of 85.18%. In the presence of both the teacher and assistant model in subsequent training, the overall model accuracy increases to 89.19%. This paper has experimented with three more recent and precise networks like Inception net V3, Efficient Net B4 and VGG-19 as a teacher model. All the performances have done with one strong assistant network Convolutional LSTM. Finally, we have used a small convolutional network as a student model. Figure 6 shows the visual representation of the accuracy obtained by the student network when it is trained with different methods as discussed in Table 6. From the results, it can be inferred that with Inception Net V3 as the teacher network, and in the presence of the assistant model, the student model achieves the highest accuracy equal to 89.19% compared to the accuracies of other student models trained by different methods. Table 7 shows the script-wise accuracies of different methods due to other researchers and the three different student models trained based on the knowledge distillation from the three different teacher networks - Inception Net V3, VGG19 and Efficient Net-B4. The student model based on the training from Inception Net V3 has the highest overall accuracy compared to other networks. The highest accuracy corresponding to each script is shown in bold in the table.

5   Conclusion

In this paper, we have studied the effect of knowledge transfer of three different states of the art deep neural networks on a student network for the task of script identification in natural scene text images. We can conclude by our experiments that the teacher network with the highest accuracy, which in our case is Inception Net v3, leads to better knowledge transfer in a student network. Through our experiments, we can also conclude that some languages have difficulties due to colour contrasts and fonts Kannada being one of them. Future work on this will be to improve the assistant and the student networks so that a better knowledge transfer is achieved.

References

1. Bhunia, A.K., Konwer, A., Bhunia, A.K., Bhowmick, A., Roy, P.P., Pal, U.: Script identification in natural scene image and video frames using an attention based convolutional-LSTM network. Pattern Recogn. **85**, 172–184 (2019)
2. Breuel, T.M.: High performance text recognition using a hybrid convolutional-LSTM implementation. In: 2017 14th IAPR International Conference on Document Analysis and Recognition (ICDAR), vol. 1, pp. 11–16. IEEE (2017)
3. Chen, G., Choi, W., Yu, X., Han, T., Chandraker, M.: Learning efficient object detection models with knowledge distillation. In: Advances in Neural Information Processing Systems, vol. 30, pp. 742–751 (2017)
4. Cho, J.H., Hariharan, B.: On the efficacy of knowledge distillation. In: Proceedings of the IEEE International Conference on Computer Vision, pp. 4794–4802 (2019)

5. Deng, J., Dong, W., Socher, R., Li, L.J., Li, K., Fei-Fei, L.: ImageNet: a large-scale hierarchical image database. In: CVPR 2009 (2009)

6. Gomez, L., Nicolaou, A., Karatzas, D.: Improving patch-based scene text script identification with ensembles of conjoined networks. Pattern Recogn. **67**, 85–96 (2017)

7. Hinton, G., Vinyals, O., Dean, J.: Distilling the knowledge in a neural network. arXiv preprint arXiv:1503.02531 (2015)

8. Huang, G., Liu, Z., Van Der Maaten, L., Weinberger, K.Q.: Densely connected convolutional networks. In: Proceedings of the IEEE Conference on Computer Vision and Pattern Recognition, pp. 4700–4708 (2017)

9. Jin, X., et al.: Knowledge distillation via route constrained optimization. In: Proceedings of the IEEE International Conference on Computer Vision, pp. 1345–1354 (2019)

10. Mirzadeh, S.I., Farajtabar, M., Li, A., Levine, N., Matsukawa, A., Ghasemzadeh, H.: Improved knowledge distillation via teacher assistant. In: Proceedings of the AAAI Conference on Artificial Intelligence, vol. 34, pp. 5191–5198 (2020)

11. Romero, A., Ballas, N., Kahou, S.E., Chassang, A., Gatta, C., Bengio, Y.: FitNets: hints for thin deep nets. arXiv preprint arXiv:1412.6550 (2014)

12. Sharma, N., Mandal, R., Sharma, R., Pal, U., Blumenstein, M.: ICDAR 2015 competition on video script identification (CVSI 2015). In: 2015 13th International Conference on Document Analysis and Recognition (ICDAR), pp. 1196–1200. IEEE (2015)

13. Shi, B., Bai, X., Yao, C.: Script identification in the wild via discriminative convolutional neural network. Pattern Recogn. **52**, 448–458 (2016)

14. Son, W., Na, J., Hwang, W.: Densely guided knowledge distillation using multiple teacher assistants. arXiv preprint arXiv:2009.08825 (2020)

15. Szegedy, C., Vanhoucke, V., Ioffe, S., Shlens, J., Wojna, Z.: Rethinking the inception architecture for computer vision. In: Proceedings of the IEEE Conference on Computer Vision and Pattern Recognition, pp. 2818–2826 (2016)

16. Tan, M., Le, Q.V.: EfficientNet: rethinking model scaling for convolutional neural networks. arXiv preprint arXiv:1905.11946 (2019)

17. Wang, X., Zhang, R., Sun, Y., Qi, J.: KDGAN: knowledge distillation with generative adversarial networks. In: Bengio, S., Wallach, H., Larochelle, H., Grauman, K., Cesa-Bianchi, N., Garnett, R. (eds.) Advances in Neural Information Processing Systems, vol. 31, pp. 775–786. Curran Associates, Inc. (2018). https://proceedings.neurips.cc/paper/2018/file/019d385eb67632a7e958e23f24bd07d7-Paper.pdf

18. Xu, Z., Hsu, Y.C., Huang, J.: Training shallow and thin networks for acceleration via knowledge distillation with conditional adversarial networks (2018)

19. Yim, J., Joo, D., Bae, J., Kim, J.: A gift from knowledge distillation: fast optimization, network minimization and transfer learning. In: Proceedings of the IEEE Conference on Computer Vision and Pattern Recognition, pp. 4133–4141 (2017)

20. Zagoruyko, S., Komodakis, N.: Paying more attention to attention: improving the performance of convolutional neural networks via attention transfer. arXiv preprint arXiv:1612.03928 (2016)

A Machine Learning Based Fertilizer Recommendation System for Paddy and Wheat in West Bengal

Uditendu Sarkar[1], Gouravmoy Banerjee[2], and Indrajit Ghosh[2(✉)]

[1] National Informatics Centre, Ministry of Electronics and Information Technology, Government of India, Jalpaiguri 735101, West Bengal, India
[2] Department of Computer Science, Ananda Chandra College, Jalpaiguri 735101, West Bengal, India

Abstract. Agricultural soil provides the nutrients to the crop, and over time, the nutrient contents deplete with continued cultivation. The adequate quantity and quality of fertilizers provide the essential nutrients to the soil for the sustained production of crops. Paddy and wheat are the two major crops cultivated by most rural farmers in West Bengal, India. As the agricultural experts are very scarce and expensive, the layman farmers apply the chemical fertilizers with poor technical knowledge. To mitigate the lack of experts and assist the rural farmers, an intelligent machine learning based fertilizer recommendation system for paddy and wheat is very noteworthy. This work proposes a machine learning-based fertilizer recommendation system for this purpose.

Instead of a single classifier, the machine learning component is designed with an assembly of multiple classifiers. Each classifier's performance is evaluated in terms of two well established accuracy metrics; percentage accuracy and Cohen's kappa. The output of the best performing classifier is always accepted as the final recommendation. The system incorporated the Soil Test Crop Response protocol suggested by the Indian Council of Agricultural Research for the recommendation of fertilizers. It allows the farmers to choose any one of four alternative combinations of fertilizers depending on the local availability and cost. To the best of the authors' knowledge, no such comprehensive fertilizer recommendation system has been suggested using Soil Test Crop Response protocol. This work is a pioneer in this field.

Keywords: Fertilizer recommendation system · Machine learning · AI in agriculture

1 Introduction

Agriculture is one of the prime sectors for the sustained economic progress of the developing nations including, India. About 70% of India's rural population depends on agriculture and allied industries for their livelihood [1]. In West Bengal, agriculture provides livelihood to around 7.12 million families [2]. In 2013–14, West Bengal contributed more

© Springer Nature Switzerland AG 2021
P. Dutta et al. (Eds.): CICBA 2021, CCIS 1406, pp. 163–174, 2021.
https://doi.org/10.1007/978-3-030-75529-4_13

than a 25% share in Gross State Value Added (GSVA) and ranked first and ninth among Indian states to produce paddy and wheat, respectively [3]. Afterward, an average fall in the total share in GSVA is observed due to a decline in productivity [3], as presented in Fig. 1.

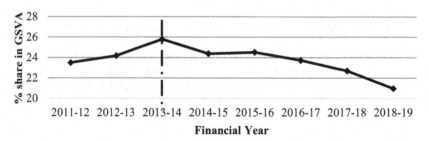

Fig. 1. Share of agriculture in the GSVA of West Bengal

Several factors were responsible for this decline of production which includes crop loss due to the infestation of insect pests and diseases [4, 5], migration of farmers to other profitable professions, decrease in cultivable land, the decline in soil fertility etc. Amongst them, adequate soil fertility is also an important precondition for paddy and wheat production along with other crops [6].

Though, soil provides the nutrients to the crop, over time, the nutrient contents deplete with continued cultivation. To keep pace with the requirement of the nutrient, external chemical fertilizers are applied. According to the United Nations Food and Agriculture Organization (FAO), chemical fertilizers play a significant role in better crop yield in India [7]. Plant growth is a very complicated process that requires nutrients and other auxiliary parameters. The auxiliary parameters are organic carbon (Oc), soil pH, electrical conductivity (Ec), crop type (Cp), the season of farming (Sf), duration of farming (Df), and irrigation type (Ir). Nutrients are of two types; macro and micro. Nitrogen (N), Phosphorous (P) and Potassium (K) are the three macronutrients that are required in large quantities and having a direct impact on plant growth [8]. The micronutrients are generally not used by the farmers because they are less concern to the well-being of a crop [9] but the auxiliary parameters play a significant role in fertilizer management [10].

It is reported that in West Bengal, soil fertility is gradually decreasing from 2015–16 [11]. One of the major causes of this decline may be the improper application of fertilizer. The adequate quantity and quality of fertilizers provide the essential nutrients to the soil for better production of crops [12]. In West Bengal, paddy and wheat are the two major crops cultivated over a widespread area by most rural farmers. The layman farmers are applying the chemical fertilizers by their own choice with poor technical knowledge. On the other hand, agricultural experts are very scarce and expensive to cover such widespread cultivation. This results in a gradual deterioration of both the quantity and quality of the paddy and wheat produced.

The application of machine learning based recommendation system in agriculture has a long history [13]. Several machine learning-based decision support systems were suggested to solve various agriculture related problems, including fertilizer management. In 1997, Broner and Comstock suggested a nitrogen based general fertilizer dosage recommendation system for malting barley using neural networks [14]. A similar approach was taken up by Moreno et al., in 2018 while employing different soil specific parameters to design a general fertilizer dosage application system for pasture crops [15]. In 2010, Yu et al. used NPK to build an ensemble neural network for fertilization modelling [16]. Hoskinson et al. and Pampolino et al. used an expert system approach to develop a nutrient management system for potato and cereal crops, respectively [17, 18]. Tremblay et al. proposed a fuzzy logic-based system for suggesting the optimal rate of nitrogen use for corn [19]. Some researchers have also used fuzzy logic to develop fertilizer recommendation system such as Ashraf et al., Chougule et al., and Prabhakaran et al. [20–22]. The other fertilizer recommendation systems include Suchitra et al., Pratap et al., and Sumaryanti et al. [23–25]. All the systems considered different soil parameters as inputs, but they suggested only the blanket dosage of fertilizers. Instead of blanket application, this system recommends the fertilizers as per the ICAR recommended STCR protocol, which is much more scientific and site-specific than a general blanket dosage.

To mitigate the lack of experts and assist the farmers in West Bengal, an intelligent machine learning based fertilizers recommendation system for paddy and wheat is very noteworthy. This work proposes a machine learning-based fertilizers recommendation system for paddy and wheat in West Bengal. The system deals with the location-specific NPK content in soil and auxiliary parameters which are equally important, as inputs for a precise recommendation. The NPK and the other auxiliary parameters are available from the soil health cards provided by the Department of agriculture and farmers welfare, Govt. of India [26]. The models' performance has been evaluated in terms of two well established standard metrics to select the best recommendation.

The data collection methods, system architecture, performance analysis and various combinations of the fertilizers are described in Sect. 2. The Sect. 3 contains the results and discussion. Finally, conclusions are provided in Sect. 4.

2 Materials and Methods

2.1 Collection of Soil Data

To train a machine learning based intelligent system, reliable data sets are required as inputs. For the proposed system, the amounts of macronutrients currently available in the soil and the auxiliary parameters are considered as the inputs. To train the system, input data sets are collected from the soil health cards provided by the Government of India [26]. The soil health card data contains the amounts of macronutrients (NPK) available in the soil of an area along with the auxiliary parameters.

The soil health card data were collected from the three districts; Jalpaiguri, Malda and South 24 Parganas in West Bengal. These three districts have been chosen based on three different geographical locations with different environments. Jalpaiguri lies in the northern terai regions of the state, Malda lies in the middle of the Gangetic plain and South 24 Parganas in the Sundarban delta area near the Bay of Bengal.

The final fertilizers requirement for each sample in the respective soil health card database was obtained by using the Soil Test Crop Response (STCR) protocol [27]. The

(STCR) protocol has been developed by the Indian Council for Agricultural Research (ICAR) that provides a mechanism to evaluate the quantity of fertilizers required by the crop based on the available nutrient in the soil and the auxiliary parameters [28]. Studies have proved that the STCR protocol is efficient enough and reduces fertilizer misuse [29, 30]. The data obtained from the soil health card were considered as the inputs and the fertilizers suggested by STCR were used as the target values for training and testing the system. The system has been designed to consider all the varieties of paddy and wheat grown in West Bengal.

2.2 Designing the System

The proposed fertilizers recommendation system has been designed for paddy and wheat cultivation in West Bengal. Based on the macro nutrients available in the soil along with other auxiliary parameters, the system recommends suitable fertilizers as outputs. This is basically a classification type of problems with supervised learning.

The system has been designed with four components; the input section, classier assembly, performance evaluator and the output selector. A block diagram of the system architecture is presented in Fig. 2.

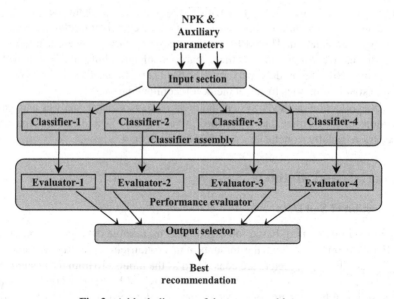

Fig. 2. A block diagram of the system architecture

The input section accepts and feeds the NPK values (in Kg/Ha) and auxiliary parameters as inputs to the classifier assembly. The classifier assembly consists of four different classifiers, i.e., decision tree, multilayer perceptron, support vector machine and k-nearest neighbor that use four popular learning techniques; non-metric learning, multilayer neural network, linear discriminant and non-parametric learning, respectively [31–34]. These different classifiers were modelled to solve the problem using the same set of inputs but with different learning techniques. The classifiers used with different learning techniques and hyperparameters are presented in Table 1.

Initially, the entire dataset was divided into two parts a training set comprising of 70% of the records and a testing set comprising of the remaining 30% of the records. The testing set is kept aside for performance evaluation. To prevent any kind of overfitting a five-fold cross validation was performed using the training set. The training data set (70%) was partitioned into five separate blocks and then the first four blocks were used as training and the last remaining one block was considered for testing. The process was repeated five times by shifting the test block from one partition to the other, while the remaining blocks were used for training.

Table 1. Classifiers used in the classifier assembly.

Classifiers	Learning techniques	Hyperparameters
Decision Tree (DT)	Non-metric [31]	Impurity Type = Gini impurity Algorithm = CART
k-Nearest Neighbour (k-NN)	Non-parametric [32]	No. of Neighbours = 2 Algorithm = Ball Tree Based
Multilayer Perceptron (MLP)	Multilayer Neural Network [33]	No. of hidden layer = 1 No. of hidden neurons = 17 Algorithm = Stochastic Gradient Descent
Support Vector Machine (SVM)	Linear Discriminant [34]	Gamma = 0.0001 Kernel = Radial Basis Function Regularization = 1 Algorithm = One vs all

The performance evaluator section consists of four evaluators, one for each classifier. After receiving the outputs from the four classifiers, the performance evaluators evaluate the performances of each classifier in terms of two well established metrices, i.e., percentage accuracy (Ac) and Cohen's kappa (k), as explained in the Subsect. 2.3. Based on the values of the performance metrics of the four classifiers, the output selector selects the best performing classifier and its output as the best recommendation.

2.3 Performance Evaluation

To test the performances of a classifier, several metrices have been suggested [35, 36]. As a standard practice, the performance of a classifier is measured in terms of classification accuracy. To measure the classification accuracy, two well accepted metrics have been used, i.e., percentage accuracy (Ac) and Cohen's Kappa (k). More the value of Ac and k, better the performance of the model.

The percentage accuracy (Ac) can be defined as [36]:

$$A_c = \frac{1}{n} \sum_{i=1}^{n} I.(y_p = y_a) \times 100 \tag{1}$$

where n is the number of samples, y_p and y_a are the predicted and actual values respectively. The function $I.(y_p = y_a)$ is an indicator function that returns 1 if $(y_p = y_a)$ is true and zero otherwise.

Cohen's kappa (k) is a standard and well-accepted measure of the accuracy of a classifier. Basically, it measures the degree of agreement, or disagreement between two instances. The range of kappa (k) values extends from negative one to positive one. When $k = 1$, a strong agreement is observed and $k = -1$ results a strong disagreement. The mid value ($k = 0$) indicates chance-level agreement.

The generalized expression to measure kappa(k) value for m classes is [36]:

$$Cohen's\ kappa(k) = \frac{N \cdot \sum_{i=1}^{m} C_{ii} - \sum_{i=1}^{m} C_{i_{corr}} \cdot C_{i_{pred}}}{N^2 - \sum_{i=1}^{m} C_{i_{corr}} \cdot C_{i_{pred}}} \tag{2}$$

Where $\sum_{i=1}^{m} C_{ii}$ is the total number of instances correctly predicted, $C_{i_{corr}}$ is the number of instances correctly classified for class i and $C_{i_{pred}}$ is the total number of instances predicted as class i and N is the total number of patterns.

2.4 Fertilizers to Be Recommended

The objective of this work was to design a comprehensive fertilizer recommendation system that provides paddy and wheat farmers with options while choosing their fertilizers. Therefore, the availability and cost of the fertilizers in the local market is an important issue. Usually, fertilizers are divided into two categories: straight fertilizers that are made from only one of the N, P, or K elements and complex fertilizers that contain a combination of two or three of N, P, K elements. Generally, a combination of three fertilizers are suggested by experts to compensate the lack of nutrients. A recent study conducted by Visva Bharati University, projected that the most available and popular fertilizers among the farmers of West Bengal are Urea, Muriate of Potash (MOP), Single Super Phosphate (SSP), Di-ammonium Phosphate (DAP), NPK (10:26:26) and NPK (20:20:20) [37]. Out of these fertilizers Urea, MOP and SSP are straight type and the rest are complex type fertilizers. Based on the availability, four alternative combinations (C-1, C-2, C-3 and C-4) of three fertilizers have been considered for recommendation as presented in Table 2. The required quantity of fertilizers (in Kg/Ha) were calculated as per the STCR protocol [38]. The objective of providing the alternative combinations of fertilizers is to make the recommendation comprehensive and to provide the best option to choose based on local availability and cost.

Table 2. Different combinations of fertilizers used for recommendation.

Alternative combinations	1st element	2nd element	3rd element
C-1	Urea (N)	MOP (K)	SSP (P)
C-2	DAP (NP)	Urea (N)	MOP (K)
C-3	NPK (20:20:20)	Urea (N)	MOP (K)
C-4	NPK (10:26:26)	Urea (N)	MOP (K)

3   Results and Discussions

In this study, the modelling of the classifiers is implemented via Python and the performance evaluation of the system is carried out with the test data sets of three districts; Jalpaiguri, Malda and South 24 Parganas of West Bengal against each of the four fertilizer combinations. The results of performance analysis for four classifiers in terms of percentage accuracy (Ac) and Cohen's kappa (k) for four combinations C-1, C-2, C-3 and C-4 are tabulated in Table 3.

Table 3. Performance of the classifiers

Districts		Jalpaiguri		Malda		South 24 Pgs	
Metrics		Ac%	k	Ac%	k	Ac%	k
1st Combination (C-1)	DT	99.93	0.999	99.93	0.999	99.87	0.999
	k-NN	94.75	0.931	92.15	0.889	83.74	0.813
	MLP	78.72	0.719	84.97	0.79	74.93	0.703
	SVM	94.55	0.927	91.35	0.876	79.1	0.753
2nd Combination (C-2)	DT	99.53	0.994	100	1	99.8	0.998
	k-NN	91.72	0.896	89.67	0.852	73.25	0.7
	MLP	75.42	0.686	78.47	0.682	64.92	0.604
	SVM	91.99	0.897	89.74	0.85	71.24	0.676
3rd Combination (C-3)	DT	98.92	0.987	99.53	0.994	99.33	0.992
	k-NN	90.17	0.875	86.18	0.827	72.58	0.669
	MLP	76.43	0.696	72.1	0.646	62.77	0.542
	SVM	90.24	0.873	86.92	0.834	70.97	0.639
4th Combination (C-4)	DT	99.33	0.992	99.8	0.998	99.67	0.996
	k-NN	93.6	0.922	93.36	0.918	88.37	0.863
	MLP	76.57	0.704	80.75	0.76	61.83	0.544
	SVM	94.07	0.927	91.28	0.891	83.47	0.795

The values of the two metrics Ac and k for each classifier averaged over four combinations are presented in Table 4 and 5.

Table 4. Average values of percentage accuracy (Ac) of each classifier for four combinations.

District	Combination	Decision Tree	k-NN	MLP	SVM
Jalpaiguri	C-1	99.93	94.75	78.72	94.55
	C-2	99.53	91.72	75.42	91.99
	C-3	98.92	90.17	76.43	90.24
	C-4	99.33	93.6	76.57	94.07
	Average	**99.43**	92.56	76.79	92.71
Malda	C-1	99.93	92.15	84.97	91.35
	C-2	100	89.67	78.47	89.74
	C-3	99.53	86.18	72.1	86.92
	C-4	99.8	93.36	80.75	91.28
	Average	**99.82**	90.34	79.07	89.82
South 24 Parganas	C-1	99.87	83.74	74.93	79.1
	C-2	99.8	73.25	64.92	71.24
	C-3	99.33	72.58	62.77	70.97
	C-4	99.67	88.37	61.83	83.47
	Average	**99.67**	79.49	66.11	76.2

For better understanding, the performance graphs plotted using the average values of percentage accuracy (Ac) and Cohen's kappa (k) for each of the districts are depicted in the Figs. 3 and 4 respectively.

Results show that the performance graph plotted by average values of percentage accuracy (Ac) of four classifiers (Fig. 3) are nearly identical for all the three districts; Jalpaiguri, Malda and South 24 Pgs. The decision tree classifier outperforms the other classifiers. The performance of the MLP classifier is the lowest among the four. The k-NN and SVM classifiers show nearly equal performances.

Since the value of the percentage accuracy (Ac) represents the goodness of each classier, bigger the value better the classifier. The results show that the average Ac value for the decision tree is almost equal to hundred which signifies that the recommendation made by the classifier will be reliable enough.

A similar result is observed when Cohen's kappa (k) is considered as the performance metric. The only difference is that the range of values of Ac is from zero to hundred but the range of k is from zero to one.

Table 5. Average values of Cohen's kappa (k) of each classifier for four combinations.

District	Combination	Decision Tree	k-NN	MLP	SVM
Jalpaiguri	C-1	0.999	0.931	0.719	0.927
	C-2	0.994	0.896	0.686	0.897
	C-3	0.987	0.875	0.696	0.873
	C-4	0.992	0.922	0.704	0.927
	Average	**0.993**	0.906	0.701	0.906
Malda	C-1	0.999	0.889	0.79	0.876
	C-2	0.999	0.852	0.852	0.85
	C-3	0.994	0.827	0.646	0.834
	C-4	0.998	0.918	0.76	0.891
	Average	**0.997**	0.866	0.753	0.858
South 24 Parganas	C-1	0.999	0.813	0.703	0.753
	C-2	0.998	0.7	0.604	0.676
	C-3	0.992	0.669	0.542	0.639
	C-4	0.996	0.863	0.544	0.795
	Average	**0.996**	0.761	0.598	0.716

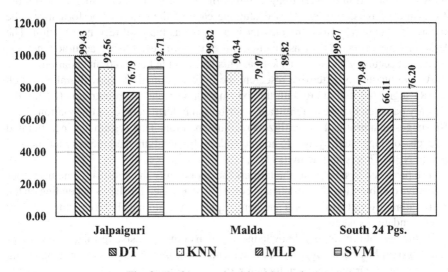

Fig. 3. Performance graph with metric Ac

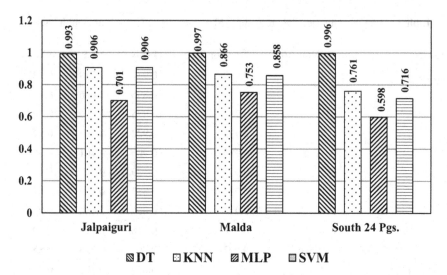

Fig. 4. Performance graph with metric *k*

4 Conclusion

The proposed system has been designed to recommend the best fertilizers for paddy and wheat cultivation in West Bengal, India. Instead of a single classifier, an assembly of classifiers has been used. After evaluating each of the classifier performances, the outcome of the best performing classier is accepted as the final recommendation. The classifiers' performance is measured in terms of two well established accuracy metrics; percentage accuracy and Cohen's kappa. This leads to the best recommendation.

As an outcome of extensive research, the Indian Council of Agricultural Research (ICAR) suggested that along with the existing soil content macronutrients (NPK), the auxiliary parameters have a significant contribution in fertilizers recommendation. They also suggested a protocol for fertilizers recommendation. This system has incorporated the protocol suggested by ICAR and considers the auxiliary parameters and the soil content NPK. This is unique in its class.

The proposed system gives the farmers the opportunity to choose any one from four alternative combinations of straight and complex NPK based fertilizers depending on the local availability and cost. This is another unique feature among all the existing fertilizer recommendation systems.

To the best of the authors' knowledge, no such comprehensive fertilizer recommendation system has been suggested to date. This work may be a pioneer in developing integrated fertilizer management tools for all other crops.

References

1. Food and Agriculture Organization: India at a glance. https://www.fao.org/india/fao-in-india/india-at-a-glance/en/. Accessed 13 July 2020

2. Mithiya, D., Bandyopadhyay, S., Mandal, K.: Measuring technical efficiency and returns to scale in Indian agriculture using panel data: a case study of West Bengal. Appl. Econ. Financ. **6**(6), 1–14 (2019)
3. GSVA/NSVA by economic activities, Ministry of Statistics and Programmer Implementation, Govt. of India. https://mospi.nic.in/GSVA-NSVA. Accessed 12 July 2020
4. Dhaliwal, G.S., Jindal, V., Dhawan, A.K.: Insect pest problems and crop losses: changing trends. Indian J. Ecol. **37**(1), 1–7 (2010)
5. Carroll, C.L., Carter, C.A., Goodhue, R.E., Lawell, C.Y.: Crop disease and agricultural productivity. National Bureau of Economic Research, Working paper 23513 (2017)
6. Gruhn, P., Goletti, F., Yudelman, M.: Integrated nutrient management, soil fertility, and sustainable agriculture: current issues and future challenges. Int. Food Pol. Res. Inst. (2000)
7. Land degradation in south Asia: Its severity, causes and effects upon the people, FAO. https://www.fao.org/3/v4360e/V4360E05.htm. Accessed 15 May 2020
8. Hossain, M.A., Kamiya, T., Burritt, D., Tran, L., Fujiwara, T.: Plant Macronutrient Use Efficiency: Molecular and Genomic Perspectives in Crop Plants. Academic Press, London (2017)
9. Sillanpää, M.: Micronutrients and the Nutrient Status of Soils: a Global Study, vol. 48. FAO, Finland (1982)
10. Fertilizer use by crop in India: Land and Plant Nutrition Management Service, Land and Water Development Division. FAO, Rome (2005)
11. Soil Nutrient Indices, Ministry of Statistics and Programmer Implementation, Govt. of India. https://www.mospi.gov.in/sites/default/files/reports_and_publication/statistical_publication/EnviStats/b14_Chapter%202.pdf. Accessed 12 July 2020
12. Ju, X.T., Kou, C.L., Christie, P., Dou, Z.X., Zhang, F.S.: Changes in the soil environment from excessive application of fertilizers and manures to two contrasting intensive cropping systems on the North China Plain. Environ. Pollut. **145**(2), 497–506 (2007)
13. Bannerjee, G., Sarkar, U., Das, S., Ghosh, I.: Artificial intelligence in agriculture: a literature survey. Int. J. Sci. Res. Comput. Sci. Appl. Manage. Stud. **7**(3), 1–6 (2018)
14. Broner, I., Comstock, C.R.: Combining expert systems and neural networks for learning site-specific conditions. Comput. Electron. Agric. **19**(1), 37–53 (1997)
15. Moreno, R.H., Garcia, O.: Model of neural networks for fertilizer recommendation and amendments in pasture crops. In: 2018 ICAI Workshops (ICAIW), pp. 1–5. IEEE (2018)
16. Yu, H., Liu, D., Chen, G., Wan, B., Wang, S., Yang, B.: A neural network ensemble method for precision fertilization modeling. Math. Comput. Model. **51**, 1375–1382 (2010)
17. Hoskinson, R.L., Hess, J., Fink, R.K.: A decision support system for optimum use of fertilizers (No. INEEL/CON-99-00291). Idaho National Engineering and Environmental Lab, Idaho Falls, USA (1999)
18. Pampolino, M.F., Witt, C., Pasuquin, J.M., Johnston, A., Fisher, M.J.: Development approach and evaluation of the nutrient expert software for nutrient management in cereal crops. Comput. Electron. Agric. **88**, 103–110 (2012)
19. Tremblay, N., Bouroubi, M.Y., Panneton, B., Guillaume, S., Vigneault, P., Bélec, C.: Development and validation of fuzzy logic inference to determine optimum rates of N for corn on the basis of field and crop features. Precis. Agric. **11**(6), 621–635 (2010)
20. Ashraf, A., Akram, M., Sarwar, M.: Fuzzy decision support system for fertilizer. Neural Comput. Appl. **25**(6), 1495–1505 (2014). https://doi.org/10.1007/s00521-014-1639-4
21. Chougule, A., Jha, V.K., Mukhopadhyay, D.: Crop suitability and fertilizers recommendation using data mining techniques. In: Progress in Advanced Computing and Intelligent Engineering, pp. 205–213. Springer, Singapore (2019). https://doi.org/10.1007/978-981-13-0224-4_19

22. Prabakaran, G., Vaithiyanathan, D., Ganesan, M.: Fuzzy decision support system for improving the crop productivity and efficient use of fertilizers. Comput. Electron. Agric. **150**, 88–97 (2018)

23. Suchithra, M. S., Pai, M.: Improving the performance of sigmoid kernels in multiclass SVM using optimization techniques for agricultural fertilizer recommendation system. In: Zelinka, I., Senkerik, R., Panda, G., Lekshmi Kanthan, P.S. (eds.) ICSCS 2018. CCIS, vol. 837, pp. 857–868. Springer, Singapore (2018). https://doi.org/10.1007/978-981-13-1936-5_87

24. Pratap, A., Sebastian, R., Joseph, N., Eapen, R.K., Thomas, S.: Soil fertility analysis and fertilizer recommendation system. In: Proceedings of International Conference on Advancements in Computing & Management (ICACM), pp. 287–292. SSRN, Rajasthan (2019)

25. Sumaryanti, L., Lamalewa, L., Istanto, T.: Implementation of fuzzy multiple criteria decision making for recommendation paddy fertilizer. Int. J. Mech. Eng. Technol. **10**(3), 236–243 (2019)

26. Soil health card database, Govt. of India. https://soilhealth.dac.gov.in/. Accessed 17 May 2020

27. Sarkar, A., Deb Roy, P.: Computation of fertilizer requirement based on Soil Test Crop Response concept to enhance nutrient use efficiency (NUE) and land productivity. https://www.dowrodisha.gov.in/TrainingProgramme/2018/FEBRUARY/ICAR/materials/dy3/. Accessed 17 May 2020

28. Soil test crop response (STCR) equations, AICPR on STCR, ICAR, Government of India. https://aicrp.icar.gov.in/stcr/activities/. Accessed 25 May 2020

29. Singh, S.R.: Soil test crop response: concepts and components for nutrient use efficiency enhancement. In: Biofortification of Food Crops, pp. 237–246. Springer, New Delhi (2016). https://doi.org/10.1007/978-81-322-2716-8_18

30. Suri, V.K., Choudhary, A.K.: Effect of vesicular Arbuscular-Mycorrhizal fungi and phosphorus application through soil-test crop response precision model on crop productivity, nutrient dynamics, and soil fertility in soybean–wheat–soybean crop Sequence in an acidic Alfisol. Commun. Soil Sci. Plant Anal. **44**(13), 2032–2041 (2013)

31. Duda, R.O., Hart, P.E., Stork, D.G.: Pattern Classification, 2nd edn. John Wiley, Delhi (2012)

32. Haykin, S.: Neural Networks and Learning Machines, 3rd Edn. Pearson Education India (2010)

33. Panigrahy, R.: An improved algorithm finding nearest neighbor using Kd-trees. In: Laber, E.S., Bornstein, C., Nogueira, L.T., Faria, L. (eds.) LATIN 2008. LNCS, vol. 4957, pp. 387–398. Springer, Heidelberg (2008). https://doi.org/10.1007/978-3-540-78773-0_34

34. Sivanandam, S.N., Sumathi, S., Deepa, S.N.: Introduction to neural networks using Matlab 6.0. McGraw-Hill Education (India), Delhi (2006)

35. Cohen, J.: A coefficient of agreement for nominal scales. Educ. Psychol. Meas. **20**(1), 37–46 (1960)

36. Tallón-Ballesteros, A.J., Riquelme, J.C.: Data mining methods applied to a digital forensics task for supervised machine learning. In: Computational Intelligence in Digital Forensics: Forensic Investigation and Applications, pp. 413–428. Springer (2014). https://doi.org/10.1007/978-3-319-05885-6_17

37. Datta, V., Mondal, D.K., Ghosh, S., Mukherjee, R., Chattopadhyay, K.S., Chakrabarti, S.: Adoption of Recommended Doses of Fertilizers on Soil Test Basis by Farmers, Study No. 179, Agro-Economic Research Centre, Visva-Bharati University, Santiniketan (2015)

38. STCR Report, Soil health card. https://soilhealth.dac.gov.in/Report/STRCReport/STCRReport. Accessed 25 May 2020

Gauging Stress Among Indian Engineering Students

Astha Singh and Divya Kumar[✉]

Computer Science and Engineering Department, Motilal Nehru National Institute
of Technology, Allahabad, India
{astha,divyak}@mnnit.ac.in

Abstract. Engineering has become one of the most chosen streams for graduation. In the recent past, many cases have been reported which increases the concern about mental health of students during the undergraduate engineering program. The aim of this study is to determine the level and source of stress and its severity. Stress is a necessary part of our lives and can have both beneficial and negative effects. The pressure response of stress is determined by our perception of an event, change, or problem. Controlling and balancing our lives in order to deal with stress can be a challenging task. An important first step is to identify the extent to which people are affected under stress in their lives and looking for strategies to improve. In this article, we have proposed a Perceived Stress Scale based model and methodology to gauge different types of stress levels among the engineering students. Further, co-relation between the calculated stress levels and the demographic income classes is established.

Keywords: Stress · Diagnostic test · Effect of stress · Perceived Stress Scale · Ardell wellness · Demographic details

1 Introduction

Today, levels of stress among undergraduate students have been rising astonishingly high due to the pressure of their studies followed by a large amount of syllabus content for a limited period of time. This makes a boundary of stress in the student. There are always high expectations of parents and teachers from a student in his work. High-level stress and mental competition convert into depression may ultimately affect the health of the student. College life is one of the most stirring and rewarding times in any scholar's life and at this phase of life students gets exposure to a new environment and opportunities, to prepare for future and experience life in a new way. This is also a period when students are exposed to wide variety of challenges which can be due to many reasons such as academics, lifestyle, time-management, workload etc. Students are exposed to immense pressure due to these challenges and expectations from various people such as family members, relatives and teachers. All these reasons increase the chances of students developing mental illness in terms of Stress, Anxiety, Anger, Depression or even Suicidal Thoughts in the extreme cases.

© Springer Nature Switzerland AG 2021
P. Dutta et al. (Eds.): CICBA 2021, CCIS 1406, pp. 175–186, 2021.
https://doi.org/10.1007/978-3-030-75529-4_14

A healthy lifestyle is an important aspect of a person towards stress reduction. The stage of Depression occurs when the stress level exceeds its ability to cope. Depression of body makes the response to change that the body needs, mental correction, or problems. Students who pursue professional academic course, they generally face challenges in satisfies all the academic norms require fulfill his eligibility to obtain the final degree. Students who took loans for study may feel more pressure and can result into stress. These factors contribute to increase the stress which is a series of burden. A stress comes under a series of reasons varying from personal life to the professional life. Feeling of continuous frustration in academic platform may weaken a student to regain the energy for the next challenge. There are broadly two kinds of stress usually seen in a student's life i.e. acute stress and chronic stress [26]. Acute stress is a kind of stress that remains for short period of time. In students, this stress generally come when he faced little rebuke from the faculty or due to little embarrassment. This stress may quickly go away. Chronic stress is a type of stress which remain for long period of time. In students, it occurs is due to a series of continuous small stress and failure. It makes the student to think deeper. It spread more negativity in the mind and it can results in severe health issues. Just as the academic opportunities and pressures are mounting on students of the ages of 15 and 24 they are required to adjust to emotional and multifarious life changes. Thus, this is the time of onset of most depressive illnesses. At this phase of time a student faces many transitions like adulthood from adolescence; hosteller from family home; new culture/language from home country/language; open market competition from basic contests; new social environment from familiar friends. These transitions may bring many challenges like leaving home for the first time, forming new relationships, learning to live independently, sleeping irregularly in hostels and skipping regular meals [29, 30]. As a normal response to these difficult events, changes and transitions college students are more likely to have symptoms of stress. Compiled studies on various stress related researches around the world reflect the following:

- 1 out of every 4 college students suffers from some form of mental illness, including depression and stress.
- 3 out of 4 college students do not seek help for their mental health problems.
- Among the causes of death among college students, suicide is the third leading cause.
- 80% of students who either contemplate or attempt suicide show clear warning signs.
- 99% of individuals have minor or major mental health problems (not disorders) from time to time.

In the present manuscript we have tried to present a comprehensive literature review, in Sect. 2 of this manuscript, of the various studies conducted to measure the stress factors among the students. Further, in Sect. 3, we have tried to brief some of the established stress measuring scales used by the experts and psychologists around the world. In this section, we have presented the methodology and questionnaires adopted by us to measure the stress among the engineering students, also. The experiment setting, results, analysis and limitations are presented in Sect. 4. Finally, the conclusion is presented in Sect. 5.

2 Literature Review

College students are required to pass through a rigorous academic channel in which they need to study multiple subjects. The projects and assignments made the student to put extra critical analysis on the topic. Therefore, years of a student in college remain pressurized under the burden of adjustments. So, a student made to compromise with his comfort zone. Students most stayed away from their homes and so this decline the support system of the student. Table 1 show some recent studies which are conducted to gauge stress in student life.

Table 1. Studies on stress exploration

Author	Description	Methodology
Sher et al. [23]	Support system in a student life under his stress	Psychological assessment of students has been taken to evaluate stress
Jogaratnam et al. [24]	Examine exposure to stressors among student-employees	Stress level has been checked under various parameters like time pressure, social mistreatment, friendship problem, academics alienation etc.
Polson et al. [25]	Study of stress exposure in fresh student specially females	Sample based survey on graduate students. Stress level has been estimated in graduate female students enrolled in marriage under family pressure
Cahir et al. [26]	Explored the impact of financial, emotional, and academic on graduate student psychology that leads to generate stress problems	Psychology student stress questionnaire. The stress scale yield into 7 standard factors. 133 graduate psychological students were examined in this test scale
Aziz et al. [27]	Explored the organizational role in building stress in women	Organizational role stress scale. The methodology performs analysis of stress that is influenced by administrative activities of an organization

Stress levels in patients can be measured using various set of standard scales that have been proposed after thorough testing through various studies. The Holmes and Rahe Stress Scale [13] bases the sources of our mental stress to our life events, and contains a list of forty-three life events based on which a relative score is calculated. This scale has a low accuracy leading to poor overall performance. The Depression and Anxiety Scale (DASS-42) has a set of 42 questions to calculate individual scores of stress, anxiety and depression. A shorter version of this scale with 21 questions has also been constructed and verified [12]. The Hamilton Anxiety Scale [11] consists of 14 items and can measure psychic anxiety and somatic anxiety. There are various scales for measuring depression levels in patients. The Hamilton Depression Rating Scale [8], Montgomery-Asberg Depression Rating Scale (Hamilton, Schutte & Malouff, 2001), Raskin Depression Rating Scale [18] Beck Depression Inventor [3], Geriatric Depression Scale (GDS) [15], Zung Self-Rating Depression Scale [22] and the Patient Health Questionnaire (PHQ) [16] are all different scales and questionnaires that provide a score rating that gives a relative measure of depression level among patients taking the test. Various studies have also been conducted in different parts of the world to measure the stress and depression levels in students of various institutes. A study was conducted in the University of Mysore [9] to measure anxiety levels in Indian and Iranian students. A study conducted in colleges of Bangalore [17] also found high levels of stress among engineering and medical students. A study conducted by Malaysia University [19] found that low performing students tend to develop higher levels of anxiety disorders as compared to other students. Most of the universities across the globe have centers and counselors for helping students to deal with and come out of this chronic and dangerous mental illness. For example, the students and faculty of University of Michigan can access Campus Mind Works [4], which is a website containing comprehensive resources to help understand depression. University of Australia also has a similar service [5]. Successful research has been conducted based on finding Perceived Stress, Sources and Severity of Stress among medical undergraduates in a Pakistani Medical School [19]. A study conducted [2] has been conducted on a group of 1617 students using the DASS-42 standard scale. Another study [1] has assessed the properties of DASS – 42 in a sample of high school students.

3   Methodology

We have presented a model which can help students in maintaining their positive mental health. It is a mental health evaluation model that takes into account socio-economic background, and the student's response to a self-administered questionnaire (comprising questions from both pre-tested standard scales as well as new questions framed with professional help from experts). An online service is preferred as students are usually unwilling to seek help due to social stigmas related to stress. A student's family history, academic performance, and stress coping capabilities are considered for his/her mental health evaluation performed through this online service with the goal to find and evaluate at-risk students. We have aimed at classifying students into three categories:

- Class A: Students who are mentally fit and don't need any help.
- Class B: Students who are suffering from some form of stress and need counseling
- Class C: Students who have high suicidal tendencies and need immediate medical attention.

The type of diagnosis, if required, after taking the test is decided based on which category the test result indicate to. The data collected from this research has been used to draw inferences regarding the mental health of the students in general too.

The proposed methodology contains some elements from standard stress measurement techniques which are based on Perceived Stress Scale (PSS) [19] and Don Ardell's

Wellness Stress Tests [28]. The Perceived Stress Scale (PSS) is a widely used psychological tool to measure stress perception. It is a measure of the extent to which situations in a person's life are considered stressful. Don Ardell's Stress Test is a separate robust stress test to find specific stress level in a person's life. It offers a balanced assessment of varied stress sources. It finds the importance of including all aspects of life in order to understanding stress.

3.1 Diagnostic Test Description

The diagnostic test or the self-administered questionnaire comprises of questions from both pre-tested standard scales as well as new questions framed by the subject experts. We have prepared a questionnaire of thirty two questions that deal with daily stress causing problems to engineering students. These questions have been prepared by consulting subject experts in psychology and encompass all major stress factors in the daily life for an engineering student. Questions have been further divided into four subclasses that each deal with separate indicators to different kinds of stress such as acute stress, chronic stress, suicidal ideations and emotional stability. The questions for all the four categories are presented randomly and scores for each category reflect a different aspect of a person's mental health:

- A student with a high acute stress often undergoes a lot of mental stress when in a particular situation. Their stressors are triggered by the onset of a particular situation e.g. Examination pressure. This kind of stress is not alarming because of being temporarily active and thus does not require medical intervention in most cases. Thus, students with even a high acute stress will most likely lie in Class A of students.
- A student with a high chronic stress often succumbs to stress being triggered by a regular or periodic stressor. Thus, these students spend most of the time in their daily lives in stress. These students classify as Class B of students and would need proper counseling by experts who can then decide to prescribe medicines.
- A student who flags as someone with having high indicators for suicidal ideations is someone who is suffering most likely from a severe stress and has a very high suicidal tendency. Such a student would classify in Class C and would need immediate medical intervention in the form of antidepressants.
- Emotional Stability only reflects a student's ability to tackle stressful situations and is not an indicator for any kind of stress in the student, in itself.

This provides us with a systematic way to assess the scores of each student and propose an appropriate treatment plan according to their mental health condition. Considering the various categories of stress, it provides us with the ability to pinpoint the source of the stress easily which can help the doctors/counselors to continue the treatment of the students who are flagged by the system. Our method enables in finding students who need immediate attention among the vast pool of students which is a task that is almost impossible to perform manually. It provides a tool to the students to regularly track their mental health and reduces the workload on counselors by filtering out the specially flagged students by the system.

3.2 Demographic Details

Demographic information is the study of factors related to a large number of population based on their socio-economic details. It is the collection of characteristics of peoples in large population. In the proposed work, the study is aimed to take into account the socio-economic background of the students. This is done using the well-known Kuppuswamy's Scale [15] to calculate the stress parameter for each student. This scale measures the SES of an individual based on three variables named as education, occupation of the head of the family and the income of the family. Usually education and occupation of head of the family are not vary with time. However, the income may changes with time in the scale. Therefore, the scale is needed to update regularly for socioeconomic classification of study populations. We have used the revised version of income parameter for 2014 (Gururaj, 2014) to maintain the validity of the research. It is mandatory for each student to provide the demographic details before they can take the diagnostic test. The Kuppuswamy Scale [15] calculates the socio-economic status of the participant in 5 classes based on socio-economy background of peoples that is described in Table 2. This classification was used to divide test subject to different categories and perform analysis on each subclass. Analysis on each separate socio economic class helps us in finding trends between the stress levels and their socio economic background. Figure 1 shows the pictorial representation of the steps taken in this study.

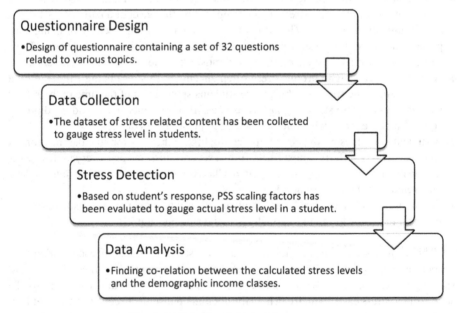

Fig. 1. The proposed methodology steps.

Table 2. Demographic classes and their respective description

Sl. no.	Class	Description
1	Upper	Class of higher managerial and administrative professionals of group A
2	Upper-middle	Intermediate managerial, professors or B grade professionals
3	Lower-middle	Supervisor and clerical peoples which may belong to group C
4	Upper-lower	Skilled workers
5	Lower	Non-technical, unskilled or semi-skilled peoples

4 Results

4.1 Participants and Setting

One hundred and two students primarily from final year B.Tech were invited to participate in this study and take the diagnostic test through the online medium. All the necessary instructions before taking the test were provided through web pages. The users were asked to sign up anonymously and thereby their identities were kept secret.

4.2 Data Collection and Analysis

The study collects 102 responses from peoples under a set of questionnaire. The dataset of participants was collected in a MySQL database and exported to be analyzed using proper statistical software. The data is geometrically analysed that contains mean score, median score and the standard deviation to perceive the various level of stress. Stress have four categories of questions namely, indicators for acute stress, indicators for chronic stress, indicators for suicidal ideations and indicators for emotional stress. The responses are divided based on the socio economic status of the participants calculated using the Kuppuswamy scale [15] and separate mean, median and standard deviation for all five categories of questions mentioned earlier were calculated for each single socio economic class. The frequency of each response to the 32 specially designed questions, with mean and median is recorded. Table 3 represents these readings. Each cell of this table represents the number of students marking a particular response based on which mean and mode values have been calculated.

The Table 3 shows the score of five responses taken in perceived stress scale. It also contains the mean and the median of stress for each questionnaire. A 32 number of general source of stress has been made that contain all the possible variation that may cause change of mind of the participant. The response scores are based on the perception of students under a given situation. The PSS scores of a person with low stress will fall in the range of 0–13, the scores of a person under moderate stress will fall in the range of 14–26. The PSS Scores ranging from 27–40 indicates high perceived

Table 3. Response pattern of the 32 stress gauging questions (rated in a scale of 0–4).

Source of stress	Never (0)	Almost never (1)	Some-times (2)	Fairly often (3)	Very often (4)	Median	Mode
Does examination scare you?	24	21	34	21	2	2	2
I find my course curriculum useless	7	16	37	25	17	2	2
I feel bored during the classes	5	12	24	36	25	3	3
I think we have enough study material for our studies	3	18	28	40	13	3	3
One day I would definitely become an engineer	5	8	22	33	34	3	4
My branch has no scope in the future	33	21	28	13	7	1	0
There are so many intelligent students in my class	6	15	33	33	15	2	*
No one is concerned with me, neither teachers nor my batch mates	13	27	32	22	8	2	2
I feel my parents have too many expectations from me	16	18	27	27	14	2	*
I am a lonely person	18	29	35	13	7	2	2
My studies are affected by my family problems	30	25	23	21	3	1	0
I miss my home	4	25	40	19	14	2	2
It is difficult for me to start a conversation with the person of the opposite sex	14	21	34	25	8	2	2
English as a study and communication medium is a problem for me	26	23	30	18	5	2	2
I am inefficient in putting my points publically	12	28	28	28	6	2	*
My hostel and the city is a boring place	10	20	31	28	13	2	2
People don't recognize my capabilities	8	33	41	15	0	2	2
Food quality of the mess is a matter of concern for me	7	15	27	33	20	3	3
I often get worried about my monthly expenses	9	27	34	22	10	2	2
Living in the city is costly for me	27	21	29	18	7	2	2
I find it difficult to have fun with my friends	27	25	26	19	5	1	0
Living conditions in the hostel are pathetic	9	24	38	27	4	2	2
I don't like to share my room with someone	22	26	18	24	12	2	1
Relationship matters do affect my mood and studies	9	23	46	21	3	2	2
I am not good looking	18	30	29	22	3	2	1
I don't get sound sleep regularly	16	18	45	19	4	2	2
I am often become sick during a semester	17	27	39	13	6	2	2
My method to tackle stress is to consume alcohol or cigarette	45	18	17	17	5	1	0
I am unable to fulfill the dreams of my parents	25	18	35	19	5	2	2
Nothing is going to change if I become an engineer	20	33	27	15	5	1	1
I want to run away from all the things	25	22	26	22	7	2	2
It is better to die than to face this situation	41	18	24	12	7	1	0

stress. The PSS ranges are the standard ranges that has adopted in many recent literatures to measure stress level in a person. The stress level can be classified from low to high by considering standard scaling range as considered standard measurement ranges given on scientific basis. Table 4 contains the stress data of five stress categories i.e. perceived, acute, chronic, suicidal, and emotional. This stress analysis has been made for all the demographic classes of society to find the co-relation between the stress levels and the income category. The Table 4 shows the five categories of stress level and the interpreted scores obtained from various classes of students involved in our experiment. Figure 2 shows the graphical representation of average stress scores of all the four economic classes. The variations of various stress (A is Perceived Stress, B is Acute Stress, C is

Chronic Stress, D is Suicidal ideation and E is Emotional Stability) with respect to the income groups is shown in Fig. 2. The upper income groups have the lowest suicidal ideation and the lower income class has the highest chronic stress. The upper class is also observed with the lowest chronic and acute stress. Suicidal tendencies are observed low among all class, but exceptionally low in the upper class. Perceived stress is the most common stress and is almost equal among irrespective of income group. For all other type of stress income category seems to have a reasonable impact. The number of observed participants in the upper-lower class is very less i.e., only five and thus their reading cannot be relied on heavily due to the lack of sufficient data.

Table 4. Various stress levels with respect the income category grouping.

Class	Category of stress	No of participants	Average	Median	Standard Deviation
Upper class	Perceived stress	33	17.81818	17	4.798792
	Acute stress	33	16.69697	16	4.369531
	Chronic stress	33	15.78788	16	3.887139
	Suicidal ideation	33	4.515152	4	3.767635
	Emotional stability	33	12.63636	12	5.389911
Upper middle class	Perceived stress	45	18.1087	19	4.403172
	Acute stress	45	17.54348	18	3.970483
	Chronic stress	45	19.65217	20	5.207761
	Suicidal ideation	45	8.130435	9	4.480122
	Emotional stability	45	17.04348	16	5.962686
Lower middle class	Perceived stress	19	20.05263	19	5.264912
	Acute stress	19	17.94737	17	3.439536
	Chronic stress	19	19.52632	20	5.004092
	Suicidal ideation	19	9.736842	9	3.739312
	Emotional stability	19	19	19	2.645751
Upper lower class	Perceived stress	5	18.5	18.5	2.081666
	Acute stress	5	18.25	18	2.217356
	Chronic stress	5	22	21.5	2.160247
	Suicidal ideation	5	9.5	10	1.732051
	Emotional stability	5	19.75	20	1.258306
Complete population	Perceived stress	102	18.39216	19	4.654726
	Acute stress	102	17.37255	17	3.947481
	Chronic stress	102	18.47059	18	5.016223
	Suicidal ideation	102	7.313725	8	4.491974
	Emotional stability	102	16.08824	16	5.724886

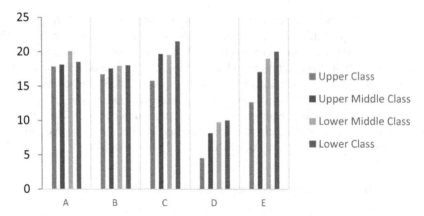

Fig. 2. Average stress scores for all economic classes

5 Conclusion

The study concludes the detection of stress in the graduate student by analyzing standard parameters and scaling factors . Stress formation depends on various factors including demography, academics, personal life, etc. The questionnaire-based study shows the effect of various reasons that indulge in building stress. It is found that about 40% of the students have reported a high level of perceived stress, and the average perceived stress of the lower middle class of students is above acceptable limits. All other categories of stress i.e., acute, chronic, suicidal ideations are well under control among all students of all categories in general. The model and question set we have developed has great intellectual as well as commercial value. Data collected further can be used to standardize the self-created thirty-two questions into a standard scale.

References

1. Afzali, A., Delavar, A., Borjali, A., Mirzamani, M.: Psychometric properties of DASS-42 as assessed in a sample of Kermanshah High School students (2007)
2. Bayram, N., Bilgel, N.: The prevalence and socio-demographic correlations of depression, anxiety and stress among a group of university students. Soc. Psychiatry Psychiatr. Epidemiol. **43**(8), 667–672 (2008)
3. Beck, A.T., Steer, R.A., Brown, G.K., et al.: Manual for the beck depression inventory-II, vol. 1, p. 82. Psychological Corporation, San Antonio (1996)
4. Wijsman, J., Grundlehner, B., Liu, H., Hermens, H., Penders, J.: Towards mental stress detection using wearable physiological sensors. In: 2011 Annual International Conference of the IEEE Engineering in Medicine and Biology Society, Boston, MA, pp. 1798–1801 (2011). https://doi.org/10.1109/IEMBS.2011.6090512
5. Zhai, J., Barreto, A.: Stress detection in computer users based on digital signal processing of noninvasive physiological variables. In: 2006 International Conference of the IEEE Engineering in Medicine and Biology Society, New York, NY, pp. 1355–1358 (2006). https://doi.org/10.1109/IEMBS.2006.259421

6. de Santos Sierra, A., Sanchez Avila, C., Guerra Casanova, J., Bailador del Pozo, G.: A stress-detection system based on physiological signals and fuzzy logic. IEEE Trans. Ind. Electron. **58**(10), 4857–4865 (2011). https://doi.org/10.1109/TIE.2010.2103538.

7. Giannakakis, G., Grigoriadis, D., Giannakaki, K., Simantiraki, O., Roniotis, A., Tsiknakis, M.: Review on psychological stress detection using biosignals. IEEE Trans. Affect. Comput. https://doi.org/10.1109/TAFFC.20192927337

8. Hamilton, M.: A rating scale for depression. J. Neurol. Neurosurg. Psychiatry **23**(1), 56–62 (1960)

9. Ghaderi, A., Salehi, M.: A study of the level of self-efficacy, depression and anxiety between accounting and management students: Iranian evidence. World Appl. Sci. **12**(9), 1299–1306 (2011)

10. Gururaj, M.: Kuppuswamy's Socio-Economic Status Scale, A Revision of Income Parameter For, pp. 1–2 (2014)

11. Hamilton, M., Schutte, N., Malouff, J.: Hamilton anxiety scale (HAMA). In: Sourcebook of Adult Assessment: Applied Clinical Psychology, pp. 154–157 (1976)

12. Henry, J.D., Crawford, J.R.: The short-form version of the depression anxiety stress scales (DASS-21): construct validity and normative data in a large non-clinical sample. Br. J. Clin. Psychols **44**(2), 227–239 (2005)

13. Holmes, T.H., Rahe, R.H.: The social readjustment rating scale. J. Psychosom. Res. **11**(2), 213–218 (1967)

14. Kee, B.S.: A preliminary study for the standardization of geriatric depression scale short form-Korea version. J. Korean Neuropsychiatr. Assoc. **35**(2), 298–307 (1996)

15. Kuppuswamy, B.: Manual of Socio-Economic Status Scale. Manasayan Publication, Delhi (1962)

16. Manea, L., Gilbody, S., McMillan, D.: Optimal cut-off score for diagnosing depression with the patient health questionnaire (PHQ-9): a meta-analysis. Can. Med. Assoc. J. **184**(3), E191–E196 (2012)

17. Naveen, S., Swapna, M., Jayanthkumar, K.: Stress, anxiety and depression among students of selected medical and engineering colleges, Bangalore-A comparative study (2015)

18. Raskin, A., Schulterbrandt, J., Reatig, N., McKEON, J.J.: Replication of factors of psychopathology in interview, ward behavior and self-report ratings of hospitalized depressives. J. Nervous Mental Dis. **148**(1), 87–98 (1969)

19. Shah, M., Hasan, S., Malik, S., Sreeramareddy, C.T.: Perceived stress, sources and severity of stress among medical undergraduates in a Pakistani medical school. BMC Med. Educ. **10**(1), 2 (2010)

20. Svanborg, P., Åsberg, M.: A comparison between the beck depression inventory (BDI) and the self-rating version of the montgomery Åsberg depression rating scale (MADRS). J. Affect. Disord. **64**(2), 203–216 (2001)

21. Vitasari, P., Wahab, M.N.A., Othman, A., Herawan, T., Sinnadurai, S.K.: The relationship between study anxiety and academic performance among engineering students. Proc.-Soc. Behav. Sci. **8**, 490–497 (2010)

22. Zung, W.W.: A self-rating depression scale. Arch. General Psychiatry **12**(1), 63–70 (1965)

23. Sher, K.J., Wood, P.K., Gotham, H.J.: The course of psychological distress in college: a prospective high-risk study. J. Coll. Student Dev. **37**(1), 42–51 (1996)

24. Jogaratnam, G., Buchanan, P.: Balancing the demands of school and work: stress and employed hospitality students. Int. J. Contemp. Hospitality Manage. **16**(4), 237–245 (2004)

25. Polson, M., Nida, R.: Program and trainee lifestyle stress: a survey of AAMFT student members. J. Marital Family Therapy **24**(1), 95–112 (1998)

26. Cahir, N., Morris, R.D.: The psychology student stress questionnaire. J. Clin. Psychol. **47**(3), 414–417 (1991)

27. Aziz, M.: Role stress among women in the Indian information technology sector. Women Manage. Rev. **19**(7), 356–363 (2004)

28. Lim, T.P., Husain, W.: Integrating knowledge-based system in wellness community portal. In: 2010 International Conference on Science and Social Research (CSSR 2010), Kuala Lumpur, Malaysia, pp. 350–355 (2010). https://doi.org/10.1109/CSSR.2010.5773798

29. Haidar, S.A., De Vries, N.K., Karavetian, M., El-Rassi, R.: Stress, anxiety, and weight gain among university and college students: a systematic review. J. Acad. Nutr. Diet. **118**(2), 261–274 (2018)

30. Hamblin, E.: Stress in College Students: Associations with Anxiety and Perfectionism (2018)

Intelligent Data Mining and Data Warehousing

Deep CNN Based Automatic Detection and Identification of Bengal Tigers

Tarun Kishore[1], Aditya Jha[1], Saurav Kumar[1], Suman Bhattacharya[2(✉)], and Mahamuda Sultana[2]

[1] Techno International New Town, Kolkata, India
[2] Guru Nanak Institute of Technology, Kolkata, India

Abstract. A system for individual identification of The Royal Bengal Tigers (Panthera tigris) is absolutely necessary not only for monitoring the population of tigers but also for saving the precious lives of those workers whose job is to count the exact number of tigers present in a particular region like Sundarban in West Bengal, India. In this paper, a solution has been proposed for individual identification of Bengal Tigers using an autonomous/manually controlled drone. In the proposed system, the drone camera will search for the tigers using a Tiger Detection Model and then the flank (the body part which contains the stripes) of the detected tiger will be passed through a Fine-tuned state-of-art network. The system based on deep CNN will detect the uncommon features for individual counting of the tiger in a particular forest. The proposed system will enhance the accuracy of tiger detection technique that will be followed by the human experts. It also reduces the risk of accidents relating to animal attacks.

Keywords: Tiger identification · Tiger detection · Deep learning · Deep CNN

1 Introduction

Different ecological field studies have used various techniques for gaining information about the animal population. These methods require the individual counting of the species which are present in a particular area. But it's not an easy task. Besides counting, tracking the tiger population is quite challenging. There are various methods of counting tigers like the pugmark method, camera trap, poop/scat method, radio collar method, etc. But these methods are either too risky or do not give favorable results. In paper [1] even though the earlier studies provided ways to formalize unique animal appearance, manual identification of individuals is a tedious job. It requires experts with specific skill sets, making the identification process prone to subjective bias. Moreover, with an increase in animal count, manual processing becomes prohibitively expensive.

Also, approaches like radio-collaring, in-field manual monitoring, and GPS tracking, minimize subjective bias and are repetitive, cost-effective, safer, and less stressful. Still, however these methods are sometimes very risky and time-consuming.

In the past few decades, with the advancement of visual pattern recognition, it is widely used to make various biometric systems like fingerprint detection [2] and facial

© Springer Nature Switzerland AG 2021
P. Dutta et al. (Eds.): CICBA 2021, CCIS 1406, pp. 189–198, 2021.
https://doi.org/10.1007/978-3-030-75529-4_15

recognition [3]. The identification process relies on visual pattern matching. In paper [4] visual biometrics has been applied to cattle to identify them from their unique features. These non-invasive techniques have a high advantage in terms of safety, cost, and convenience.

According to paper [5] each tiger stripes are distinguishable, like the fingerprints of a human. So each tiger would be individually identified by the stripes it has. Until now this method was done manually by experienced professionals, this requires extensive manpower and time. The manual identification depends on experienced operators and is highly subjective. If the number of tigers is large then, it is not suitable to identify each and every tiger individually.

Deep Learning can provide a high level of visual semantic description. However, identification using CNNs are mostly used to classify different types of species. For individual identification of a species, there are various technical challenges that need to be overcome.

The present existing research works basically depend on the manual identification, which is unsuitable for enormous datasets. Therefore, in this research work, a system is proposed in which the images of tigers should be taken from an autonomous/manually controlled drone. Considering The Royal Bengal Tiger images which would pose a training data set, a CNN model is made to distinguish individual tigers with their body stripes.

The CNN model constructed is used for automatic identification of Bengal Tigers. The model would reduce the laborious task of manual recognition. Furthermore, the technology and method are conducive to establishing a database of stripes of various tigers, which is advantageous for the conservation and management of Bengal tigers.

2 Related Work

2.1 Tiger Detection

The earliest works on automatic animal detection in the paper [7, 8] use a Haar-like & low-level features tracker. This system detects faces at multiple scales working in real-time with slight pose variations.

In paper [9] heads of different animals were detected by using shape and texture features. This approach depends on the shapes of the ear and variation in the pose from different angles. These approaches are beneficial for identifying different animals and tracking them. But they are not up to the mark because they fail in case of occlusion or significant pose variation.

In paper [10], the object or animal is found by using a background subtraction method. In the paper, [11] it is shown that it is very difficult and tedious to choose the threshold value as the background image changes periodically. The approach is called the power spectrum approach, but the work carried out in that paper shows that the approach is not up to the mark for real-time detection/identification.

2.2 Individual Tiger Identification

The estimation of the number of individuals of a species in a population is a key question in the field of ecology and wildlife conservation [12, 13]. Population estimates of any species are required for the formulation of a conservation strategy, prioritization, and allocation of resources, as well as for evaluating the success of conservation programs [14].

The first attempt to enumerate tigers from their pugmarks was made by W. J. Nicholson in Palamu district, Bihar. He developed the methodology for a census of pugmarks. The basic method is that the people with experience identify each individual tiger from their pugmark.

The early used technique of the tiger population had the following drawbacks [15]: (1) several field personnel is often inconsistent and of poor quality; (2) individual tigers are believed to be identifiable from the substandard data by supervisory officials.

The classification of different species has been dominated by convolutional neural networks [16, 17]. For automatic identification, there are various technical challenges that need to be overcome.

3 Background

The flow of the proposed system is given in Fig. 1. The proposed system consists of an autonomous/manual drone. It takes the picture of the tigers in real-time using Tensor Flow Lite and then passes the picture to the CNN model which will further predict the class of the input image.

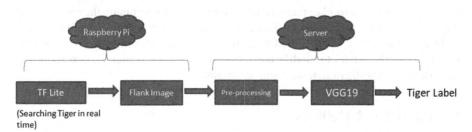

Fig. 1. Flow diagram of the proposed system

3.1 Detection Using Tensor Flow Lite and Raspberry Pi

In the proposed system a Raspberry Pi 4 Model B configured with a Camera and Tensor Flow Lite model should be attached to the drone for detecting the tigers in real-time to take their pictures.

The Raspberry Pi is an immensely compact but powerful computer having very few dimensions. Raspberry Pi uses an Advanced RISC Machines (ARM) processor. The processor in the Raspberry Pi 4 Model B system is a quad-core Arm Cortex-A72 system-on-chip (SOC) multimedia processor [18].

A Tensor Flow Lite model should be used to perform the real time tiger identification. Tensor Flow Lite supports hardware acceleration with Android Neural Network API (Application programming interface). It applies many techniques to achieve low latency, optimization kernel, pre-fused activations, and quantization kernel.

Raspberry pi in drone has been implemented in this system proposed which takes the input for detection work. All the computation for Tiger detection has been done using the Tensor Flow Lite model. After detecting the flank of the tiger, the flank image would be sent to the server where the flank image passes through the CNN model for the individual identification of the Tiger.

3.2 VGG19 Model

In 2014 Oxford's Visual Geometry group introduced VGG architectures, which achieved a top-5 error rate of 7.3% in the ILSVRC competition. The networks VGG16 and VGG19 were introduced. In which 13 and 16 convolutional layers were present in VGG16 and VGG19 respectively.

VGG19 is a pre-trained model, it has 19 layers out of which 16 are convolutional layers, 3 fully connected layers, 5 Max Pool layers, and 1 Soft max layer in its network. The model has been trained on more than millions of images of Image net datasets, having 1000 different classes [19]. As a result, the network has learned rich feature representations for a wide range of images. This model took 224 × 244 image size as the input.

In the paper [6] the authors did fine-tuning of CNN weights from a different dataset which helped them to overcome the problem of medical image scarcity. The facts shown is fine-tuning the top blocks of a CNN model can save time and computational power and produce more robust classifiers. Hence, in this system fine-tuning the top layers or fully connected layers of the VGG19 model has been made to get the desired results.

In this system, the VGG19 model has been used for network surgery that means fine-tuning of the model to modify the actual architecture, so that some parts of the network for said problem statement can be retrained.

4 Material and Methods

4.1 Data Augmentation

This is a well-known fact that a sufficient amount of data is needed to train the proposed model. The images of eight different Bengal tigers from various sources have been collected. After that, those images have been taken into consideration where the stripes of the tigers were clearly visible. While collecting the dataset various difficulties were handled such as the tilted orientation of the images. In those cases, the pictures were inclined to some angle to keep the straight orientation as much as possible.

In paper [20] and [21] various techniques have been implemented to improve image datasets for the training of the predictive model. Since the deployment of the proposed system is under-process, the sample size of the images to train a deep CNN model is not up to the mark. Precaution has been taken while increasing the dataset so that it would not hinder the result. Keeping these things in mind, some data augmentation techniques like flipping the image and rotating are applied. The fact that the captured image can be blurry for moving tigers, some pictures are also made blurred and the brightness is manipulated taking sunlight into consideration. Initially, the images of eight different tigers have been collected and there were around 3,110 images. After applying all the filters and methods in the dataset, the total size of the dataset was increased to around 18,692 images.

4.2 Detection Using Tensor Flow Lite

Both the tiger and its flank region would be detected using Tensor flow Lite (TF Lite). The network would be trained to detect 2 classes: the tiger and the flank. The images of the tiger and its flank should be taken as an input to the model.

There are three primary steps for training and deploying the Tensor Flow lite model. Using the Tensor flow models in Tensor flow Lite requires converting the models that are trained in quantized SSD net models using Tensor flow into the Saved Model format. This requires using the freeze-graph utility. Then, the Tensor flow Lite optimization converter would be used to create a Tensor flow lite model, setting flags in the model that will auto-prune computation and other graph nodes that are unnecessary at inference time.

TFLite_Detection_PostProcess operation can be used, where a variation of Non-maximum Suppression (NMS) is implemented on the model's output. Non-maximum Suppression filters many bounding boxes using set operations.

During testing time, if a single image would be taken as input. The output would be the bounding boxes around the tiger and their object ness scores.

4.3 Individual Identification Using VGG19

One of the approaches in Transfer learning called fine-tuning has been used to create the CNN model. The imported VGG19 model has been fine-tuned with the images of the Bengal tiger's flank in the training set using Keras. VGG19 has an optimum architecture for benchmarking. The pre-trained networks for VGG are available freely to the public, which can be modified and used for other similar tasks. It is also commonly used out of the box network for various applications. Weights are easily available with other frameworks like Keras so they can be tinkered with and used as one wants.

In this process, fully connected layers and the soft max layer of the VGG19 model were removed and replaced by the new layers on the top of the CNN. All the layers below the previously fully connected layers were frozen so that their weights don't get updated. After that, the network is trained using an immensely small learning rate (0.001) to warm up fully connected layers. It implies that the newly added fully connected layers would be learning patterns from the earlier CONV layers in the network and then the weights are fine-tuned to recognize the new Bengal Tiger classes.

The fine-tuned model will not classify images as one of the 1000 different classes for which it was previously trained on, but instead, it will work only to classify images of the Bengal Tigers it has been fine-tuned on.

5 Experiments and Results

The visual illustration of fine-tuned CNN architecture is given in Fig. 2. The constructed network has five convolution layers. The first block have two convolution layers having

64 filters each with a size of 3 × 3, the second block have 2 convolution layers and each convolution layers have 128 filters with a size of 3 × 3, the third block has a total of four convolution layers, having 256 filters with a size of 3 × 3, the fourth convolution block consists of four convolution layers with 512 filters of size 3 × 3 and lastly the fifth convolution block consist of four convolution layers with 512 filters of size 3 × 3. All the blocks mentioned above are separated by a Max Pooling layer. The constructed network has 139.5 million parameters with 26 layers.

The fully connected layers have been trained with Bengal Tiger images. It achieved an accuracy of 95.34% on training data and 94.26% accuracy on validation data after 20 epochs with a learning rate of 0.001, since the learning rate should be kept very small in case of fine-tuning of the pre-trained CNNs. The calculated Precision and Recall is 0.9502 and finally a micro F1-score of 0.9502 has been achieved. The mini-batch size of 300 has been taken as there are approx. 18000 images in said dataset and dividing the dataset into small mini-batches is preferable. Adams optimizer is used as it is appropriate for problems with a lot of noise or sparse gradient and also it is computationally efficient. Categorical Cross Entropy is used as it is a decent loss function for Classification Problems since it minimizes the distance between two probability distributions - predicted and actual. Accuracy and F1 score are used as a metric as it gives a good intuition about the model's performance.

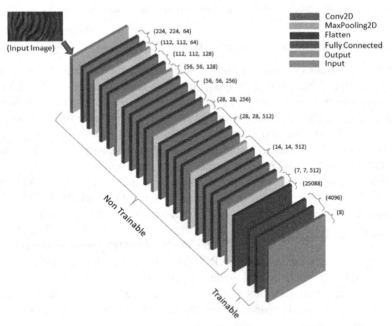

Fig. 2. Architecture of VGG19

Before initiating the process, all images were pre-processed. For this, the batches of training, validating, and testing were created by using an Image data generator from Keras. Some pre-processed images are shown in Fig. 3.

Fig. 3. Pre-processed images used for creating training, validating and testing batches.

20 epochs have been used for training the network. This was observed that the accuracy is increasing slowly after every epoch and goes up to 95.34%, while on validation data it goes up to 94.26%, and similarly as expected the loss is decreasing slowly after every epoch. Finally, it reaches 0.1725 on training data and 0.1974 on validation data. The entire process has been described through the graph in Fig. 4, 5.

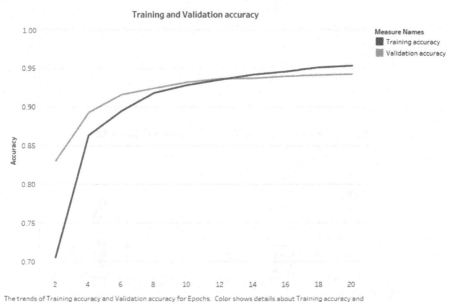

The trends of Training accuracy and Validation accuracy for Epochs. Color shows details about Training accuracy and Validation accuracy.

Fig. 4. Epoch vs accuracy graph on training & validation data

In this model, every experiment was performed in the GPU of Google Collaboratory. The training of the network takes about 155 min and the entire running time of the experiment is about 162 min.

The Confusion Matrix of the test batch is shown in Fig. 6. Approx. 3800 different images of Bengal tigers belonging to 8 different classes have been tested in batch. Through the Confusion Matrix, the fact can easily be established that the proposed model can accurately identify the total count of Bengal Tiger among images that are taken through Drone camera.

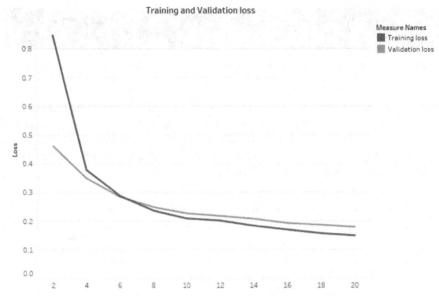

Fig. 5. Epoch vs. loss graph on training and validation data

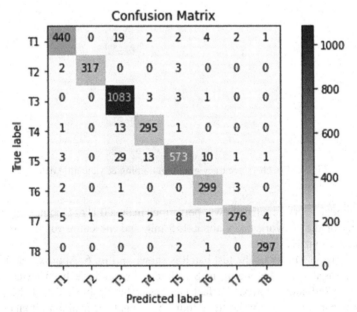

Fig. 6. Confusion matrix

6 Conclusion

In this paper, a solution is provided with the help of an autonomous/manually controlled drone which would perform the job of individual recognition and monitoring the population of Royal Bengal Tigers (Panthera Tigris) with greater efficiency. In the risk-prone regions like Sundarban Forest in West Bengal, it will be beneficial by securing the lives of the workers who used to do the counting of tigers manually. In the proposed system, a drone camera has searched the tigers using the 'Tiger Detection Model' in which the flank of the detected tiger passes through a fine-tuned state-of-art network. To summarize, the system having its base on deep CNN aims to detect the count of the tigers in a given forest and also to revolutionize the accuracy of tiger detection technique which will be followed by the human experts and to cap it all it puts a decisive edge to the scenario of the death toll due to animal attack. The future scope of this research would be implementing this method not only to tigers but also to other animal with patterns like zebra, cheetah, etc. There could be some improvement in both quality and quantity of datasets to keep track of all conditions where a tiger is probable to be found and tests can be done using better available frameworks, by following this more optimum result could be achieved.

References

1. Sharma, S., Jhala, Y., Sawarkar, V.B.: Identification of individual tigers (Panthera tigris) from their pugmarks. J. Zool. **267**, 9–18 (2005)
2. Jiang, X., Yau, W.Y.: Fingerprint minutiae matching based on the local and global structures. In: ICPR, vol. 2, pp. 1038–1041. IEEE (2000)
3. Simonyan, K., Zisserman, A.: Very Deep Convolutional Networks for Large-Scale Image Recognition. arXiv arXiv:1409.1556 (2014)
4. Kumar, S., Singh, S.: Cattle recognition: a new frontier in visual animal biometrics research. Proc. Natl. Acad. Sci. India Sect. A: Phys. Sci. **90**(4), 689–708 (2019). https://doi.org/10.1007/s40010-019-00610-x
5. Patel, R.: Real time animal detection system using HAAR like feature. Web (2015). https://www.researchgate.net/publication/281537804
6. Kandel, I., Castelli, M.: How deeply to fine-tune a convolutional neural network: a case study using a histopathology dataset, Lisboa, pp. 1070–1312 (2020)
7. Burghardt, T., Calic, J.: Real-time face detection and tracking of animals. In: Neural Network Applications in Electrical Engineering, p. 2732. IEEE (2006)
8. Burghardt, T., Calic, J., Thomas, B.T.: Tracking animals in wildlife videos using face detection. In: EWIMT (2004)
9. Mukai, N., Zhang, Y., Chang, Y.: Pet face detection, pp. 52–57 (2018). https://doi.org/10.1109/NICOINT.2018.00018
10. Thorpe, M.F., Delorme, A., Marlot, S.T.C.: A limit to the speed processing in ultra-rapid visual categorization of novel natural scene. Cogn. Neurosci. **13**, 171–180 (2003)
11. Peijiang, C.: Moving object detection based on background extraction. In: Computer Network and Multimedia Technology (CNMT) (2009)
12. Caughley, G.: Sampling in aerial survey. J. Wildlife Manag. **41**(4), 605–615 (1977). JSTOR. www.jstor.org/stable/3799980. Accessed 18 Oct 2020
13. Schwarz, C., Seber, G.: Estimating animal abundance: review III. Stat. Sci. **14** (1999). https://doi.org/10.1214/ss/1009212521

14. Chomba, C., Senzota, R., Chabwela, H., Nyirenda, V.: Lion hunting and trophy quality records in Zambia for the period 1967–2000: will the trends in trophy size drop as lion population declines? Open J. Ecol. **4**, 182–195 (2014). https://doi.org/10.4236/oje.2014.44019

15. Karanth, K., Chundawat, R., Nichols, J., Kumar, N.: Estimation of tiger densities in the tropical dry forests of Panna, Central India, using photographic capture–recapture sampling. Anim. Conserv. **7**, 285–290 (2004). https://doi.org/10.1017/S1367943004001477

16. LeCun, Y., Bengio, Y., Hinton, G.: Deep learning. Nature **521**, 436–444 (2015). https://doi.org/10.1038/nature14539

17. Farabet, C., Couprie, C., Najman, L., LeCun, Y.: Learning hierarchical features for scene labelling. IEEE Trans. Pattern Anal. Mach. Intell. **35**(8), 1915–1929 (2013). https://doi.org/10.1109/TPAMI.2012.231

18. Chaudhari, H., Shri Sant Gadge: Raspberry Pi Technology: A Review (2015)

19. Simonyan, K., Zisserman, A.: Very Deep Convolutional Networks for Large-Scale Image Recognition. arXiv 1409.1556 (2014)

20. Mikołajczyk, A., Grochowski, M.: Data augmentation for improving deep learning in image classification problem. In: 2018 International Interdisciplinary PhD Workshop (IIPhDW), Swinoujście, pp. 117–122 (2018). https://doi.org/10.1109/IIPHDW.2018.8388338

21. Shorten, C., Khoshgoftaar, T.: A survey on Image data augmentation for deep learning. J. Big Data **6**(1), 1–48 (2019). https://doi.org/10.1186/s40537-019-0197-0

AI Based Automated Model for Plant Disease Detection, a Deep Learning Approach

Aditi Ghosh[1] and Parthajit Roy[2(✉)]

[1] The Department of Master of Computer Applications, Techno India Hooghly, Chinsurah 712101, West Bengal, India
[2] The Department of Computer Science, The University of Burdwan, Purba Bardhaman 713104, West Bengal, India

Abstract. Plants can be affected by different diseases and many of them are expressed through leaves. Plant diseases are major issues in the field of agriculture and automatic detection of diseases can reduce production costs. In the present study, an automated disease detection model from leaf images has been proposed which is based on Convolutional Neural Network. Five diseases, which use leaves as one of their expression mediums, have been considered in this study. These are Early Blight, Late Blight, Esca, Isariopsis and Black Rot. The first two are mostly found in Potatoes and the rest three are in Grapes. Images of healthy and symptom expressive leaves have been taken for each species and the proposed model has been trained and tested using them. Overall efficiency of our proposed model is found to be 87.47% for Potatoes and 91.96% for Grapes. The results have been analyzed from different aspects in various scales. The efficiency of our model has also been measured against some of the existing models.

Keywords: Deep Learning · Plant disease detection · Convolutional Neural Network · Machine Learning · Image processing

1 Introduction

Physiological or structural deformities, caused by a living organism that hinders plants to carry out its maximum potential, is referred to as a plant disease. Host plant, pathogen and supportive environments [1] are the three conditions that are responsible for the development of each disease. Plant pathogens include bacteria, fungi, viruses, oomycetes etc. Leaf spot, Wilts, Blight, Cankers, Mildew, Rust etc. are the well known diseases caused by fungi whereas Mottling, Mosaic, Chlorosis etc. are caused by viruses [1,2]. Bacterial plant diseases include Blight, Wilts, Leaf spot, Soft rots etc. The symptoms of these diseases can be seen in leaf, stem, fruit or any other parts. In this research work we are interested to detect diseases from leaf images present in Potato and Grape. Two diseases Early

© Springer Nature Switzerland AG 2021
P. Dutta et al. (Eds.): CICBA 2021, CCIS 1406, pp. 199–213, 2021.
https://doi.org/10.1007/978-3-030-75529-4_16

Blight and Late Blight of potato, and three diseases Esca, Isariopsis, Black Rot
of grape have been considered in our study.

Early Blight and Late Blight of potato are the most common diseases visible
in potato. Early Blight (Ref. Fig. 1(b)) is caused by Alternaria Solani [3], a
fungal pathogen. Different parts of the plant like leaves, stem, even tubers can
be affected by this disease. Lesions, caused by early blight are dark brown to
black in color and become visible as small circular shape on leaves. Area of the
lesions increases gradually. The fungal pathogen Alternaria Solani mainly affects
the leaf tissues which are older, weak due to deficiency of nutrients or injury.
The first symptoms of early blight can be seen on leaves and if left untreated,
it will affect tubers and cause low production. Late blight [4] disease of potato
is caused by the oomycetes Phytophthora infestans (Mont.) de Bary. It is one
of the most devastating diseases that can affect the foliage as well as tubers.
Initially, the symptoms of late blight include small circular shaped spot which is
light to dark green in color (Ref. Fig. 1(c)). These lesions are gradually increased
in cool, moist weather and the color changes to dark brown or black. In this
disease also, the first symptom appears on leaves.

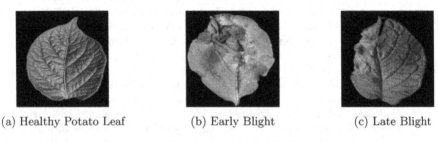

(a) Healthy Potato Leaf   (b) Early Blight   (c) Late Blight

Fig. 1. (a) Healthy Potato leaf. (b) Dark brown spot in Early Blight affected Potato
leaf. (c) Dark brown to Black spot in Late Blight affected Potato leaf. (Color figure
online)

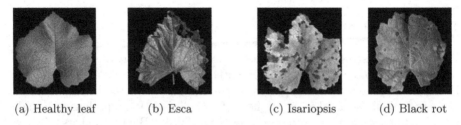

(a) Healthy leaf   (b) Esca   (c) Isariopsis   (d) Black rot

Fig. 2. (a) Healthy grape leaf. (b) Tiger strip pattern in Esca. (c) Purplish brown to
black spot in Isariopsis. (d) Reddish brown spot in Black Rot. (Color figure online)

In case of grapes, the present study has considered three types of diseases
Esca, Isariopsis and Black Rot. Esca [5], a grapevine trunk disease, is caused

by the fungi Phaeoacremonium aleophilum and Phaeomoniella chlamydospora. Esca is also known as Black Measles. Symptoms of this disease are light green rounded or irregular spots along the leaf margins or between the veins (Ref. Fig. 2(b)), which gradually becomes yellow brown or red brown and forms a tiger stripes pattern. Isariopsis [6] leaf spot, a disease in grape, is caused by the fungi Pseudocercospora vitis. Initially some small irregular chlorotic patches are formed and turned into larger lesions of purplish brown to black (Ref. Fig. 2(c)). Black rot [7] disease of grape is caused by the fungi Guignardia bidwellii in hot and humid weather. Lesions formed by this disease are irregular, reddish brown, surrounded by a black margin (Ref. Fig. 2(d)). Young leaves are affected by this disease. Figure 2 shows the healthy grape leaf along with three types of disease affected leaves.

Traditional agriculture uses some laboratory based methods to detect plant diseases. Among those, Polymerase Chain Reaction (PCR) technique has been used extensively to detect microbial pathogen. Similarly the other techniques like Enzyme-Linked immunosorbent Assay (ELISA), Immunofluorescence (IF) [8] etc. have also been used. Application of these methods are time consuming, need domain experts and laboratory setup. Also, these methods are expensive. Therefore, our aim is to build an Artificial Intelligence (AI) based model for disease detection which is cost effective and free from domain experts.

Modern technology brings a revolution in the field of agriculture. The task involving plant classification, disease detection, weed detection etc. has now become easier by the use of Machine Learning (ML) [2] technology and image processing [2]. Image processing is required for image pre-processing, image segmentation and extract features from those. The task of image pre-processing includes conversion in gray scale or binary or in other color space, filtering images, background elimination, morphological transformation like opening, closing etc.

After extracting features via image processing techniques, it is needed to feed the classifier with these extracted feature values. Here we need ML technology. Learning methods of ML can be supervised, unsupervised or semi supervised. Different classifiers are also available based on these techniques.

One of the main drawback of any ML based model is that it requires featurized data as input for its classifier. These features can be extracted via complex image processing techniques. Not only that, there are so many type of features like shape, color, texture, vein etc., out of which selection of appropriate feature is also difficult. Depending on the use of appropriate feature vector, the accuracy of the classifier will depend. Therefore, it will be beneficial for us if we don't require this featurize data as input. It is possible only because of the Deep Learning (DL) technology used today. DL is a sub field of ML where we can use multiple layers to extract higher level features from the raw input. In this research work, our aim is to detect plant diseases using Convolutional Neural Network (CNN). CNN [9–11] is a class of DL architecture specially designed for image analysis.

Now we shall discuss some of the previous research work done by others for automatic plant disease detection. Kuo-Yi Huang [12] proposed a model to detect Phalaenopsis seedling disease. To classify three types of diseases he used some color and texture features. Back Propagation Neural Network (BPNN) was used as a classifier and the average accuracy was 89.6%. The authors in [13] proposed an automatic disease detection model for detecting Brown Spot and Frog Eye diseases of Soybean. After image pre-processing and image segmentation, shape features were extracted and then K Nearest Neighbour (KNN) classifier was used to detect the diseases. Classification rate was 70% for Brown Spot and 80% for Frog Eye. Cotton leaf disease identification using Pattern Recognition techniques proposed by Rothe et al. [14] used image segmentation and Hu invariant moment features for detecting diseases like Bacterial leaf Blight, Alternaria etc. BPNN was used as classifier and the classification accuracy was 85%. To classify different diseases of tomato, Sabrol et al. [15] introduced a model which was based on decision tree classifier. According to this model, image segmentation, feature extraction and normalization were done before using the classifier. Extracted features were then given to the decision tree classifier for classification. Average accuracy was 78%. Rice blast, Rice Sheath Blight and Brown spot diseases were identified by Anthonys et al. [16] through the image processing techniques. After digitization and image segmentation, texture, shape and color features were extracted. They defined membership function for each class for classification. Overall accuracy was 70%. Ferdouse et al. [17] proposed a novel approach to detect tomato diseases using deep CNN. They proposed a CNN model consisting of 15 layers and the efficiency was 76%. In 2020, Emma Harte [11] proposed plant disease detection system using a pre-trained ResNet34 model. Different types of diseases of present in potato, tomato and rice leaves were detected with an impressive accuracy.

From the above discussions, it can be noted that most of the research work have used traditional ML. Some though have used modern DL technique, the accuracy is not satisfactory. Therefore there is still a need to build a CNN model which will give us better accuracy. In this research work we propose a CNN model for detecting different types of potato and grape diseases along with healthy leaves, which gives us better accuracy.

As of now we have given a brief introduction as well as the literature review. The remaining part of this paper is oriented as follows. Section 2 gives a brief discussion of CNN. This section discusses different layers of CNN and their working principles. Section 3 presents the proposed model. Experimental setup i.e. data set, indexes for measurement etc. have been given in Sect. 4 where as the results and the discussions have been explored in Sect. 5. The conclusion and the references come thereafter.

2   Brief Overview of CNN

DL is a sub field of ML, the core of which is the multi layered Artificial Neural Network (ANN). Popular DL architecture includes CNN, Recurrent Neural Network (RNN) etc. CNN is most commonly used to analyse images. CNN consists of convolution layer, pooling layer and fully connected layer, each of which is described below.

Convolution Layer. One of the most important layers in any CNN architecture is the convolution layer [9,18]. This layer is mainly used for feature extraction from the raw input images. It can detect the edges present in the image by the linear operation called convolution. Convolution operation is performed between an input image and a kernel. Corresponding elements between the image and the kernel have been multiplied and then we obtain a single value by summing up all the product values together. Then we move the kernel to the right and then bottom until we reach the boundary of the image and perform the same multiplication and addition operation to obtain the output.

Sometimes, the output of this layer can be lesser than the size of the input image. In that case, if we want to keep the output size same as the input size, we need to do padding, i.e. inserting extra rows and columns around the input image. The values of these cells are usually set to 0, but it can have other values as well. Another important feature related to this convolution operation is stride. Stride determines the distance between two consecutive kernel positions. Usually this value is 1, but it can be greater than 1 if required. Size of the feature map of an M*M*1 gray scale image is,

$$\left(\frac{M+2P-N}{S}+1\right)*\left(\frac{M+2P-N}{S}+1\right)*F$$

where $N*N$ is the kernel size, P is padding, S is stride and F is the number of filter.

While training a CNN, the values of kernel in the convolution layer are updated and the kernel that performs best have been identified according to a given task. Therefore, the parameter of the convolution layer is the kernel values while the kernel size, padding, stride value, number of filters act as the hyper parameter values. This layer is mainly responsible for detecting low level features like edges, color, gradient orientation etc. In each convolution layer, an activation function is used. Rectified Linear Unit (ReLU) [9] is the most popular one. ReLU is a non linear activation function which is defined using Eq. 1.

$$f(x) = max(0, x) \tag{1}$$

Maxpooling Layer. After convolution layer, the next important layer is the pooling layer [9,18]. It is used to reduce the computational complexity of the network by reducing the number of learning parameters. Main responsibility of the pooling layer is to perform down sampling operation. Down sampling is an operation, which is applied on to the feature map to reduce its dimensionality by reducing spatial resolution. Maxpooling is one of the most common pooling operations. Maximum value from the selected region of the feature map which is covered by the pre defined filter has been taken to form the new feature map. Down sampling operation in this layer reduces the size of the feature map by a factor of 2.

Fully Connected Layer. Feature map, obtained from the final convolution or pooling layer has been flattened [9, 18]. After flattening, we get a one dimensional vector which is connected to one or more fully connected layers (also called dense layer) [9, 18]. This is same as simple ANN. Where every neuron of the previous layer is connected to the every other neuron of the next layer. The activation function which is used for last layer in case of multi class classification is softmax. Mathematical formulation of the softmax function has been given in Eq. 2 [19].

$$\sigma(\boldsymbol{x})_p = \frac{e^{x_p}}{\sum_{q=1}^{k} e^{x_q}} \tag{2}$$

where $\boldsymbol{x}$ is the input vector, e^{x_p} is the standard exponential function for input vector, e^{x_q} is the standard exponential function for output vector, k is the number of classes.

3   Description of the Proposed Model

This section describes the required steps of our proposed model. Before applying the input images to the CNN, we need to collect the images and pre-process those images. Disease detection of leaf images consists of the following steps. 1) Image Acquisition 2) Image Pre-processing 3) Classification.

3.1   Image Acquisition

We have taken entire dataset from Plant Village dataset. It is a very well known and huge collection of different type of diseases belonging to different categories. From this dataset we have taken healthy and unhealthy leaves of grape and potato. All these images are color image.

3.2   Image Pre-processing

All the leaf images that have been collected from the Plant Village dataset are of dimension 256*256. In this step we resize the images to reduce the dimension and make it 100*100. After that, we convert those color images to the gray scale image. Equation 3 [20] is used for this step. Figure 3 the resulting images obtained from the image pre-processing step.

$$G = c_1 + c_2 + c_3 \tag{3}$$

where $c_1 = 0.2989 * R$, $c_2 = 0.5870 * G$ and $c_3 = 0.1140 * B$.

3.3   Classification Using CNN

Convolution Layer: In our model we have used three convolution layers with 64 filters in the 1st convolution layer, 128 in the 2nd convolution layer and 256 in the 3rd convolution layer. Kernel size is 3*3 in each case with stride as 1. As

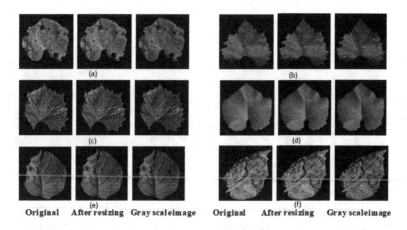

Original After resizing Gray scale image   Original After resizing Gray scale image

Fig. 3. Resulting images obtained from the image pre-processing step.

the images are of size 100*100, the size of the feature map of the 1st convolution layer is 98*98*64 which is clearly shown in Fig. 4. In this layer we have used ReLU activation function. Similarly, in the second convolution layer, the size of the feature map becomes 47*47*128 and for the third convolution layer it becomes 21*21*256. This is also shown is Fig. 4. ReLU activation function has been used in this two layers also.

Maxpooling Layer: Each convolution layer is followed by a maxpooling layer. In our model we have used pool size as (2,2) and stride of 2. Maxpooling layer performs the dimensionality reduction. Therefore, in the first maxpooling layer, the size of the feature map becomes 49*49*64 which is shown is Fig. 4. Similarly, for the second and third maxpooling layer, the size of the feature map becomes 23*23*128 and 10*10*256 respectively.

Fully Connected Layer: In our model, we have used two fully connected layers. In the first layer, there is 64 neurons and in the final layer there is 4 neurons for grape and 3 neurons for potato. This is because number of classes for potato is 3 and for grape it is 4. As it is a multi class classification problem, we have used softmax activation function in the final layer (output layer). Overall architecture of our model has been shown in Fig. 4.

4 Experimental Setup

Now we are ready to present the performance of the proposed model. To judge the performance of a model, we need three things. 1. A benchmark dataset, 2. Standard indexes for measurement of accuracy and 3. Existing models for comparative studies. This section explores each of them.

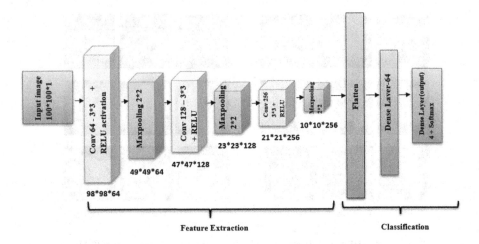

Fig. 4. Architecture of the proposed model.

Dataset: We have taken Plant Village dataset [21] for our study. It is a large dataset containing different images of plant leaf diseases. Among those, potato and grape have been taken. For potato, the diseases like Early Blight and Late Blight have been classified along with healthy leaves. Similarly for grape, diseases like Esca, Isariopsis, and Black Rot have been identified along with healthy leaves. Total number of samples of each category has been shown in the Table 1. Among those, 80% have been used as training samples and 20% as test samples. Total number of training and test samples have also been shown in Table 1.

Standard Indexes: After fixing the dataset, it is important to choose the performance measurement indexes to measure the accuracy of the model. As it is a multi class classification problem and the dataset is imbalanced, we have taken Precision, Recall and F1 score for measuring accuracy. Equations 4, 5, 6 describes the mathematical formulation of the Precision, Recall and F1 score [22].

$$Precision = \frac{TS}{(TS + FS)} \tag{4}$$

$$Recall = \frac{TS}{(TS + FR)} \tag{5}$$

$$F1 - Score = \frac{2 * (Precision * Recall)}{(Precision + Recall)} \tag{6}$$

where TS is the True Selection [22], FS is the False Selection [22] and FR is the False Rejection [22].

Table 1. Description of the dataset [21]. In this work, Healthy and Unhealthy leaves of Potato and Grape taken from the Plant Village dataset, have been used. Total 2152 Potato leaves and 3359 Grape leaves have been used. Out of which, approximately 80% have been used for training and 20% for testing.

Name of the disease	Sample Image	No. of Sample	No. of training sample	No. of test sample
Potato Early Blight		1000	805	195
Potato Late Blight		1000	792	208
Potato Healthy		152	124	28
Esca		1168	918	250
Isariopsis		876	697	179
Black Rot		976	796	180
Grape Healthy		339	276	63

Existing Models for Comparative Study: We have also compared the performance of the proposed model with that of ten other existing models. To make the comparison more realistic, we have divided the set of existing models in two categories. In the first category, we have put those models that used the same dataset that we have taken as well as grape diseases that we have considered. DCNN-1 [17], DCNN-2 [23], Hybrid Intelligent System [24], SVM [25] and Fuzzy Set Theory [26] come in this category. In the second category, those models have been taken where the standard dataset is not same but their focus is leaf image based disease detection. Models BPNN+HU [14], Decision Tree [15], Membership Function [16], Genetic Algorithm [27] and ANN [28] come in this category.

5   Results and Discussions

Once the dataset and performance measurement indices have been fixed up, in this section we have discussed the outcome of the classification. We have used

CNN to detect different types of diseases of potato and grape. Figure 5 shows the resulting images obtained as output from the first convolution layer. It is clear from this figure that convolution layer tries to detect the edges present in the input images. As we have used 64 filters in this layer, we are getting 64 images.

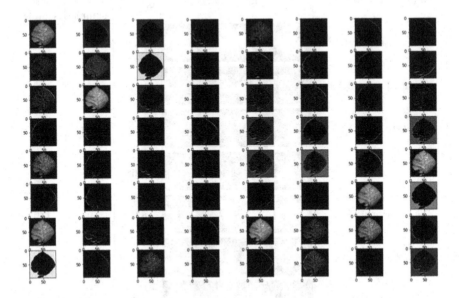

Fig. 5. Resulting images obtained from the 1st convolution layer

Similarly Fig. 6 shows the output obtained from the first maxpooling layer. This layer is used to reduce the dimensionality of the feature map. In this figure we can see that the dimension of the feature map is reduced to 50*50 from 100*100. It shows the most prominent features obtained from the previous feature map.

Table 2 shows the accuracy metrics precision, recall and F1-score of the potato leaf diseases. It is clear from this table that the Precision value of Potato Late Blight is 0.90 which is maximum among all others. This indicates low FS rate. Recall value of Potato Late Blight is also maximum and it indicates low FR rate. F1-score of the Potato Late Blight is 0.91 which is the Harmonic progression of Precision and Recall value. Precision, Recall and F1-score of Potato is moderate. On the other hand, Potato healthy leaf achieves the lowest Precision, Recall and F1-score. It means that FS and FR rate is high in this case.

Similarly, Table 3 shows the Precision, Recall and F1 score of the grape leaf diseases. Precision value of Black Measles is 0.99 which is maximum among all others. It indicates low FS rate. Recall value of Black Measles is 0.97 which is

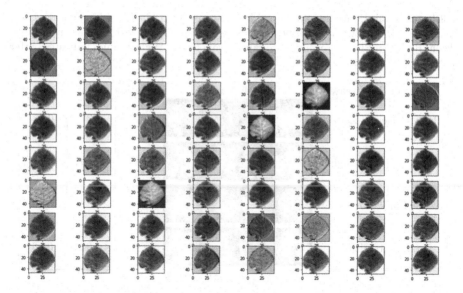

Fig. 6. Resulting images obtained from the 1st maxpooling layer

Table 2. Details of accuracy of Potato leaf diseases. Three classes of Potato leaf - Early Blight, Late Blight and Healthy leaves have been identified with high accuracy. Precision, Recall and F1-score values are ranges from 0 to 1. Higher values indicates better accuracy.

Name of the disease	Sample Image	Precision	Recall	F1 score
Potato Early Blight		0.86	0.87	0.87
Potato Late Blight		0.90	0.91	0.91
Potato Healthy		0.75	0.64	0.69

also good and indicates a low FR rate. Grape healthy leaves also achieve high Precision, Recall and F1-score and these are 0.95, 0.97 and 0.96 respectively. These values are moderate in case of grape Black rot disease. Lowest accuracy have been obtained in case of grape Leaf Blight.

Confusion matrix of Potato and Grape diseases have been shown in Fig. 7. The diagonal elements of the confusion matrix are the TS values. Total TS values of potato is $(170+189+18) = 377$ where as for grape it is $(174+161+222+61) = 618$. Sum of each row of the confusion matrix gives the total number of test set of the corresponding class. For example, total test set of Potato early blight is $(170 + 20 + 5) = 195$. If we subtract the TS value from this, we obtain FR value.

Table 3. Details of accuracy of Grape leaf diseases. Four classes of Grape leaf - Esca, Isariopsis, Black Rot and Healthy leaves have been identified with high accuracy. Precision, Recall and F1-score values are ranges from 0 to 1. Higher values indicates better accuracy.

Name of the disease	Sample Image	Precision	Recall	F1 score
Esca (Black Measles)		0.99	0.97	0.98
Isariopsis (Leaf Blight)		0.85	0.89	0.87
Black Rot		0.92	0.89	0.90
Grape Healthy		0.95	0.97	0.96

So, the FR value of each class of potato are 25, 19 and 10 respectively and for grape this values are 5, 19, 28 and 2 respectively. Similarly sum of each column excluding TS is the FS value. 28, 20, 24 are the FS value of each class of potato whereas 2, 29, 20 and 3 are the FS value of each class of grape.

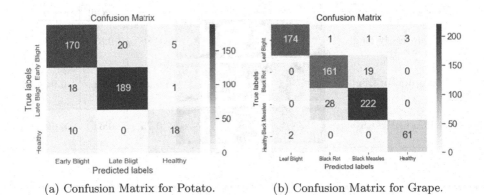

(a) Confusion Matrix for Potato.   (b) Confusion Matrix for Grape.

Fig. 7. (a) Confusion matrix of Potato. (b) Confusion matrix of Grape. The colors indicate the number of points in the cell. The more deeper blue the color, the more number of points in the cell. The more whitish the color, the less the number of points. (Color figure online)

A graphical representation of Train-Test accuracy with number of epochs for potato and grape have been shown in the Fig. 8(a) and 8(b) respectively. Accuracy obtained while training the dataset is termed as training accuracy.

Test accuracy means the accuracy obtained on test dataset. It is clear from the Fig. 8 that Grape diseases give better accuracy than Potato.

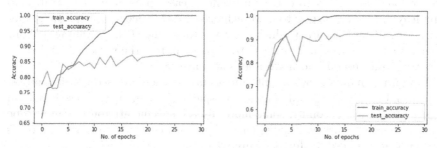

(a) Training and testing accuracy of potato (b) Training and testing accuracy of grape.

Fig. 8. (a) Training and testing accuracy of potato. (b) Training and testing accuracy of grape. The blue color line show the training accuracy and the orange color line show the testing accuracy. (Color figure online)

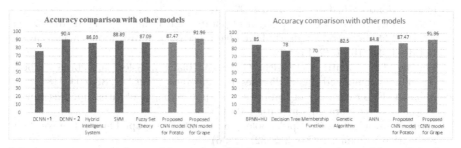

(a) Accuracy comparison with models that use either Plant Village Dataset or Grape leaf.

(b) Accuracy comparison with models that use other dataset of leaf images for detecting plant diseases.

Fig. 9. (a) Accuracy of our model measured against DCNN [17], DCNN [23], Hybrid Intelligent System [24], SVM [25] and Fuzzy Set Theory [26]. (b) Accuracy of our model measured against BPNN+HU [14], Decision Tree [15], Membership Function [16], Genetic Algorithm [27] and ANN [28].

Figure 9 shows the graphical representation of the accuracy of different models along with our proposed one. Figure 9(a) compares our models with others where either Plant Village dataset or Grape leaves have been used. In Fig. 9(b), the comparison is among the models that use different dataset with our proposed one. Accuracy of our proposed model for grape disease detection is the best among all others. Also, the accuracy of the proposed model for potato is best in Fig. 9(b) and better than three existing models out of five in Fig. 9(a).

6   Conclusion and Future Scope

Automated plant disease detection model plays an important role in agriculture. Here we have used CNN to detect different diseases present in the potato and grape leaves. In case of potatoes we achieved 87.47% accuracy and for grapes we achieved 91.96% accuracy which is satisfactory. One of the advantages of our model is that it requires no feature extraction step. It is the responsibility of the layers to extract useful information for classification.

Though the model shows significant accuracy, there are scopes of improvements also. First of all instead of images in spatial domain, one can use images in frequency domains. Secondly, some more disease specific attributes can also be added for better accuracy. Finally, more sophisticated machine learning models can also be introduced for further improvements.

References

1. Kimberly, L., Kelly, J., Smith, R., Gauthier, N.: Plant diseases (2016)
2. Kaur, S., Pandey, S., Goel, S.: Plants disease identification and classification through leaf images: a survey. Arch. Comput. Methods Eng. **26**(2), 507–530 (2018). https://doi.org/10.1007/s11831-018-9255-6
3. Waals, J.E.: A review of early blight of potato. Afr. Plant Prot. **7**, 91–102 (2001)
4. Arora, R., Sharma, S., Singh, B.: Late blight disease of potato and its management. Potato J. **41**, 16–40 (2014)
5. Mugnai, L., Graniti, A., Surico, G.: Esca (black measles) and brown wood-streaking: two old and elusive diseases of grapevines. Plant Dis. **83**, 404–418 (1999)
6. Mehmet, F.: Occurrence of isariopsis leaf spot or blight of vitis rupestris caused by pseudocercospora vitis in Turkey (2017)
7. Jermini, M., Gessler, C.: Epidemiology and control of grape black rot in southern Switzerland. Plant Dis. **80**, 322–325 (1996)
8. Fang, Y., Ramasamy, R.: Current and prospective methods for plant disease detection. Biosensors **5**, 537–561 (2015)
9. Yamashita, R., Nishio, M., Do, R., Togashi, K.: Convolutional neural networks: an overview and application in radiology. Insights Imaging **9**, 06 (2018)
10. Boulent, J., Foucher, S., Théau, J., St-Charles, P.-L.: Convolutional neural networks for the automatic identification of plant diseases. Front. Plant Sci. **10**, 941 (2019)
11. Harte, E.: Plant disease detection using CNN. Ph.D. thesis, September 2020
12. Huang, K.-Y.: Application of artificial neural network for detecting phalaenopsis seedling diseases using color and texture features. Comput. Electron. Agric. **57**(1), 3–11 (2007)
13. Shrivastava, S., Hooda, D.S.: Automatic brown spot and frog eye detection from the image captured in the field. Am. J. Intell. Syst. **4**(4), 131–134 (2014)
14. Rothe, P.R., Kshirsagar, R.V.: Cotton leaf disease identification using pattern recognition techniques. In: 2015 International Conference on Pervasive Computing (ICPC), pp. 1–6 (2015)
15. Sabrol, H., Kumar, S.: Intensity based feature extraction for tomato plant disease recognition by classification using decision tree. Int. J. Comput. Sci. Inf. Secur. **14**, 622–626 (2016)

16. Anthonys, G., Wickramarachchi, N.: An image recognition system for crop disease identification of paddy fields in Sri Lanka, December 2009
17. Ferdouse Ahmed Foysal, Md., Shakirul Islam, M., Abujar, S., Akhter Hossain, S.: A novel approach for tomato diseases classification based on deep convolutional neural networks. In: Uddin, M.S., Bansal, J.C. (eds.) Proceedings of International Joint Conference on Computational Intelligence. AIS, pp. 583–591. Springer, Singapore (2020). https://doi.org/10.1007/978-981-13-7564-4_49
18. Hussain, M., Bird, J., Faria, D.: A study on CNN transfer learning for image classification, June 2018
19. Agarap, A.F.: Deep learning using rectified linear units (ReLU), March 2018
20. Wu, S.G., Bao, F.S., Xu, E.Y., Wang, Y.-X., Chang, Y.-F., Xiang, Q.-L. : A leaf recognition algorithm for plant classification using probabilistic neural network (2007)
21. Mohanty, S.P., Hughes, D.P., Salathé, M.: Using deep learning for image-based plant disease detection. Front. Plant Sci. **7**, 1419 (2016)
22. Fawcett, T.: An introduction to ROC analysis. Pattern Recogn. Lett. **27**(8), 861–874 (2006). ROC Analysis in Pattern Recognition
23. Wang, G., Sun, Y., Wang, J.: Automatic image-based plant disease severity estimation using deep learning. Comput. Intell. Neurosci. **2017**, 1–8 (2017)
24. Meunkaewjinda, A., Kumsawat, P., Attakitmongcol, K., Srikaew, A.: Grape leaf disease detection from color imagery using hybrid intelligent system. In: 2008 5th International Conference on Electrical Engineering/Electronics, Computer, Telecommunications and Information Technology, vol. 1, pp. 513–516 (2008)
25. Padol, P.B., Yadav, A.A.: SVM classifier based grape leaf disease detection. In: 2016 Conference on Advances in Signal Processing (CASP), pp. 175–179 (2016)
26. Kole, D.K., Ghosh, A., Mitra, S.: Detection of downy mildew disease present in the grape leaves based on fuzzy set theory. In: Kumar Kundu, M., Mohapatra, D.P., Konar, A., Chakraborty, A. (eds.) Advanced Computing, Networking and Informatics- Volume 1. SIST, vol. 27, pp. 377–384. Springer, Cham (2014). https://doi.org/10.1007/978-3-319-07353-8_44
27. Xu, G., Zhang, F., Shah, S., Ye, Y., Mao, H.: Use of leaf color images to identify nitrogen and potassium deficient tomatoes. Pattern Recogn. Lett. **32**, 1584–1590 (2011)
28. Majumdar, D., Kole, D., Chakraborty, A., Majumder, D.: An integrated digital image analysis system for detection, recognition and diagnosis of disease in wheat leaves, August 2015

Gene Expression-Based Prediction of Lung Cancer-Associated Protein-Protein Interactions

Lopamudra Dey[1](✉) and Anirban Mukhopadhyay[2]

[1] Computer Science and Engineering Department, Heritage Institute of Technology, Kolkata, India
lopamudra.dey@heritageit.edu

[2] Computer Science and Engineering Department, University of Kalyani, Kayani, India

Abstract. The most prevalent form of cancer in the world is lung cancer. Although many qualitative and quantitative studies screened the proteins related to lung cancer over the years, protein-protein interactions (PPIs) related to lung cancer are not identified until now. Therefore in this article, we have aimed to analyze specific PPIs in lung cancer tissues using a microarray gene expression dataset. To identify the genes that are up-regulated and down-regulated during lung cancer progression in the human body, firstly, the differentially expressed genes are extracted from the lung cancer microarray dataset. Then, the PPI network of these proteins is constructed using the STRING web server. After this, we have collected pairwise features, like, sequence similarity score, gene ontology(GO)-based semantic score, domain-domain similarity score and, average shortest path length (ASPL) of the interacting protein pairs. Finally, a total of 10042 PPIs from HPRD, related to lung cancer are predicted using the NNET algorithm. In addition, this projected human PPI network's literature filtering and KEGG pathway of the hub proteins are studied and reported in the paper. Although many hub proteins related to lung cancer has been analyzed over the years, we have identified a new set of hub proteins of lung cancer in this study.

1 Introduction

Lung cancer, especially in America and China, has become one of the leading threats worldwide. According to the American Lung Association, the number of newly diagnosed patients affected by lung cancer is around 2.1 million in 2018, as well as 1.8 million deaths. Based on the size of the affected cell, lung cancer is mainly of two types, small cell lung cancer (SCLC) and non-small cell lung cancer (NSCLC). NSCLC accounts for 85% of all patients, while SCLC accounts for the remaining 15%. Despite the advancement of new therapeutic strategies as well as surgical techniques, most patients diagnosed with lung cancer finally die of this disease [1]. Therefore, it is very important to understand the molecular

© Springer Nature Switzerland AG 2021
P. Dutta et al. (Eds.): CICBA 2021, CCIS 1406, pp. 214–228, 2021.
https://doi.org/10.1007/978-3-030-75529-4_17

mechanisms of lung cancer and its progression pathway in the human body to develop some optimal anti-cancer therapy.

To date, various researches are going on to identify the hub proteins and pathways of lung cancer. In [2], Tingting Guo et al., using 4 GEO datasets (GSE118370, GSE85841, GSE43458, and GSE32863) discovered 11 hub genes related to LUAD. Mengwei Ni et al. explored 5 significant genes (TOP2A, CCNB1, CCNA2, UBE2C, and KIF20A) associated with NSCLC using 4 GEO datasets (GSE18842, GSE19804, GSE43458, and GSE62113) in [3]. A biometric analysis was performed in [5] on various cancer microarrays data like bladder, colon, kidney, and thyroid. They showed that PPIs from different cancer types have common functions across all cancers. In [6], Zhang et al. have used network-based topologies to identify the similarity and difference between NSCLC and SCLC pathogenesis. They demonstrated that except for the average shortest path length (ASPL), all the other network properties are the same in NSCLC and SCLC. This indicates that the two types of lung cancer play a similar function in the human body.

Protein-protein interaction (PPI) plays a major role in understanding the biological and molecular functions linked with different disease networks like cancer. Proteins are the products of genes. Therefore, a microarray gene expression dataset can provide useful information for PPI [7]. It provides the rate of expression of thousands of genes at a given time and condition in the tumor as well as in normal cells. It has been widely used to predict drug targets for different cancer diseases [2].

We attempted to predict the PPIs associated with lung cancer in this work from the HPRD database based on the pairwise features like sequence similarity score, gene ontology related semantic score, domain-domain similarity score and ASPL of the protein pairs. Finding the potential target PPIs relevant to a particular cancer disease is very important to understand their tumor-promoting functionality. Different supervised learning algorithms like KNN (K-nearest Neighbor), Random Forst (RF), Support Vector Machine (SVM), and Neural Network (NNET) are examined for prediction. Using 10-fold cross-validation, replicated 10 times, the outcomes of the supervised machine learning algorithms are assessed. The NNET algorithm works more efficiently than the other algorithms. Therefore, we have predicted a large set of lung cancer-related PPIs using the combined features of the human PPI database and the NNET technique. In addition, a set of statistically significant 7 hub proteins and 11 key proteins is identified in the current research. Most of these hub proteins are not predicted in earlier researches. Experimental findings will further verify these predicted associations, as well as hub and key proteins.

2 Data and Proposed Methodology

2.1 Experimental Dataset

The lung cancer gene expression dataset, GSE1987, is taken from [44]. The microarray dataset contains the gene expression data of 10541 genes and 34 samples. These 34 samples consist of 25 lung cancer samples, including 17 squamous cell carcinoma and 8 lung adenocarcinoma, and 9 normal tissue samples. We have considered both these lung cancer types into one.

2.2 Differential Gene Expression Dataset

The microarray data includes the patterns of expression at various environments of thousands of different genes. The differential gene expressions are calculated when a statistically significant change is observed in expression levels between two experimental conditions, like, disease state and healthy state. Therefore, finding the differential expressed genes (DEGs) is very important to identify the genes that are up-regulated or down-regulated during the invasion of a particular disease in the human body.

2.3 Identification of DEGs

Investigation of the DEGs associated with lung cancer is a very powerful way to understand the functions of the genes and their potential control structures for the emergence and development of diseases. In this research, we have analyzed the DEGs between lung cancer and normal tissues by edgeR [8] and limma package [9] of R. The criteria of $\log_2 |FC|$ with a threshold of 1.5 and $p \leq 0.05$ were used to determine the significant DEGs. We found that out of 10541 genes, 402 are up-regulated ($\log_2 |FC| \geq 1.5$ and $p \leq 0.05$), while 681 are down-regulated ($\log_2 |FC| \leq -1.5$ and $p \leq 0.05$). There are some genes (413) whose expression level is high throughout all samples (both cancer and normal tissue). These genes are placed in both up-regulated and down-regulated gene list. The detailed number of differentially expressed genes in lung cancer is presented in Table 1. The most important DEGs are listed in Table 2. From the 1882 DEGs, 134 genes have a 4-fold change in the frequency of expression, including 11 DEGs that have a 10-fold change in the level of their expression. The complete list of up-regulated, down-regulated and highly expressed genes are given in Supplementary File S1.

Table 1. The number of genes in lung cancer that are differentially expressed.

Genes	Up-regulated	Down-regulated
Total- 10541	402	681
After adding 413 highly expressed genes and removing overlapping genes	824	1058

Table 2. Ten top-ranked DEGs in lung cancer.

Gene symbol	Up-regulated DEGs Log2FC	p-value	Gene symbol	Down-regulated DEGs Log2FC	p-value
COL11A1	4.602	0.0018	FABP4	−4.092	2.12E-06
MMP12	4.1239	0.0002	WIF1	−3.6739	1.07E-05
SPP1	3.9797	5.89E-07	AGER	−3.5039	1.81E-05
TFAP2A	3.9349	0.00339	GDF10	−3.454	1.16E-07
SERPINB5	3.336	0.0285	EXOSC7	−3.313	8.83E-06
S100A2	3.2598	0.0025	ADH1A	−3.291	7.17E-05
KRT6C	3.151	0.0378	CLSN18	−3.20 3	.0058
KRT6A	3.078	0.0323	FHL1	−3.116	1.89E-08
UGT1A4	3.038	0.0032	MYH11	−3.096	1.34E-07
UGTA10	3.0118	0.0160	AD1RF	−3.092	7.36E-05

2.4   Analysis of DEGs Using KEGG Pathway

KEGG pathway analysis reveals the possible disease that can occur due to the involved protein set. We have performed KEGG pathway analysis on the DEGs having 4-fold-change using DAVID https://david.ncifcrf.gov/ and mentioned in Table 3. In [10], the roles of the P53 signaling pathway, ECM-receptor interaction, Oocyte meiosis, and the cell cycle in the pathologic process of lung cancer, especially in NSCLC, have been confirmed and studied extensively. Smoking is associated with the development of lung cancer, which endangers smokers to a range of carcinogenic chemicals such as cytochrome P450 [11]. In [12], the authors had reported a case of a 66-year old patient diagnosed with the dilated Phase of Hypertrophic Cardiomyopathy as a side effect of lung cancer. Therefore, these underlying up-regulated proteins, namely, CCNB1, CDK1, CCNE1, CCNB2, PTTG1, COL11A1, THBS2, HsT2645, HIST2H2AA3, HIST1H2BD and HIST1H2AE and down-regulated proteins, such as ADH1C, ADH1B, ADH1A, AOC3, FMO2, DES, TNNC1, TTN, SGCA, CLDN18, CLDN5, JAM3, and CDH5 can be treated as key proteins of lung cancer progression in the human body.

Table 3. KEGG pathway analysis of DEGs having 4-fold change related to Lung
Cancer

Expression	Term	Gene	P value
Up-regulation	hsa04115:p53 signaling pathway	CCNB1, CDK1, CCNE1, CCNB2, SERPINB5	8.9E-5
	hsa04114:Oocyte meiosis	CCNB1, CDK1, CCNE1, CCNB2, PTTG1	6.3E-4
	hsa04110:Cell cycle	CCNB1, CDK1, CCNE1, CCNB2, PTTG1	9.5E-4
	hsa04512:ECM-receptor interaction	COL11A1, THBS2, HsT2645	3.9E-2
	hsa04914:Progesterone-mediated oocyte maturation	CCNB1, CDK1, CCNB2	3.9E-2
	hsa05322:Systemic lupus erythematosus	HIST2H2AA3, HIST1H2BD, HIST1H2AE	8.4E-3
Down-regulation	hsa00350:Tyrosine metabolism	ADH1C, ADH1B, ADH1A, AOC3	1.3E-3
	hsa00982:Drug metabolism - cytochrome P450	FMO2, ADH1C, ADH1B, ADH1A	8.6E-3
	hsa05410:Hypertrophic cardiomyopathy (HCM)	DES, TNNC1, TTNI3, SGCA	1.3E-2
	hsa05414:Dilated cardiomyopathy	DES, TNNC1, TTNI3, SGCA	1.5E-2
	hsa04670:Leukocyte transendothelial migration	CLDN18, CLDN5, JAM3, CDH5	3.5E-2

2.5 Survival Analysis of Key Proteins

We evaluated the survival curves of each key proteins to determine the prognostic importance of these proteins further using the Kaplan – Meier plotter analytics platform http://kmplot.com. We have considered a hazard ratio (HR) of 95% confidence intervals and log-rank P having < 0.05 values are considered as the cutoff value. Among the 23 key proteins, 11 proteins satisfied the said cutoff criteria and mentioned in Fig. 1. It can be noted from the figure, 10 up-regulated proteins (CCNB1, CDK1, CCNE1, CCNB2, PTTG1, COL11A1, HsT2645, HIST2H2AA3, HIST1H2BD, and HIST1H2AE) and 1 down-regulated protein (TNNI3) are significantly associated with the poor overall surviva of lung cancer patients. The rest of the proteins have a p-value greater than 0.05. Therefore, those proteins are not included in the final key protein list.

2.6 Building of PPI Network

The final set of up-regulated and down-regulated genes are mapped to corresponding proteins, and those proteins are utilized to create the PPI network from the STRING [45] database with a score of 0.7 as the threshold. We got 1228 and 792 PPIs from up-regulated and down-regulated proteins, respectively (Supplementary File S2).

3   Features

We have collected a total of 6 pairwise features of all these PPIs. For all features, the missing values are replaced by the mean value of the corresponding feature's missing values. These 6 feature sets are described below.

3.1 Pairwise Sequence Similarity Score

The sequence similarity score has been commonly used in several experiments in PPI prediction [13]. Here, a pairwise sequence similarity score is calculated between the interacting proteins of humans. We have applied the Smith-Waterman algorithm to calculate the local alignment of two protein sequences. The alignment criteria, namely the gap penalty and fines for penalties of 10 and 0.5, respectively, and the BLOSUM62 matrix, are used for calculating the score.

3.2 Pairwise Semantic Similarity Score

One of the most common resources to compute the biological significance of PPI is Gene Ontology (GO). In many research work, the semantic similarity of GO-based genes was efficiently used to estimate gene-to-gene interactions [14]. A high semantic similarity score reveals that two proteins have identical cellular components (CC), molecular functions (MF) and are involved in similar biological processes (BP). There are multiple methods to calculate the semantic similarity of two GO terms, like, Wang [15], Resnik [16], Jiang [12], Lin [17], and Schlicker [18], etc. In this study, we have used the Wang method to calculate the three semantic similarity scores, i.e., GO-CC, GO-MF, and GO-BP between the interacting proteins.

3.3 Pairwise Domain-Domain Similarity Score

Domains are the basic building blocks of proteins. They are responsible for the overall role of a protein, e.g., the particular function and interaction, etc. We have collected the domain information of all proteins of our dataset from UniProt. Then we have calculated the domain-domain similarity score using the Jaccard similarity index between the domains of two proteins using the following formula:

$$J = \frac{\text{intersection of domains of interacting human proteins}}{\text{union of all domains of interacting human proteins}}$$

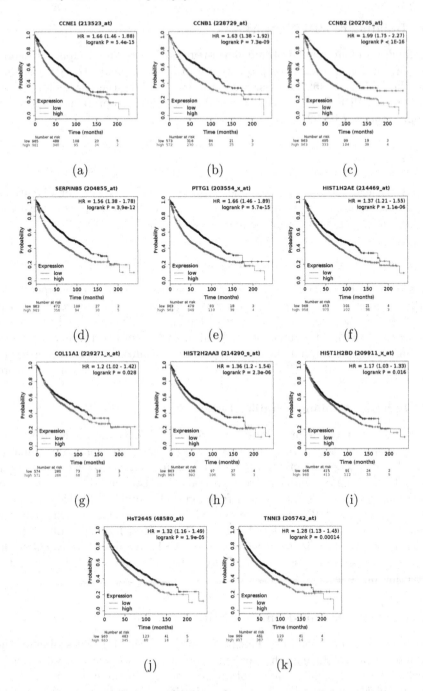

Fig. 1. Kaplan-Meier curves depicting the overall survival of key genes identified in this study. (a) CCNE1 (b) CCNB1 (c) CCNB2 and (d) SEPINB5 (e) PTTG1 (f) HIST1H2AE (g) COL11A1 and (h) HIST2H2AA3 (i) HIST1H2BD (j) HsT2645 and (k) TNNI3 are obtained using K-M plotter.

3.4 ASPL

ASPL, a topological feature, is used in many studies to demonstrate the functional cohesiveness of the proteins [19]. It shows the compactness of the network. It is calculated as the shortest path between two proteins, i.e., a path where the length of the interacting protein pair is minimum possible in the network [6]. In this study, we have calculated the ASPL of the PPIs of our dataset with respect to all the PPI of the HPRD database using the igraph package of R.

4 Results and Discussion

4.1 Construction of 1:1 Balanced Training Dataset

The PPI network constructed from DGEs consists of 1228 and 792 PPIs corresponding to the up-regulated and down-regulated proteins, respectively. We have considered these up-regulated interactions as our positive dataset and down-regulated interactions as our negative dataset. As the number of interactions in both classes is not the same, it generates the class imbalance problem. Standard classifiers like KNN, RF, Decision Tree, etc. are biased towards classes that have more instances. Therefore, there remains a high probability of misclassification of the classes [20]. To handle this problem, we have applied the K-means clustering algorithm independently to both positive and negative PPIs based on their GO-MF, GO-CC, GO-BP, and sequence similarity score. Then we have extracted 460 PPI from each of the datasets based on the proportional stratified sampling of the clusters. Now, this 1:1 positive and negative dataset is used as the training dataset for prediction.

4.2 The Classifiers' Efficiency Analysis

There are various machine learning methods used for predicting PPIs. To test efficiency based on 10-fold cross-validation techniques, we have implemented four classifiers, KNN, SVM, RF, and NNET (Table 4) on the 1:1 training dataset. The results showed that the NNET-based approach produces better average accuracy (86.92%) and kappa (73.84%) compared to traditional algorithms like KNN, SVM and RF.

The test (blind dataset) dataset is implemented before the NNET algorithm is applied to estimate potential human PPI linked to lung cancer. From (Table 5) it can be noted that better precision (75.67%), sensitivity (76.27%), F1 score (74.58%) and accuracy (70.06%) over KNN, SVM and RF classifiers are obtained by the NNET-based algorithm. Therefore, using the NNET classifier, unknown possible targets of lung cancer-related PPI have been predicted.

Table 4. Average accuracy calculation on 1:1 positive and negative training dataset using KNN, SVM, RF and NNET algorithm.

Classifier	Accuracy	Kappa
KNN	74.39	64.66
SVM	82.31	68.63
RF	84.82	70.64
NNET	**86.92**	73.84

Table 5. Analysis of different performance metrics on blind dataset using KNN, SVM, RF and NNET algorithm.

Classifier	Accuracy	Sensitivity	Specificity	F1 Score	Precision
KNN	59.45	62.45	60.67	61.03	62.32
SVM	62.39	68.42	56.67	60.71	65.38
RF	71.09	74.21	56.67	66.02	69.23
NNET	**75.67**	**76.27**	54.42	**74.58**	**70.06**

4.3 Prediction of Lung-Cancer Related PPIs

Identification of the PPI related to a particular cancer type is very crucial to analyze their pathway and other disease-promoting functionality [21]. The HPRD database update 9 has been downloaded for this, and all human PPIs from the HPRD that are not present in the training dataset are considered as testing data. With the assistance of R, the 6 combined features of these human PPIs are determined. Then, we have applied the NNET-based classifier and predicted 10042 PPI relevant to lung cancer. The predicted PPIs are given in Supplementary File S3. The flowchart of the whole methodology is shown in Supplementary File S5.

4.4 Analysis of the Predicted PPIs

To examine the biological significance of the predicted PPI relevant to lung cancer, we have calculated the degree of the proteins of the predicted PPI network using Cytoscape and identified the hub proteins. Then the relation and functionality between these hub proteins with lung cancer are further investigated with the help of published literature and the KEGG pathway.

Literature Filtering of Hub Proteins. We have searched PUBMED for exploiting some current research recognizing the influence of the hub proteins in lung cancer disease and mentioned in Supplementary File S4. Table 6 shows the top 10 hub proteins with their degree, lung cancer types, PUBMED ID, and references. All these hub proteins are either related to NSCLC or SCLC or both. The highest degree protein, CCDC85B associated with NSCLC progression and causes invasion of lung cancer cells through the oncogenic signaling pathway of active AKT/GSK3β/β-catenin [22]. In [23], the biologists collected a total of 111 patients' data of tumor and non-cancerous tissues with NSCLC. They found that the MDFI protein acts as a promoter in NSCLC, especially to females, non-smokers, and people having ages greater than 65. Pei-Fang Hung et al. found that SUMO proteins play a critical role in NSCLCs using yeast-hybrid screening [24]. TP53, the tumor suppressor protein, is the most frequently mutated protein in many human cancer diseases. The research showed that the irregularity of the TP53 protein plays a crucial function in tumor occurrence in lung epithelial cells [25]. The expression of SETDB1 is amplified in both NSCLC and SCLC cells and this over-expression causes tumor invasiveness [26]. The microRNA miR-509-5p serves as a tumor suppressor in various types of cancer and causes NSCLC by targeting YWHAG [27]. In [28], the authors showed that GRB2 protein invades in lung cancer cell lines through metastatic progression, especially in NSCLC. CREBBP mutated in SCLC and acts as an influential tumor suppressor [29]. The evidence of the association of the rest of the hub proteins with lung cancer is listed in file S4. Therefore, these hub proteins might be considered as novel targets for NSCLC and SCLC treatment.

Table 6. The top 10 hub proteins with their degree, lung cancer type, Pubmed ID and Reference.

Hub Proteins	Degree	Lung Cancer Type	PUBMED ID	Reference
CCDC85B	60	NSCLC	30242906	[30]
MDFI	55	NSCLC	29805634	[31]
SUMO4	54	NSCLC	30612578	[32]
TP53	53	NSCLC and SCLC	21331359	[33]
SETDB1	43	NSCLC and SCLC	23770855	[34]
YWHAG	40	NSCLC	27894843	[35]
GRB2	39	NSCLC	30087284	[36]
KRTAP4-12	39	NSCLC	28081052	[37]
SMAD9	38	NSCLC and SCLC	26323359	[38]
CREBBP	38	SCLC	N/A	[39]

KEGG Pathway Analysis. KEGG pathway analysis reveals the possible disease that can occur due to the involved protein set. The KEGG pathway of the 30 high-degree human proteins from predicted PPIs are calculated using DAVID 6.8 [40]. Table 7 lists the top 7 KEGG pathways with a corrected p-value (Benjamini-Hochberg) smaller than 0.05 along with human proteins. The involvement of these proteins with NSCLC and SCLC are already established in the previous section. From the table, we can note that these proteins are engaged in NSCLC along with several other types of cancers, like, prostate cancer, pancreatic cancer, etc. Research shows that viruses and other infectious

Table 7. The important KEGG pathways of the estimated top 30 lung cancer-related human proteins.

KEGG Pathways	Protein count	Human proteins
Hepatitis B (p = 1.6E-14)	14	PRKCA, GRB2, TGFBR1, STAT5A, CREBBP, TP53, RB1, STAT3, SRC, MAPK1, CASP3, EP300, MAPK3, PCNA
Viral carcinogenesis (p = 2.6E-11)	13	MAPK1, TRAF2, CASP3, YWHAG, EP300, GRB2, STAT5A, CREBBP, MAPK3, TP53, RB1, SRC, STAT3
Pathways in cancer (p = 3.7E-8)	13	PRKCA, MAPK1, TRAF2, CASP3, EP300, GRB2, STAT5A, TGFBR1, CREBBP, MAPK3, TP53, RB1, STAT3
Chronic myeloid leukemia (p = 3.3E-6)	6	MAPK1, GRB2, TGFBR1, MAPK3, TP53, RB1
Non-small cell lung cancer (p = 1.8E-5)	6	PRKCA, MAPK1, GRB2, MAPK3, TP53, RB1
Prostate cancer (p = 7.5E-6)	7	MAPK1, EP300, GRB2, MAPK3, CREBBP, TP53, RB1
Pancreatic cancer (p = 3.0E-5)	6	MAPK1, TGFBR1, MAPK3, TP53, RB1, STAT3

agents are responsible for nearly 20% of all human cancers worldwide. In [41], the authors have established the fact that some potential infectious agents cause NSCLC. They also analyzed that the patients having tumors containing viral DNA gone through better long-term survival compared with patients with viral DNA-negative tumors [41]. Chronic myeloid leukemia (CML) and cancer disease are closely related to each other as patients who suffered from CML, have a 30% higher risk of developing secondary cancer like lung cancer, thyroid cancer, prostate cancer, etc. [42]. Although the relation between hepatitis B and lung cancer still not identified [43], these proteins can fill this gap and help to understand the infection pathway. Therefore, the recent analysis of genetic markers for lung cancer provides more new perspectives than the hub genes provided by the currently available report.

4.5   Survival Analysis of Hub Genes

We have analyzed the prognostic value of these hub proteins using K–M plotter. The cutoff value is assumed to be the Hazard Ratio (HR) with 95% percent and log-rank p with < 0.05 values. We found that among the 30 genes, 23 genes are not significantly correlated with the prognosis of lung cancer whereas 7 genes are reported to be statistically significant with the occurrence of lung cancer,

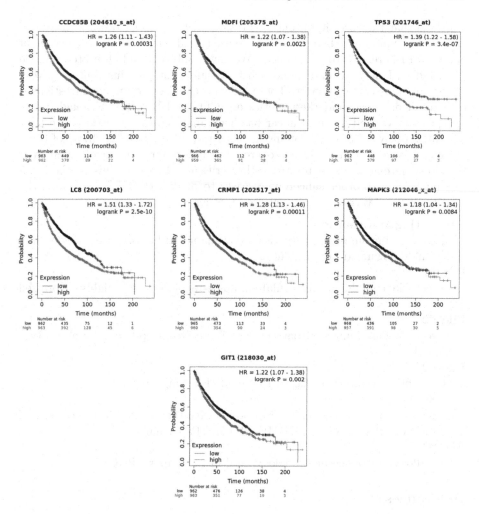

Fig. 2. In this figure, Kaplan-Meier curves indicate the overall survival of the 7 hub genes. HR: hazard ratio

considering 1925 patients' data (Fig. 2). The survival curve indicates a downward slope with an increase in time. If the slope is higher then it implies a lower survival rate.

5 Conclusion

In this study, we have identified 11 proteins as key proteins, including 10 up-regulated proteins (CCNB1, CDK1, CCNE1, CCNB2, PTTG1, COL11A1, HsT2645, HIST2H2AA3, HIST1H2BD, and HIST1H2AE) and 1 down-regulated protein (TNNI3). The survival analysis based on the expression of these proteins indicated that they are significantly associated with the poor overall survival of lung cancer patients. Then, the NNET-based prediction reveals a large set of potential PPIs related to lung cancer. We have analyzed the hub proteins of the predicted PPI network and found a list of significant proteins that play very important roles in lung cancer. These hub proteins can be further investigated for clinical diagnosis and therapeutics of SCLC and NSCLC. Although many hub proteins related to lung cancer has been analyzed over the years, we have identified a new set of hub proteins in this study. The KEGG pathway of these proteins has also been analyzed to provide support for their involvement and functional interconnection towards other critical pathways. This method can also be applied to other cancerous diseases to predict the PPIs as well as the relation of these various cancers with each other.

Supporting Information

The following supplementary files are available at: https://sites.google.com/site/conffilesdownload/supplementary

File S1

Excel file containing up-regulated, down-regulated and highly expressed genes.

File S2

Excel file containing PPI dataset constructed from up-regulated and down-regulated proteins.

File S3

Excel file containing predicted PPI related to lung cancer.

File S4

Excel file containing top 30 hub proteins with their degree in predicted PPI network, lung cancer types, PUBMED ID and Paper name.

File S5

The flowchart of the methodology used in this paper. (PNG)

References

1. Zhang, Y., Zhang, G., Li, X., Li, B., Zhang, X.: The effect of ribosomal protein s15a in lung adenocarcinoma. PeerJ **4**, e1792 (2016)
2. Guo, T., Ma, H., Zhou, Y.: Bioinformatics analysis of microarray data to identify the candidate biomarkers of lung adenocarcinoma. PeerJ **7**, e7313(2019)
3. Ni, M., et al.: Identification of candidate biomarkers correlated with the pathogenesis and prognosis of non-small cell lung cancer via integrated bioinformatics analysis. Front. Genet. **9**, 469 (2018)
4. Wu, C., Zhu, J., Zhang, X.: Integrating gene expression and protein-protein interaction network to prioritize cancer-associated genes. BMC Bioinform. **13**(1), 182 (2012)
5. Guda, P., Chittur, S.V., Guda, C.: Comparative analysis of protein-protein interactions in cancer-associated genes. Genomics Proteomics Bioinform. **7**(1–2), 25–36 (2009)
6. Zhang, W., Zhang, Q., Zhang, M., Zhang, Y., Li, F., Lei, P.: Network analysis in the identification of special mechanisms between small cell lung cancer and non-small cell lung cancer. Thorac. Cancer **5**(6), 556–564 (2014)

7. Liu, W., Rajapakse, J.C.: Fusing gene expressions and transitive protein-protein interactions for inference of gene regulatory networks. BMC Syst. Biol. **13**(2), 37 (2019)
8. Robinson, M.D., McCarthy, D.J., Smyth, G.K.: edgeR: a bioconductor package for differential expression analysis of digital gene expression data. Bioinformatics **26**(1), 139–140 (2010)
9. Smyth, G.K.: Limma: linear models for microarray data. In: Gentleman, R., Carey, V.J., Irizarry, R.A., Dudoit, S. (eds.) Bioinformatics and Computational Biology Solutions Using R and Bioconductor. Statistics for Biology and Health, pp. 397–420. Springer, New York (2005). https://doi.org/10.1007/0-387-29362-0_23
10. Tovar, C., et al.: Small-molecule MDM2 antagonists reveal aberrant p53 signaling in cancer: implications for therapy. Proc. Natl. Acad. Sci. **103**(6), 1888–1893 (2006)
11. Oyama, T., et al.: Cytochrome p450 in non-small cell lung cancer related to exogenous chemical metabolism. Front. Biosci. (Schol. Ed.) **4**, 1539–46 (2012)
12. Jiang, J.J., Conrath, D.W.: Semantic similarity based on corpus statistics and lexical taxonomy. arXiv preprint cmp-lg/9709008 (1997)
13. Yu, H., et al.: Annotation transfer between genomes: protein-protein interologs and protein-DNA regulogs. Genome Res. **14**(6), 1107–1118 (2004)
14. Peng, J., et al.: Improving the measurement of semantic similarity by combining gene ontology and co-functional network: a random walk based approach. BMC Syst. Biol. **12**(2), 18 (2018)
15. Wang, J.Z., Du, Z., Payattakool, R., Yu, P.S., Chen, C.-F.: A new method to measure the semantic similarity of go terms. Bioinformatics **23**(10), 1274–1281 (2007)
16. Resnik, P.: Semantic similarity in a taxonomy: an information-based measure and its application to problems of ambiguity in natural language. J. Artif. Intell. Res. **11**, 95–130 (1999)
17. Lin, D., et al.: An information-theoretic definition of similarity. In: ICML, vol. 98, pp. 296–304. Citeseer (1998)
18. Schlicker, A., Domingues, F.S., Rahnenführer, J., Lengauer, T.: A new measure for functional similarity of gene products based on gene ontology. BMC Bioinform. **7**(1), 302 (2006). https://doi.org/10.1186/1471-2105-7-302
19. Embar, V., Handen, A., Ganapathiraju, M.K.: Is the average shortest path length of gene set a reflection of their biological relatedness? J. Bioinform. Comput. Biol. **14**(06), 1660002 (2016)
20. Sabinasz, D.: Dealing with unbalanced classes in machine learning. Deep Ideas (2017)
21. Li, Z.: The OncoPPi network of cancer-focused protein-protein interactions to inform biological insights and therapeutic strategies. Nat. Commun. **8**, 14356 (2017)
22. Feng, Y.: CCDC85B promotes non-small cell lung cancer cell proliferation and invasion. Mol. Carcinog. **58**(1), 126–134 (2019)
23. Ma, H., et al.: Hypermethylation of MDFI promoter with NSCLC is specific for females, non-smokers and people younger than 65. Oncol. Lett. **15**(6), 9017–9024 (2018)
24. Hung, P.-F., et al.: Hypoxia-induced slug SUMOylation enhances lung cancer metastasis. J. Exp. Clin. Cancer Res. **38**(1), 5 (2019)
25. Mogi, A., Kuwano, H.: TP53 mutations in nonsmall cell lung cancer. BioMed Res. Int. **2011** (2011)
26. Rodriguez-Paredes, M., et al.: Gene amplification of the histone methyltransferase SETDB1 contributes to human lung tumorigenesis. Oncogene **33**(21), 2807 (2014)

27. Wang, P., Deng, Y., Fu, X.: MiR-509-5p suppresses the proliferation, migration, and invasion of non-small cell lung cancer by targeting YWHAG. Biochem. Biophys. Res. Commun. **482**(4), 935–941 (2017)

28. Mitra, P., Kalailingam, P., Tan, H., Thanabalu, T.: Overexpression of GRB2 enhances epithelial to mesenchymal transition of A549 cells by upregulating snail expression. Cells **7**(8), 97 (2018)

29. Jia, D., et al.: Crebbp loss drives small cell lung cancer and increases sensitivity to HDAC inhibition. Cancer Discov. **8**(11), 1422–1437 (2018)

30. Oughtred, R., et al.: The BioGRID interaction database: 2019 update. Nucleic Acids Res. **47**(D1), D529–D541 (2018)

31. Xenarios, I., Rice, D.W., Salwinski, L., Baron, M.K., Marcotte, E.M., Eisenberg, D.: DIP: the database of interacting proteins. Nucleic Acids Res. **28**(1), 289–291 (2000)

32. Chatr-Aryamontri, A., et al.: Mint: the molecular interaction database. Nucleic Acids Res. **35**(suppl_1), D572–D574 (2006)

33. Zahiri, J., Hannon Bozorgmehr, J. and Masoudi-Nejad, A.: Computational prediction of protein-protein interaction networks: algorithms and resources. Current Genomics **14**(6), 397–414 (2013)

34. Dong, J., Horvath, S.: Understanding network concepts in modules. BMC Syst. Biol. **1**(1), 24 (2007)

35. Albert, I., Albert, R.: Conserved network motifs allow protein-protein interaction prediction. Bioinformatics **20**(18), 3346–3352 (2004)

36. Ma'ayan, A.: Insights into the organization of biochemical regulatory networks using graph theory analyses. J. Biol. Chem. **284**(9), 5451–5455 (2009)

37. Yook, S.-H., Oltvai, Z.N., Barabási, A.-L.: Functional and topological characterization of protein interaction networks. Proteomics **4**(4), 928–942 (2004)

38. Zhang, L.V., et al.: Motifs, themes and thematic maps of an integrated saccharomyces cerevisiae interaction network. J. Biol. **4**(2), 6 (2005)

39. Liu, S., Liu, C., Deng, L.: Machine learning approaches for protein-protein interaction hot spot prediction: progress and comparative assessment. Molecules **23**(10), 2535 (2018)

40. Dennis, G.: DAVID: database for annotation, visualization, and integrated discovery. Genome Biol. **4**(9), R60 (2003)

41. Robinson, L.A.: Molecular evidence of viral DNA in non-small cell lung cancer and non-neoplastic lung. Br. J. Cancer **115**(4), 497 (2016)

42. Miranda, M., et al.: Secondary malignancies in chronic myeloid leukemia patients after imatinib-based treatment: long-term observation in CML study IV. Leukemia **30**(6), 1255 (2016)

43. Song, C., et al.: Associations between hepatitis B virus infection and risk of all cancer types. JAMA Netw. Open **2**(6), e195718–e195718 (2019)

44. Dehan, E., et al.: Chromosomal aberrations and gene expression profiles in non-small cell lung cancer. Lung Cancer **56**(2), 175–184 (2007)

45. Szklarczyk, D., et al.: STRING v11: protein-protein association networks with increased coverage, supporting functional discovery in genome-wide experimental datasets. Nucleic Acids Res. **47**(D1), D607–D613 (2019)

ValveCare: A Fuzzy Based Intelligent Model for Predicting Heart Diseases Using Arduino Based IoT Infrastructure

Kaustabh Ganguly, Amiya Karmakar, and Partha Sarathi Banerjee[(✉)]

Kalyani Government Engineering College, Kalyani, West Bengal, India
{kaustabh.ganguly,amiya.karmakar}@kgec.edu.in

Abstract. IoT-based portable medical diagnostic tools like smartwatches, health monitors, etc. are extensively used for real-time data collection and monitoring. There are a plethora of options available for tech stacks to be used and open source frameworks for managing a complete internet of things system. Recognizing the pattern of fluctuation of medical data and making a decision on the probability of disease before the onset of any symptom, puts forth a big challenge for the medical practitioners. We propose our model ValveCare which leverages the power of machine learning to find patterns in the data for finding thresholds of optimal values of each parameter and use those thresholds to predict with a certain probability whether a subject is going to have cardiovascular diseases (CVD) in near future. We have opted to use fuzzy logic to find the probability of chances of CVD of the user directly in an android app. ValveCare uses an Arduino based microcontroller to take the heart rate of a subject through a pulse sensor, and temperature through a temperature sensor. The Arduino is linked with our ValveCare app where the user inputs other details like total cholesterol levels, age, and other relevant parameters and our model computes and shows the inference instantly in the app with the likelihood of the subject having CVD in the future.

Keywords: Arduino · CVD · IoT · Machine learning

1 Introduction

Sensor based wearable devices are extensively used nowadays for measuring various physiological parameters like heart beat, blood pressure etc. These devices usually provide recorded data on real-time basis but are unable to read the pattern of the data and predict the probability of any disease. Manisha et al. [5] and Li et al. [6] has shown the use of smart monitoring systems that can reduce the risk of heart attack and heart-related ailments by constant monitoring of sensed data. Similar works are found in [40]. With the advent of new smart-watches, data collection has been quite easy and hence literatures based on smart devices like [7] have been increased in numbers. Our proposed model ValveCare is a cheap and effective alternative to the likes of the AppleWatch and Fitbit. It can be built with a fraction of a cost using an Arduino microcontroller and an android app that is used to connect to the microcontroller. The IoT can be referred to

© Springer Nature Switzerland AG 2021
P. Dutta et al. (Eds.): CICBA 2021, CCIS 1406, pp. 229–242, 2021.
https://doi.org/10.1007/978-3-030-75529-4_18

as a miniature version of edge computing which harnesses the power of small, efficient, computers that can compute and act upon electrical input stimuli from the sensors to which it is connected to. Big Data [1] is very much necessary in storing a huge amount of sensor data recordings efficiently which can be further processed by the intelligent layers. In our model, we have tried to push boundaries by integrating this future tech into the medical domain; to make a better lifestyle for users and predict the chances of cardiovascular diseases quickly and efficiently.

2 IoT System Architecture

2.1 Design

We are using an Arduino Uno board which is acting as our microcontroller, and we are using a pulse sensor and a temperature sensor module that connects to the Arduino board. The board is connected to the internet with a wifi ESP8266 module. The app ValveCare is an android based application (we plan on extending the app to iOS in the future) that works closely with the Arduino and interacts through the cloud. It collects data from the two sensors and uploads the data to a remote server. It then fetches the data through an API call and stores it in the device for further processing. and further prompts the user to input their total cholesterol level, age, gender, if they have any breathing problem (yes/no), and if they do regular exercise (yes/no). Then the app uses the sensor data and these input data to infer the probability of having CVD in the future using Fuzzy Logic (Fig. 1).

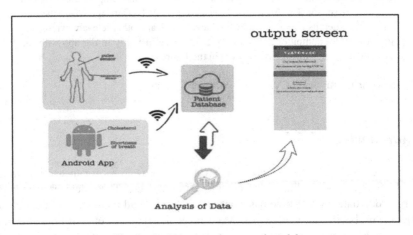

Fig. 1. Architecture of proposed model

2.2 Software

To connect to the cloud we used google spreadsheet, where the sensor data is being uploaded in a specific cell in the spreadsheet and we are fetching the data from the sheet using API calls in the app. We are using Google Spreadsheet for its ease of use and demo purposes. Once the system is integrated on the scale, a dedicated server can be used. We have trained our data with independent variables - Cholesterol, Heart Rate, Breathing Trouble(binary), Temperature, Age, Gender, Regular Exercise (binary). Our dependent variable is our target (binary) value which signifies the onset of CVD in the future. The algorithm we chose is XGBoost with cross-validation [17] because it gives good results in a small dataset [13] and it performs slightly better than Random Forest Classifier (based on our empirical observations) [14]. The other algorithms we tested are the Support Vector Machine (SVM) Classifier [15] and the Naive Bayes Classifier [16]. All of which gave less accurate results. Our model's accuracy is 94% butit will vary depending on the quantity of data. As we had fewer imbalanced data, we synthetically augmented with SMOTE. But having greater quantities of already balanced data will give better results. Once our model is trained, we extracted the F-Score from the XGBoost model which gives us an idea about the most important features. Our results show the most important parameters are cholesterol, age, temperature, and regular exercise (ranked from most important to least). Gender and breathing trouble showed a very negligible correlation as we can see in Fig. 2.

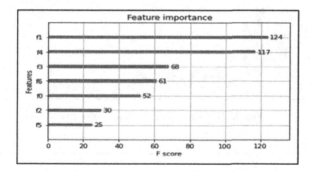

Fig. 2. Most important features

In Fig. 2, Y-axis has some variables which are respectively - f0 = heart rate, f1 = cholesterol, f2 = Breathing Trouble, f3 = temperature, f4 = age, f5 = gender, f6 = regular exercise. The F score or F1 score [29] of the parameters are as follows (in Y axis): f1 > f4 > f3 > f6 > f0 > f2 > f5.

We get the thresholds of cholesterol, heart rate, and temperature by making a custom test set containing all possible values of these three parameters while keeping other parameters constant at normal levels (explained in the detail in Sect. 3 - Detailed Analysis - C. Threshold Finding). According to our model gender is playing an insignificant role in predicting the results. And we kept the age parameter constant because, each individual is different and with different ages, different thresholds will be significant. Our model can be expanded to test all the different ages and their threshold of cholesterol, heart rate, and body temperature. After we got our thresholds, we followed the method of Ephzibah et al. [18] and created three triangular membership functions, defined by three zones according to our threshold which we put in the model manually. It outputs the probability by fuzzy logic. The most important features are only relevant to thresholds. The machine learning model is not predicting the CVD instead, the fuzzy logic we implemented using the thresholds is used to predict the chances of CVD and there the features are not weighted as we see in Fig. 2. The fuzzy logic we used is defined in detail in Sect. 3.4.

3   Detailed Analysis

Our data has 8 columns namely, Person ID, Heart Rate, Total Cholesterol, Breathing Trouble (Yes/No), Temperature, Age, Gender, Regular Exercise (Yes/No), and CVD.

3.1   Preprocessing

To understand the data we plot three major columns - Total Cholesterol (Fig. 3), Heart Rate (Fig. 4), and Temperature (Fig. 5) as histogram charts.

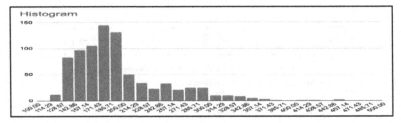

Fig. 3. Histogram plot of Total Cholesterol

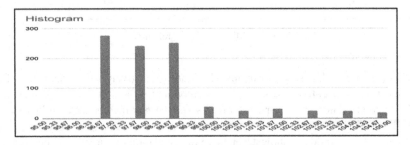

Fig. 4. Histogram plot of Heart Rate (BPM)

We can see the skewed normal distribution nature of the data. In the above diagrams (Fig. 3, Fig. 4, and Fig. 5) we can see classic histogram charts of the input data of our subjects. We plotted the data to understand the patterns of the distribution which is as expected - a slightly skewed normal distribution. In Fig. 3 - on the X-axis we have the cholesterol value in mg/dL as points and on the Y-axis we have the number of subjects having those. Now when we plot the histogram charts, we can see the majority of the people fall in the 140–200 mg/dL range and as the values in the x-axis extend towards

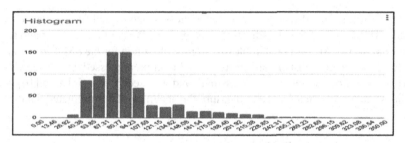

Fig. 5. Histogram plot of Temperature

the extremities, the number of people decreases exponentially. Now, coming to Fig. 4, - on the X-axis we took the points of heart rate in bpm, and on the Y-axis we took the number of people having them. We can see the majority of the people fall in the 60–100 bpm range and as the bpm goes towards extremities, the bars representing several people diminishes exponentially. Further coming to Fig. 5. - on the X-axis we can see the temperature points measured in Fahrenheit. And on the Y-axis we put the number of people as points. Now, in this plot, as the temperature has a very little variance, we can see the majority of temperature values measured are in the normal body temperature zone with some very few outliers in extremities.

All of these give us a deeper understanding of the data we are dealing with and in the next sections, we have used the data to build a machine learning model to find the threshold values for implementing the fuzzy membership function. We use this limited data and use under-sampling and oversampling to create a bigger augmented dataset for training our model. To achieve this we first compared SMOTE [20] and ADASYN [21] algorithms and settled with SMOTE and implemented a custom model with an ensemble of Borderline SMOTE [22], SVMSMOTE [23], and SMOTE ENN [24] (by Batista et al.) to soothe out the imbalanced dataset. Zeng et al. show in their paper [25] how SMOTE works wonderfully on imbalanced medical data.

3.2 Model

We split the data into a training set and a test set in the ratio of 8:2. Now for the classification task, we tried and tested several algorithms including naive Bayes classifier, support vector machine classifier, and random forest classifier, [14–16]. We directly used the opensource library scikit learn for our experimentation [41]. We also tried Tianqi Chen and Carlos Guestrin's 2016 SIGKDD conference paper [11] which implements a robust decision tree model (CART - Classification and Regression Trees) [11], bagging (using multiple ensembles of independent trees to make decision process), Random Forest [14], gradient boosting (as demonstrated by Friedman et al. [26]). We chose XGBoost because it is a gradient boosting machine [26] that fundamentally implements parallelization of inner loops and uses parallel threads to train the model which results in blazing fast execution. It also implements a greedy tree pruning algorithm which improves computational performance. It also optimizes the hardware by allocating internal buffers in each thread to store gradient statistics. Also, it adds regularization (both L1 and L2) [27] to prevent overfitting and also adds sparsity awareness which is vital for imbalanced medical data. The details of the classification strategy are - We split the training and testing on the ratio of 9:1. We used the "imblearn" library of python for the SMOTE variations. Then we used the XGBoost classifier directly to fit our preprocessed data. Then we used the cross-validation estimator as a "classifier" and we used cross-validation [16] with a splitting strategy parameter as 10 to measure the accuracy of our predicted data.

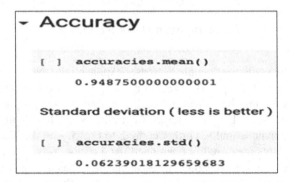

Fig. 6. Accuracy of the trained model with a standard deviation

After we fine-tuned hyperparameters we got around 94% accuracy (Fig. 6).

3.3 Threshold Finding

We made a custom test set to find out the upper threshold of each parameter (Total Cholesterol, Heart Rate, etc. when keeping other parameters constant). We took a range of values of heart rate (40–150), Cholesterol (80–300), and temperature (96.5–103.5) mutually exclusive while keeping other parameters at a normal level based on published research on normal values, [2–4]. The normal level is defined as in Table 1.

Table 1. Normal values that we took

Heart rate	Cholesterol	Breathing trouble	Temperature	Age	Gender	Regular exercise
72	150	0	98.7	40	0	0

The concept that we used is that, we will sequentially input data starting from minimum and going to maximum, if we see the prediction is positive for CVD for consecutive test entries, then we will consider the first of the three entries as our upper threshold. For example, keeping the other 6 parameters constant, we input heart rate starting from 40 and increment it by 1, and check when the prediction becomes positive. If it starts to become positive then we will take the base value. After inputting our custom data, we got a list of upper threshold values that we will use in our fuzzy model in the next step.

An important thing to note is that we took the age as 40, but as CVD depends also on age, we can use this technique to find the thresholds for all ages. For simplicity, we took the age as 40. The upper threshold values that we got are:

Heart Rate: 76, Cholesterol: 289, Temperature: 100.02

Similarly, we found the lower threshold values by varying the test data and checking when the negative outcome becomes positive, and it came out as:
Heart Rate: 72, Cholesterol: 142, Temperature: 98.3.

3.4 Fuzzy Model

In this proposed model inputs are given to fuzzifier. Fuzzifier fuzzify the crips inputs. Based on fuzzy rules output is generated. Defuzzificaton is applied on the output. As per our findings, the lower threshold is 72 bpm for heart rate and the upper threshold is 76 bpm. The lower threshold for our Cholesterol level is 142 mg/dl and the upper limit is 289 mg/dl. We define a fuzzy membership logic where we categorize three ranges - low, medium, and high (Fig. 7 and Fig. 8). The ranges overlap and create a probabilistic output. The fuzzy logic model is inspired by the works of Ephzibah et al. [30, 31] and Zimmermann, Hans-Jürgen's [32].

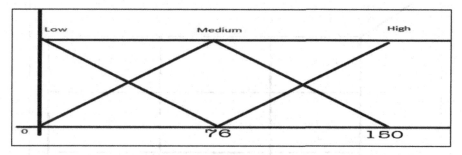

Fig. 7. Fuzzy Membership diagram for heart rate

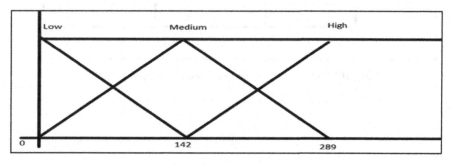

Fig. 8. Fuzzy Membership diagram for cholesterol

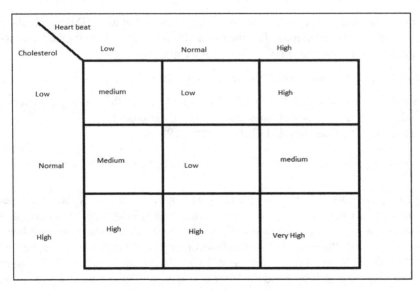

Fig. 9. Fuzzy matrix for people with shortness of breath

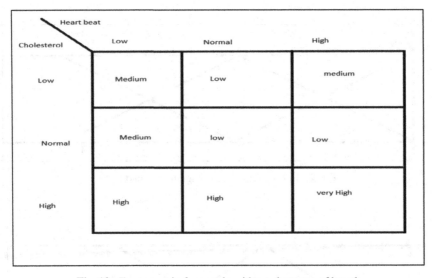

Fig. 10. Fuzzy matrix for people without shortness of breath

Our model takes the input from the app and tallies it with the matrix (Fig. 9 and Fig. 10). It then calculates the probability and then it outputs the probability as a result.

If the user has shortness of breath, the matrix defined in Fig. 9 comes into play, the matrix defined in Fig. 10 comes into play. Based on the above fuzzy matrices fuzzy, the system output is generated as presented in Fig. 11.

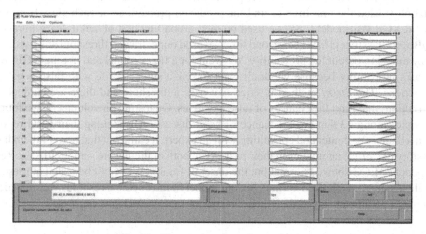

Fig. 11. The results of our fuzzy system

4   Output Architecture

The sensors collect the temperature and heart rate from the user and then the user inputs his/her total cholesterol levels in the ValveCare app and then our fuzzy model loaded with the thresholds predicts the result and shows in the app instantly. It shows helpful links in managing health (internet connection is needed for that) as presented in Fig. 12.

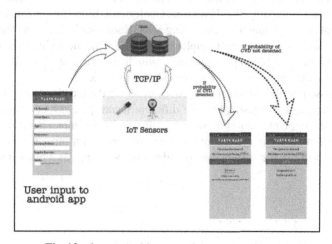

Fig. 12. Output Architecture of the proposed model

5   Testing

To test our model we created some testing data based on real-world samples. In our 50 rows of test data, each subject's CVD probability was recorded two times. The logistic function is used the first time to find the predicted probability of each class from the trained XGBoost model [28] (we used predict_proba function of scikit_learn library's XGBoost Classifier [16]). The second time we used our extracted threshold and used our fuzzy model to output the probability. We went for a fuzzy model and not the XGBoost model's probability because we don't want to risk a subject's life with false-negative predictions. The Fuzzy method is safer as it uses a threshold and there are hardcoded instructions that limit the chances of false negatives. On testing on volunteers, we found 2 people among 13 that have a chance of heart disease. After taking their ECG report from a diagnostic center and consulting with an expert, it came out that both of them had a history of cardiac anomalies in their past. Also, both of them were senior citizens. Rest 11 people's ECG showed normal but the onset of future CVD can't be tested at present but their symptoms showed normal. So, our model found out the thresholds within which if a user's parameter stayed then their chances of future CVD gets decreased.

6   Comparison with Other Works

The strategy we used was to find thresholds of different health parameters that lead to CVD in the future. The exact same type of work has not been done, but there are three particularly interesting workswe that have similar goals but with a different approach. We are going to compare similar works done by others, with our model. We have chosen three models proposed by Sanjeev et al. [33], M. Kowsigan et al. [34], and NeeruPathania et al. [35]. We refer to them by Model 1, Model 2, and Model 3 respectively. The comparison has been based on a SWOT strategic analysis method [36] which will show us the Strengths, Weaknesses, Opportunities, and Threats of the proposed models.

Model 1 uses Chest pain, Blood Pressure, Cholesterol, Blood Sugar, Maximum Heart Rate, Old Peak as input data, Corresponding SWOT analysis is shown in Table 2.

Model 3 uses almost similar principles as model 1. This model has used data in the form of chest pain type, blood pressure, maximum heart rate, and old peak. The SWOT analysis corresponding to model 3 has been shown in Table 3.

Our proposed model Valvecare improves upon all the existing models with 94% accuracy in finding the threshold of the different health parameters. We propose the hardware-based implementation as well as software-based implementation. The proposed model covers complete end-to-end infrastructure from input to output and the end-user who will use the system can treat the inner workings as a black box and treat

Table 2. SWOT analysis of Model 1 [33] and Model 2 [34]

Strengths	Weaknesses
1. Lab database. They collected and sampled quality data 2. They used the Mamdani inference method [37] 3. 90% accuracy according to expert	1. The model is very general and based on global threshold values. No method to segregate threshold values according to age 2. No implementation details were discussed 3. Artificial Neural Network is mentioned but no application is discussed
Opportunities	Threats
1. Used to gauge real-time patient metrics, in hospitals around Punjab, India 2. Very naive implementation and easy to implement	1. IoT systems integrated with Artificial Intelligence will replace this old model 2. Hardware implementation is not discussed properly, so wrong implementation can lead to different results

Table 3. SWOT analysis of Model 3 [35]

Strengths	Weaknesses
1. Worked on the dataset taken from various hospitals of Amritsar 2. 92% accuracy compared to experts	1. The model is very general and based on global threshold values. No method to segregate threshold values according to age 2. Blood sugar level has very little correlation to cardiovascular diseases. The effects are still in research 3. Genetic algorithms and neural networks are mentioned as better alternatives but never used in any implementation
Opportunities	Threats
1. Used to gauge real-time patient metrics, in hospitals around Amritsar 2. Very naive implementation and easy to implement	1. IoT systems integrated with Artificial Intelligence will replace this old model 2. Hardware implementation not discussed properly. The wrong implementations can lead to drastically different results

the system as a diagnostic tool. Our model predicts the future onset of CVD, as we discussed in Sect. 5 - "Testing" until we wait for few years to test the subjects we tested on in our study we can't accurately measure the success rate of our predictions (Table 4).

Table 4. Comparison with other models based on parametric values

Parameters	Model 1 [33]	Model 2 [34]	Model 3 [35]	Proposed model
Parameters that require invasive methods	2	2	2	1
The technique used to find the threshold	No method to segregate threshold values. Threshold values are given manually	No method to segregate threshold values. Threshold values are given manually	No method to segregate threshold values. Threshold values are given manually	Threshold values are calculated from the Previous dataset
Accuracy	90%	90%	92%	94%

7 Conclusion

ValveCare is a new direction towards robust edge computing which is one step closer in the direction of smart medical infrastructure. With the modern sensors and medical devices launching every single month, collecting data and using our ValveCare ecosystem to estimate the likelihood of CVD will hopefully save millions of lives. If the collected data set is small numbers, synthetic data generation algorithms like SMOTE [20] or ADASYN [21] can be used to create data points as we did in our work. Artificial Neural Networks (ANN) can also be used and we are working on that. Our proposed model is tested in a small research environment and the results we obtained may vary depending on the quality of data collected, mainly focused on demographic, patient age group, and tools to collect data. We are further working on our model to include more features and fine-tuning it for better usability.

References

1. Chen, M., Mao, S., Liu, Y.: Big data: a survey. Mob. Netw. Appl. **19**(2), 171–209 (2014)
2. Sniderman, A., et al.: Association of coronary atherosclerosis with hyperapobetalipoproteinemia [increased protein but normal cholesterol levels in human plasma low density (beta) lipoproteins]. Proc. Natl. Acad. Sci. **77**(1), 604–608 (1980)
3. Acharya, R., et al.: Heart rate analysis in normal subjects of various age groups. Biomed. Eng. Online **3**(1), 24 (2004)
4. Sund-Levander, M., Forsberg, C., Wahren, L.K.: Normal oral, rectal, tympanic and axillary body temperature in adult men and women: a systematic literature review. Scand. J. Caring Sci. **16**(2), 122–128 (2002)
5. Manisha, M., et al.: IoT on heart attack detection and heart rate monitoring. Int. J. Innov. Eng. Technol. (IJIET) **7**(2), 459 (2016). ISSN 2319-1058
6. Li, C., Hu, X., Zhang, L.: The IoT-based heart disease monitoring system for pervasive healthcare service. Proc. Comput. Sci. **112**, 2328–2334 (2017)
7. Hsiao, K.-L.: What drives Smartwatch adoption intention? Comparing Apple and non-Apple watches. Library Hi Tech (2017). https://www.emerald.com/insight/content/doi/10.1108/LHT-09-2016-0105/full/html

8. Palaniappan, S., Awang, R.: Intelligent heart disease prediction system using data mining techniques. In: 2008 IEEE/ACS International Conference on Computer Systems and Applications. IEEE (2008)

9. Soni, J., et al.: Predictive data mining for medical diagnosis: an overview of heart disease prediction. Int. J. Comput. Appl. **17**(8), 43–48 (2011)

10. Jabbar, M.A., Deekshatulu, B.L., Chandra, P.: Heart disease prediction using lazy associative classification. In: 2013 International Mutli-Conference on Automation, Computing, Communication, Control and Compressed Sensing (iMac4s). IEEE (2013)

11. Chen, T., Guestrin, C.: XGBoost: a scalable tree boosting system. In: Proceedings of the 22nd ACMSIGKDD International Conference on Knowledge Discovery and Data Mining (2016)

12. Torlay, L., Perrone-Bertolotti, M., Thomas, E., Baciu, M.: Machine learning–XGBoost analysis of language networks to classify patients with epilepsy. Brain Inform. **4**(3), 159–169 (2017). https://doi.org/10.1007/s40708-017-0065-7

13. Liaw, A., Wiener, M.: Classification and regression by randomForest. R News **2**(3), 18–22 (2002)

14. Keerthi, S.S., et al.: Improvements to Platt's SMO algorithm for SVM classifier design. Neural Comput. **13**(3), 637–649 (2001)

15. Rish, I.: An empirical study of the Naive Bayes classifier. In: IJCAI 2001 Workshop on Empirical Methods in Artificial Intelligence, vol. 3, no. 22 (2001)

16. Kohavi, R.: A study of cross-validation and bootstrap for accuracy estimation and model selection. IJCAI **14**(2), 1137–1145 (1995)

17. Ephzibah, E. P., Sundarapandian, V.: A fuzzy rule based expert system for effective heart disease diagnosis. In: Meghanathan, N., Chaki, N., Nagamalai, D. (eds.) CCSIT 2012. LNICST, vol. 85, pp. 196–203. Springer, Heidelberg (2012). https://doi.org/10.1007/978-3-642-27308-7_20

18. Liu, W., et al.: Large-margin softmax loss for convolutional neural networks. ICML **2**(3), 7 (2016)

19. Chawla, N.V., et al.: SMOTE: synthetic minority over-sampling technique. J. Artif. Intell. Res. **16**, 321–357 (2002)

20. Das, R., Turkoglu, I., Sengur, A.: Effective diagnosis of heart disease through neural networks ensembles. Expert Syst. Appl. **36**(4), 7675–7680 (2009)

21. He, H., et al.: ADASYN: adaptive synthetic sampling approach for imbalanced learning. In: 2008 IEEE International Joint Conference on Neural Networks (IEEE World Congress on Computational Intelligence). IEEE (2008)

22. Han, H., Wang, WY., Mao, B.H.: Borderline-SMOTE: a new over-sampling method in imbalanced data sets learning. In: Huang, D.S., Zhang, X.P., Huang, G.B. (eds.) ICIC 2005. LNCS, vol. 3644, pp. 878–887. Springer, Berlin, Heidelberg (2005). https://doi.org/10.1007/11538059_91

23. Taneja, S., Suri, B., Kothari, C.: Application of balancing techniques with ensemble approach for credit card fraud detection. In: 2019 International Conference on Computing, Power and Communication Technologies (GUCON). IEEE (2019)

24. Batista, G.E.A.P.A., Prati, R.C., Monard, M.C.: A study of the behavior of several methods for balancing machine learning training data. ACM SIGKDD Explor. Newslett. **6**(1), 20–29 (2004)

25. Zeng, M., et al.: Effective prediction of three common diseases by combining SMOTE with Tomek links technique for imbalanced medical data. In: 2016 IEEE International Conference of Online Analysis and Computing Science (ICOACS). IEEE (2016)

26. Safavian, S.R., Landgrebe, D.: A survey of decision tree classifier methodology. IEEE Trans. Syst. Man Cybern. **21**(3), 660–674 (1991)

27. Friedman, J.H.: Greedy function approximation: a gradient boosting machine. Ann. Stat. **29**, 1189–1232 (2001)

28. Girosi, F., Jones, M., Poggio, T.: Regularization theory and neural networks architectures. Neural Comput. **7**(2), 219–269 (1995)

29. Wang, X., Yan, X., Ma, Y.: Research on user consumption behavior prediction based on improved XGBoost algorithm. In: 2018 IEEE International Conference on Big Data (Big Data). IEEE (2018)

30. https://xgboost.readthedocs.io/en/latest/python/python_api.html

31. Goutte, C., Gaussier, E.: A probabilistic interpretation of precision, recall and F-score, with implication for evaluation. In: Losada, D.E., Fernández-Luna, J.M. (eds.) Advances in Information Retrieval. LNCS, vol. 3408, pp. 345–359. Springer, Heidelberg (2005). https://doi.org/10.1007/978-3-540-31865-1_25

32. Ephzibah, E.P.: Cost effective approach on feature selection using genetic algorithms and fuzzy logic for diabetes diagnosis. arXiv preprint arXiv:1103.0087 (2011)

33. Ephzibah, E.P., Sundarapandian, V.: A neuro fuzzy expert system for heart disease diagnosis. Comput. Sci. Eng. **2**(1), 17 (2012)

34. Zimmermann, H.-J.: Fuzzy Set Theory—And Its Applications. Springer, Dordrecht (2011). https://doi.org/10.1007/978-94-010-0646-0

35. Kumar, S., Kaur, G.: Detection of heart diseases using fuzzy logic. Int. J. Eng. Trends Technol. (IJETT) **4**(6), 2694–2699 (2013)

36. Kowsigan, M., et al.: Heart disease prediction by analysing various parameters using fuzzy logic. Pak. J. Biotechnol .**14**(2), 157–161 (2017)

37. Pathania, N., Ritika: Implementation of fuzzy controller for diagnose of patient heart disease. Int. J. Innov. Sci. Eng. Technol. **2**(4), 694–698 (2015)

38. Hill, T., Westbrook, R.: SWOT analysis: it's time for a product recall. Long Range Plann. **30**(1), 46–52 (1997)

39. Iancu, I.: A Mamdani type fuzzy logic controller. In: Fuzzy Logic: Controls, Concepts, Theories and Applications, pp. 325–350 (2012)

40. Kowsigan, M., Balasubramanie, P.: An improved job scheduling in cloud environment using auto-associative-memory network. Asian J. Res. Soc. Sci. Humanit. **6**(12), 390–410 (2016)

41. Kooshki, A., Mohajeri, N., Movahhedi, A.: Prevalence of CVD risk factors related to diet in patients referring to Modarres Hospital in Tehran IN 1379 (1999), 17–22 (2003)

42. Diwakar, M., et al.: Latest trends on heart disease prediction using machine learning and image fusion. Mater. Today: Proc. **37**, 3213–3218 (2020)

43. Pedregosa, F., et al.: Scikit-learn: machine learning in Python. J. Mach. Learn. Res. **12**, 2825–2830 (2011)

Abstractive Text Summarization Approaches with Analysis of Evaluation Techniques

Abdullah Faiz Ur Rahman Khilji⬤, Utkarsh Sinha⬤, Pintu Singh⬤,
Adnan Ali⬤, and Partha Pakray^(✉)⬤

Department of Computer Science and Engineering,
National Institute of Technology Silchar, Silchar, Assam, India
{abdullah_ug,utkarsh_ug,pintu_ug,adnan_ug,partha}@cse.nits.ac.in

Abstract. In today's world where all the information is available at our fingertips, it is becoming more and more difficult to retrieve vital information from large documents without reading the whole text. Large textual documents require a great deal of time and energy to understand and extract the key components from the text. In such a case, summarized versions of these documents provide a great deal of flexibility in understanding the context and important points of the text. In our work, we have attempted to prepare a baseline machine learning model to summarize textual documents, and have worked with various methodologies. The summarization system takes the raw text as an input and produces the predicted summary as an output. We have also used various evaluation metrics for the analysis of the predicted summary. Both extractive and abstractive based text summarization have been described and experimented with. We have also verified this baseline system on three different evaluation metrics i.e. BLEU, ROUGE, and a textual entailment method. We have also done an in-depth discussion of the three evaluation techniques used, and have systematically proved the advantages of using a semantic-based evaluation technique to calculate the overall summarization score of a text document.

Keywords: Text summarization · Abstractive · Evaluation · Entailment · Adversarial · Attention

1 Introduction

Automatic text summarization is a technique to generate a concise and fluent summary that captures the main idea of a given text so that humans can understand the essence of long documents in comparatively lesser time. Broadly speaking, two different approaches are used for text summarization. The first one is an extractive approach in which only the important sentences, keywords, or phrases from the original text are identified, extracted, and combined to produce a summary. The second approach is abstractive summarization. This is in

P. Dutta et al. (Eds.): CICBA 2021, CCIS 1406, pp. 243–258, 2021.
https://doi.org/10.1007/978-3-030-75529-4_19

contrast to the extractive approach wherein only the sentences that are present in the original text are used. Here, the original sentence might not be present in the summarized text. It produces a more powerful, human-like summary by generating new keywords, phrases, or sentences and combining them to form a summary.

Apart from experimenting with our baseline model on benchmark datasets, we have tabulated results on major evaluation techniques used to evaluate those summaries. In addition to BLEU and ROUGE scores, we have also used a textual entailment method to evaluate those summaries and have discussed the benefits of using a semantic-based evaluation system.

The rest of the paper is divided into the following sections. Related works are briefly discussed in Sect. 2. The dataset description and data statistics are given in Sect. 3. The experimental setup is described in Sect. 4 and experimentation is discussed in Sect. 5. Section 6 discusses the different evaluation techniques used. The obtained result and its analysis are tabulated in Sect. 7. And finally, we conclude with discussion and conclusion in Sect. 8. We also include the future works in this last section.

2   Related Works

Upon investigating different methodologies for text summarization, we found two popular approaches as discussed by [33] viz. extractive summarization [32] and abstractive summarization [5]. Some works have also shown an ensemble model using both the methodologies to leverage the textual corpora [15]. The work on extractive text summarization dates long back to 1958, wherein [29] used word and phrase frequencies to detect important sentences in the document. A similar approach was used by [7], which used a log-likelihood ratio test to detect defining words of the to-be-produced abstract. The work by [9] leveraged latent semantic analysis to garner frequency distribution features and to perform singular value decomposition. The generated matrix was then used to predict the sentence which would be present in the summary. Later works by [39,45] used machine learning-based techniques to classify the source sentences into "is" summary or "is not" summary. Graph-based techniques using the modified versions of the text rank algorithm were used by [30]. The work by [8] and [32] showed similar techniques but used different weighting formulas. The work by [27], utilized a generative model for summary generation using bidirectional LSTM and a discriminative model as a binary classifier that distinguishes the summary generated by machines from the ones generated by humans. There has also been sufficient work done to use pre-trained encoders for summary generation [28].

A bottom-up tree-based technique based on sentence fusion is provided by [3]. A template-based summarization module was provided by [12]. Many researchers have also proposed various ontology-based methods to perform document summarizations [22]. Semantic role labeling has been used by [16]. Some of the summarization techniques has also been discussed by [21]. Text summarization is an essential tool that can be used in a variety of downstream tasks like question-answering [18, 19, 23], review summarization [49] and also in healthcare [17]. Since this summarization task has large number of applications, it's evaluation is necessary. Thus, for evaluation too, there are many measures with which we can evaluate the summary [44]. Some of them include content-based measures like cosine similarity, unit overlaps, pyramids [35], bilingual evaluation understudy (BLEU) [37] score, recall-oriented understudy for gisting evaluation (ROUGE) [26]. In our work for the baseline system, we have used extractive and abstractive based text summarization consisting of encoders and decoders. Further details regarding the model are discussed in Sect. 4.

For evaluation, we have used BLEU [37], ROUGE [26] and a textual entailment technique to determine how good the accuracy really is. Respective scores can be viewed in Tables 4, 5, 6, 7, 8, 9, 10, 11, 13 and 14.

Table 1. Gigaword dataset

	Train	Validation	Test
Count	287,227	13,368	11,490
Size	1.2 GB + 92 MB	52 MB + 4.8 MB	45 MB + 3.9 MB

Table 2. DUC 2003

	Train
Count	624
Size	44 KB

Table 3. DUC 2004

	Test
Count	500
Size	36 KB

3   Dataset

In order to prepare the baseline system of the extractive based text summarization model, we have used the TextRank algorithm on the Amazon fine food reviews[1] dataset. This algorithm uses a graph-based unsupervised approach to summarize the raw text into a summary. The data consists of half a million reviews collected over a period of 10 years. Each review has an average length of 75 words and also has a user-specified title. Since this dataset has very small textual summaries or titles, we used this dataset only for extractive text summarization.

For the abstractive text summarization model, following [25], we have used the Gigaword [10] dataset and the Document Understanding Conferences (DUC) [36] corpora for training, evaluation, and testing the model. The Gigaword is a summarization dataset based on the annotated Gigaword[2] corpora. Only one sentence i.e. the first sentence is extracted from various news with headlines, to form a sentence summary pair. The dataset statistics for the Gigaword corpus is as shown in Table 1. In our experiments, we have also used the DUC-2003[3] and DUC-2004[4] corpora [36], DUC-2003 is used only for training and DUC-2004 is used only for testing purposes. Details regarding training and evaluation are discussed in depth in Sect. 5 and 6 respectively. The Gigaword dataset was downloaded as prepared by [42].

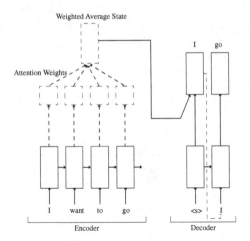

Fig. 1. Seq2seq LSTM with Attention

4 Experimental Setup

For developing an abstractive model we have undertaken the following pre-processing steps as described in Sect. 4.1 and the experimental setup is devised as mentioned in Sects. 4.2 and 4.3.

---

[1] https://www.kaggle.com/snap/amazon-fine-food-reviews.
[2] https://catalog.ldc.upenn.edu/ldc2012t21.
[3] https://www-nlpir.nist.gov/projects/duc/data/2003_data.html.
[4] http://duc.nist.gov/duc2004.

4.1 Pre-processing

To prepare the data for training, we have undertaken pre-processing steps which include removal of stop words, Hypertext Markup Language (HTML) tags, numbers, special characters, expanding of contracted words, lemmatization, stemming, tokenization of words, and creating word embeddings using global vectors for word representation GloVe[5] [38], developed by Stanford. It is an unsupervised learning algorithm that is used to create a vector representation of words.

The data set is further divided into training, validation, and test set so that it could be used for different phases of training and evaluation. Detailed dataset statistics are as shown in Table 1, 2 and 3.

4.2 Sequence to Sequence Based Networks

To develop and train the models, we have used OpenNMT[6] [20] an open source available for neural machine translation (NMT). This can also be used for sequence learning based on deep neural architecture. The system is Massachusetts Institute of Technology (MIT) licensed and its initial versions had principal contributions from Harvard NLP and SYSTRAN Paris.

Here, we have trained the model using long short-term memory (LSTM) [14] encoder-decoder. Apart from the vanilla LSTM layers, LSTM with attention [46] mechanism has also been employed using the default experimental settings of ONMT[7]. We have also used a pretrained model for one of our experiments with LSTM using attention mechanism.

4.3 Generative Adversarial Based Networks

In order to experiment with our models on the generative adversarial-based architecture [50] we have followed the experimental setup of [48], and the method used by [31] is used for adversarial training. The overall model consists of a generator, a discriminator, and a reconstructor. Both the generator and the re-constructor are based on seq2seq pointer-generator networks [43], which can decide either to copy the words from the encoder or generate from the vocabulary. On the other hand, the discriminator takes a sequence as an input.

To train the reconstructor, the cross-entropy loss is computed between the output sequence generated by the reconstructor and the original source text. The loss L_{recon} can be given by the Eq. 1. Here i and j, denote the source and target texts respectively. l_s is the log-likelihood of the source text which is negatively conditioned.

$$L_{recon} = \sum_{d=1}^{D} l_s(i, j) \tag{1}$$

---

[5] https://github.com/stanfordnlp/GloVe.

[6] http://github.com/opennmt/opennmt.

[7] The models were trained on Quadro P2000 GPU which has a total of 5 GB GPU RAM.

Table 4. ROUGE Scores on TextRank

	Recall	Precision	F Score
ROUGE 1	19.91	5.88	8.17
ROUGE 2	5.13	1.62	2.21
ROUGE L	18.7	6.01	8.15

In our adversarial model, the reconstructor and the generator form an auto-encoder. In spite of this, the output of the generator is not directly fed to the reconstructor but is first discretely sampled. But since the discrete samples are non-differentiable, we used the reinforcement algorithm as a loss function. Here the generator is seen as an agent with a reward equivalent to l_s. In order to maximize the reward, our agent tries to decrease the loss. The generator parameters are updated using the Monte Carlo [11] estimates of policy gradients.

Since the agent works on the sampled discrete values, the loss is not continuous and varies from sample to sample. To smoothen the curve, a baseline is used to reduce the training. The reward is modified and the difference is stabilized by applying self-critical sequence training [41]. Following [31] maximum likelihood estimation (MLE) [34], is used.

Table 5. BLEU Scores on TextRank

BLEU 1	1.5
BLEU 2	0.2

Table 6. Textual Entailment Score on TextRank

Entailment	5.15
Neutral	93.56
Contradiction	39.95

Table 7. BLEU Scores on LSTM

Training Data	Test Data	BLEU 1	BLEU 2	BLEU 3	BLEU 4	BLEU Average
Gigaword	Gigaword	11.4	3.1	0.9	0.3	3.925
Gigaword	DUC 2004	8.4	2.1	0.5	0.2	2.8
DUC 2003	Gigaword	1.8	0	0	0	0.45
DUC 2003	DUC 2004	5.2	0.8	0.3	0.1	1.6

Table 8. ROUGE Scores on LSTM

Training Data	Test Data	ROUGE 1			ROUGE 2			ROUGE L		
		Recall	Precision	F Score	Recall	Precision	F Score	Recall	Precision	F Score
Gigaword	Gigaword	43.12	13.85	20.28	13.16	4.04	5.97	37.14	11.95	17.48
Gigaword	DUC 2004	45.76	16.01	23.42	14.84	4.91	7.29	38.75	13.54	19.82
DUC 2003	Gigaword	2.437	2.8	2.528	0.035	0.053	0.041	2.334	2.707	2.432
DUC 2003	DUC 2004	7.229	6.73	6.916	1.289	1.247	1.259	6.371	5.933	6.095

Table 9. BLEU Scores on LSTM with Attention

Training Data	Test Data	BLEU 1	BLEU 2	BLEU 3	BLEU 4	BLEU Average
Gigaword + DUC 2003	Gigaword	39.5	19.9	11.3	7.2	19.475
Gigaword + DUC 2003	DUC 2004	20.5	6.9	3	1.1	7.875

Table 10. ROUGE Scores on LSTM with Attention

Training Data	Test Data	ROUGE 1			ROUGE 2			ROUGE L		
		Recall	Precision	F Score	Recall	Precision	F Score	Recall	Precision	F Score
Gigaword + DUC 2003	Gigaword	41.915	32.748	35.506	20.452	16.081	17.373	39.158	30.612	33.174
Gigaword + DUC 2003	DUC 2004	36.358	23.193	27.766	15.212	9.604	11.483	39.678	25.239	30.259

Table 11. ROUGE Scores on Adversarial Network

Training Data	Test Data	ROUGE 1			ROUGE 2			ROUGE L		
		Recall	Precision	F Score	Recall	Precision	F Score	Recall	Precision	F Score
Gigaword	Gigaword	25.77	24.33	24.18	8.33	7.70	7.68	23.19	21.84	21.72

5 Experimentation

For training the model using the abstractive approach, we have used the experimental setup as discussed in Sect. 4. Further details regarding training the model to generate the summaries are mentioned in Sects. 5.1 and 5.2.

5.1 Sequence to Sequence Based Model

For our experiments, we have used seq2seq based 2-layer LSTM [14] as the encoder with a hidden layer size of 500 dimensions. The 2 layered decoder also gives an output of 500. Both the encoder and the decoder have a dropout of 0.3. The words are embedded in 100 dimensions. We have also trained our models on 2-layer LSTM with attention [46] mechanism, with a hidden size of 500, similar to the plain LSTM architecture as shown in Fig. 1.

5.2   Generative Adversarial Based Model

For training the generative adversarial network, as discussed in Sect. 4, we have used the experimental settings of [31]. The discriminator has been trained up to 1,700 epochs and the generator is trained up to 2,000 epochs. Other settings are used following the work of [48].

6   Evaluation

For evaluating the performance of our model, we have used ROUGE [26], BLEU [37] and a textual entailment method based on semantics. BLEU scores are calculated using the `multi-bleu.perl` script available at the mosesdecoder repository[8]. The ROUGE score is calculated using the `files2rouge` codebase[9].

Table 12. Types of Entailment

S. No.	Text	Sentence Pair	Relation
1	Text 1	I went to the gym yesterday	Positive Entailment
	Text 2	The gym wasn't empty yesterday	
2	Text 1	I went to the gym yesterday	Negative Entailment
	Text 2	The gym was empty yesterday	
3	Text 1	I went to the gym yesterday	Neutral Entailment
	Text 2	The gym is quite good	

For evaluating the model using textual entailment [6] we have used the implementation of [13]. Textual entailment is usually used to determine whether a sentence can be deciphered from the other sentence or not. If the other sentence can be derived from the original sentence, then we say that they have a "positive entailment" among them. The scenario of the sentences having stark opposite meanings is termed as "negative entailment" whereas the pair having no "positive" or "negative" sense is termed as "neutral" [2]. The positive entailment implies the hypothesis, negative contradicts and the neutral statement cannot prove or disprove the given statement. For example, the sentence "I went to the gym yesterday" logically implies "The gym wasn't empty yesterday", and thus the pair forms a case of "positive entailment". Whereas the pair "I went to the gym yesterday" and "The gym was empty yesterday" are contradictory in nature and hence form the case of "negative entailment". An example of "neutral entailment" can be seen with the pair "I went to the gym yesterday" and "The gym is quite good". Clearly, with the amount of context known, the two sentences have no correlation whatsoever. The example is as shown in Table 12.

---

[8] https://github.com/moses-smt/mosesdecoder/blob/master/scripts/generic/multi-bleu.perl.

[9] https://github.com/pltrdy/files2rouge.

Table 13. Result Comparison between Entailment, BLEU and ROUGE scores

S. No.	Approach	Train	Test	Entailment	Neutral	Contradiction
1	PageRank (Extractive)	Amazon Reviews	Amazon Reviews	5.15	93.56	39.95
2	LSTM	Gigaword	Gigaword	24.47	50.61	−28.01
3	LSTM	Gigaword	DUC 2004	47.93	36.05	−18.31
4	LSTM	DUC 2003	Gigaword	−8.23	66.37	−12.57
5	LSTM	DUC 2003	DUC 2004	10.32	48.03	−2.33
6	LSTM + Attention	Gigaword + DUC 2004	Gigaword	7.74	46.96	9.90
7	LSTM + Attention	Gigaword + DUC 2004	DUC 2003	41.82	17.17	14.73
8	Adversarial Network	Gigaword	Gigaword	−38.05	52.24	1.66

Table 14. Result Comparison between Entailment Percentage, BLEU and ROUGE scores

S. No.	Approach	Train	Test	BLEU 1	ROUGE-L (Precision)	Entailment Percentage
1	PageRank (Extractive)	Amazon Reviews	Amazon Reviews	1.5	6.01	25.25
2	LSTM	Gigaword	Gigaword	3.1	11.95	39.56
3	LSTM	Gigaword	DUC 2004	2.1	13.54	37.8
4	LSTM	DUC 2003	Gigaword	1.8	2.7	2.87
5	LSTM	DUC 2003	DUC 2004	5.2	5.93	4.2
6	LSTM + Attention	Gigaword + DUC 2004	Gigaword	39.5	30.61	11.94
7	LSTM + Attention	Gigaword + DUC 2004	DUC 2003	20.5	23.19	14.42
8	Adversarial Network	Gigaword	Gigaword	23	21.84	5.48

Table 15. ROUGE F1 Score Comparison Among Different Papers

S. No.	Year	Paper Name	ROUGE 1	ROUGE 2	ROUGE L
1	2015	A Neural Attention Model for Sentence Summarization, [40]	28.18	8.49	23.81
2	2016	Abstractive Sentence Summarization with Attentive Recurrent Neural Networks, [4]	33.78	15.97	31.15
3	2018	Entity Commonsense Representation for Neural Abstractive Summarization, [1]	37.04	16.66	34.93
4	2018	Incorporate Entailment Knowledge into Abstractive Sentence Summarization, [24]	35.33	17.27	33.19
5	2019	Simple Unsupervised Summarization by Contextual Matching, [51]	26.48	10.05	24.41
6	–	LSTM	20.28	5.97	17.48
7	–	LSTM + Attention	35.5	17.37	33.17
8	–	Adversarial	24.18	7.68	21.72

In our approach, we have used the pre-trained GloVe [38] word vectors for word vectorization and an LSTM network with dropout on the initial and final layers to calculate the entailment score for the generated summary. The loss function used is a variation of the softmax loss function provided by TensorFlow. Some regularization losses are added as well, along with an optimizer to help the model learn to reduce the net loss. The score has three parts for a single pair of summaries i.e. entailment, neutral, and contradiction. For training the entailment evaluation model, we have used "The Stanford Natural Language

Inference (SNLI) Corpus"[10] [47]. For calculating the entailment percentage, each sentence pair is classified as entailed or not entailed. A score of 1 is given if the sentence pair is entailed and 0 otherwise. The sum of all such scores is calculated and hence, the percentage score is determined. Raw entailment, neutral, and contradiction scores are calculated by simply averaging all the probability values across all the sentences in the dataset. The entailment percentage is tabulated in Table 14 and average entailment score is as given in Table 13.

The obtained score using BLEU, ROUGE and entailment techniques are tabulated in the Tables 4, 5, 6, 7, 8, 9, 10, 11, 13 and 14.

7 Results and Analysis

As discussed in Sect. 5, we have tabulated the generated results in Tables 4, 5, 6, 7, 8, 9, 10, 11, 13 and 14. BLEU, ROUGE and entailment techniques are used to generate this score. From Table 14, it can be seen that according to the most used evaluation metrics i.e. BLEU and ROUGE, the best model here is the LSTM with Attention mechanism, while still offering an entailment score comparable to that of the vanilla LSTM. In some instances, the simple LSTM outperforms LSTM with Attention even though it has a comparatively less BLEU score.

It is to be noted that the extractive approach used here (PageRank) directly extracts textual excerpts from the text and has a high neutral entailment (as shown in Table 13). By tuning these parameters viz. entailment, neutral, and contradiction, we can measure whether the generated summary is close to human language or not. It can also be shown whether the summary can be inferred from the original summary or not.

Table 16. Example Sentences with Entailment, BLEU and ROUGE scores

	Sentence	Entailment	Neutral	Contradiction	BLEU 1	ROUGE L (Precision)
Actual	Sri lanka closes schools as war escalates	21.81	−16.09	−38.59	22	33
Predicted	Sri lankan government schools with tamil separatists escalated in					
Actual	Repatriation of bosnian refugees postponed	−37.17	33.96	−45.92	50	50
Predicted	Repatriation of at refugees to return					

---

[10] https://nlp.stanford.edu/projects/snli/.

8   Discussion and Conclusion

In our work, we have worked with various algorithms and deep learning techniques for the given text summarization task. We have also validated the result of our baseline system on various metrics including BLEU, ROUGE, and a semantic-based evaluation technique. Given the tabulated results in Table 14, we can make a comparative analysis of the three evaluation techniques used. The BLEU 1 score and the ROUGE-L precision score are based on the syntactical structure of the sentence, whereas the entailment percentage is based on the semantics of the sentence. The score based on the sentence structure may not always give good results. Considering the semantics of the sentence and similarity between word vectors is also necessary while calculating the final score. The second example given in Table 16 can be taken as an example here, wherein the information obtained from the predicted sentence is in no way related to the actual summary. But theoretically, the sentence has a high BLEU 1 score of 50 and a ROUGE-L precision score of 50. Also, a low BLEU 1 or ROUGE score may not necessarily mean that the prediction is bad, as can be seen from the first example in Table 16. The sentence here has a comparatively low BLEU and ROUGE score, but we can gain some information from the prediction (at least better than the second sentence having a disproportionately high BLEU and ROUGE scores). Here, the entailment score gives a better picture of the predicted summarization, by giving the first sentence a higher entailment score of 21.81 and a negative score of -37.17 to the second. A good summary must give a semantically fit sentence for a correct summary and have the required fluency and adequacy.

Thus, from the above observations in Table 16, we can understand that in a task like a summary generation, semantic metrics are necessary and can contribute a part to generating the overall score. Table 15 lists our baseline model accuracy comparison with summarization tasks on the same Gigaword dataset.

The present baseline system uses only text data to generate a one-line summary. Future works will include multi-modal summarization approaches to leverage the visual features, and a semantic-based evaluation system considering the entailment and the neutrality of the text (i.e. whether the generated summary is more like human-written or not) to calculate a score. Such a loss function can also be devised which can help the model converge into producing a more optimal summary.

Acknowledgment. We would like to thank Department of Computer Science and Engineering and Center for Natural Language Processing (CNLP) at National Institute of Technology Silchar for providing the requisite support and infrastructure to execute this work. The work presented here falls under the Research Project Grant No. IFC/4130/DST-CNRS/2018-19/IT25 (DST-CNRS targeted program).

References

1. Amplayo, R.K., Lim, S., Hwang, S.: Entity commonsense representation for neural abstractive summarization. In: Proceedings of the 2018 Conference of the North American Chapter of the Association for Computational Linguistics: Human Language Technologies, NAACL-HLT 2018, New Orleans, Louisiana, USA, 1–6 June 2018, Volume 1 (Long Papers), pp. 697–707. Association for Computational Linguistics (2018). https://doi.org/10.18653/v1/n18-1064

2. Androutsopoulos, I., Malakasiotis, P.: A survey of paraphrasing and textual entailment methods. J. Artif. Intell. Res. **38**, 135–187 (2010). https://doi.org/10.1613/jair.2985

3. Barzilay, R., McKeown, K.R.: Sentence fusion for multidocument news summarization. Comput. Linguist. **31**(3), 297–328 (2005). https://doi.org/10.1162/089120105774321091

4. Chopra, S., Auli, M., Rush, A.M.: Abstractive sentence summarization with attentive recurrent neural networks. In: NAACL HLT 2016, The 2016 Conference of the North American Chapter of the Association for Computational Linguistics: Human Language Technologies, San Diego California, USA, 12–17 June 2016, pp. 93–98. The Association for Computational Linguistics (2016). https://doi.org/10.18653/v1/n16-1012

5. Cohan, A., et al.: A discourse-aware attention model for abstractive summarization of long documents. In: Proceedings of the 2018 Conference of the North American Chapter of the Association for Computational Linguistics: Human Language Technologies, NAACL-HLT, New Orleans, Louisiana, USA, 1–6 June 2018, Volume 2 (Short Papers), pp. 615–621. Association for Computational Linguistics (2018). https://doi.org/10.18653/v1/n18-2097

6. Dagan, I., Roth, D., Sammons, M., Zanzotto, F.M.: Recognizing Textual Entailment: Models and Applications. Synthesis Lectures on Human Language Technologies. Morgan & Claypool Publishers (2013). https://doi.org/10.2200/S00509ED1V01Y201305HLT023

7. Dunning, T.: Accurate methods for the statistics of surprise and coincidence. Comput. Linguist. **19**(1), 61–74 (1993)

8. Erkan, G., Radev, D.R.: LexRank: graph-based lexical centrality as salience in text summarization. CoRR abs/1109.2128 (2011). http://arxiv.org/abs/1109.2128

9. Gong, Y., Liu, X.: Generic text summarization using relevance measure and latent semantic analysis. In: SIGIR 2001: Proceedings of the 24th Annual International ACM SIGIR Conference on Research and Development in Information Retrieval, New Orleans, Louisiana, USA, 9–13 September 2001, pp. 19–25. ACM (2001). https://doi.org/10.1145/383952.383955

10. Graff, D., Kong, J., Chen, K., Maeda, K.: English gigaword. Linguistic Data Consortium, Philadelphia **4**(1), 34 (2003)

11. Hammersley, J.: Monte Carlo Methods. Springer, Heidelberg (2013)

12. Harabagiu, S.M., Lacatusu, F.: Generating single and multi-document summaries with gistexter. In: Document Understanding Conferences, pp. 11–12 (2002)

13. Hewitt, S.: Textual entailment with tensorflow, July 2017. https://www.oreilly.com/content/textual-entailment-with-tensorflow/

14. Hochreiter, S., Schmidhuber, J.: Long short-term memory. Neural Comput. **9**(8), 1735–1780 (1997). https://doi.org/10.1162/neco.1997.9.8.1735

15. Hsu, W.T., Lin, C., Lee, M., Min, K., Tang, J., Sun, M.: A unified model for extractive and abstractive summarization using inconsistency loss. In: Proceedings of the 56th Annual Meeting of the Association for Computational Linguistics. ACL 2018, Melbourne, Australia, 15–20 July 2018, Volume 1: Long Papers, pp. 132–141. Association for Computational Linguistics (2018). https://doi.org/10.18653/v1/P18-1013, https://www.aclweb.org/anthology/P18-1013/

16. Khan, A., Salim, N., Kumar, Y.J.: Genetic semantic graph approach for multi-document abstractive summarization. In: 2015 Fifth International Conference on Digital Information Processing and Communications (ICDIPC), pp. 173–181. IEEE (2015)

17. Khilji, A.F.U.R., Laskar, S.R., Pakray, P., Kadir, R.A., Lydia, M.S., Bandyopadhyay, S.: HealFavor: dataset and a prototype system for healthcare chatbot. In: 2020 International Conference on Data Science, Artificial Intelligence, and Business Analytics (DATABIA), pp. 1–4, July 2020. https://doi.org/10.1109/DATABIA50434.2020.9190281

18. Khilji, A.F.U.R., et al.: CookingQA: answering questions and recommending recipes based on ingredients. Arab. J. Sci. Eng. **46**, pages3701–3712 (2021). https://doi.org/10.1007/s13369-020-05236-5

19. Khilji, A.F.U.R., Manna, R., Laskar, S.R., Pakray, P., Das, D., Bandyopadhyay, S., Gelbukh, A.: Question classification and answer extraction for developing a cooking QA system. Computación y Sistemas **24**(2) (2020)

20. Klein, G., Kim, Y., Deng, Y., Senellart, J., Rush, A.M.: OpenNMT: open-source toolkit for neural machine translation. In: Proceedings of the 55th Annual Meeting of the Association for Computational Linguistics, ACL 2017, System Demonstrations, Vancouver, Canada, 30 July–4 August, pp. 67–72. Association for Computational Linguistics (2017). https://doi.org/10.18653/v1/P17-4012

21. Kumari, H., Sarkar, S., Rajput, V., Roy, A.: Comparative analysis of neural models for abstractive text summarization. In: Bhattacharjee, A., Borgohain, S.K., Soni, B., Verma, G., Gao, X.-Z. (eds.) MIND 2020. CCIS, vol. 1241, pp. 357–368. Springer, Singapore (2020). https://doi.org/10.1007/978-981-15-6318-8_30

22. Lee, C., Jian, Z., Huang, L.: A fuzzy ontology and its application to news summarization. IEEE Trans. Syst. Man Cybern. Part B **35**(5), 859–880 (2005). https://doi.org/10.1109/TSMCB.2005.845032

23. Lee, M., et al.: Beyond information retrieval - medical question answering. In: American Medical Informatics Association Annual Symposium, AMIA 2006, Washington, DC, USA, 11–15 November 2006. AMIA (2006). http://knowledge.amia.org/amia-55142-a2006a-1.620145/t-001-1.623243/f-001-1.623244/a-094-1.623466/a-095-1.623463

24. Li, H., Zhu, J., Zhang, J., Zong, C.: Ensure the correctness of the summary: incorporate entailment knowledge into abstractive sentence summarization. In: Proceedings of the 27th International Conference on Computational Linguistics, COLING 2018, Santa Fe, New Mexico, USA, 20–26 August 2018, pp. 1430–1441. Association for Computational Linguistics (2018). https://www.aclweb.org/anthology/C18-1121/

25. Li, P., Lam, W., Bing, L., Wang, Z.: Deep recurrent generative decoder for abstractive text summarization. In: Proceedings of the 2017 Conference on Empirical Methods in Natural Language Processing, EMNLP 2017, Copenhagen, Denmark, 9–11 September 2017, pp. 2091–2100. Association for Computational Linguistics (2017). https://doi.org/10.18653/v1/d17-1222

26. Lin, C.Y.: Rouge: a package for automatic evaluation of summaries. In: Text Summarization Branches Out, pp. 74–81 (2004)

27. Liu, L., Lu, Y., Yang, M., Qu, Q., Zhu, J., Li, H.: Generative adversarial network for abstractive text summarization. In: Proceedings of the Thirty-Second AAAI Conference on Artificial Intelligence, (AAAI-18), the 30th innovative Applications of Artificial Intelligence (IAAI-18), and the 8th AAAI Symposium on Educational Advances in Artificial Intelligence (EAAI-18), New Orleans, Louisiana, USA, 2–7 February 2018, pp. 8109–8110. AAAI Press (2018). https://www.aaai.org/ocs/index.php/AAAI/AAAI18/paper/view/16238

28. Liu, Y., Lapata, M.: Text summarization with pretrained encoders. In: Proceedings of the 2019 Conference on Empirical Methods in Natural Language Processing and the 9th International Joint Conference on Natural Language Processing, EMNLP-IJCNLP 2019, Hong Kong, China, 3–7 November 2019, pp. 3728–3738. Association for Computational Linguistics (2019). https://doi.org/10.18653/v1/D19-1387

29. Luhn, H.P.: The automatic creation of literature abstracts. IBM J. Res. Dev. **2**(2), 159–165 (1958). https://doi.org/10.1147/rd.22.0159

30. Mallick, C., Das, A.K., Dutta, M., Das, A.K., Sarkar, A.: Graph-based text summarization using modified TextRank. In: Nayak, J., Abraham, A., Krishna, B.M., Chandra Sekhar, G.T., Das, A.K. (eds.) Soft Computing in Data Analytics. AISC, vol. 758, pp. 137–146. Springer, Singapore (2019). https://doi.org/10.1007/978-981-13-0514-6_14

31. de Masson d'Autume, C., Mohamed, S., Rosca, M., Rae, J.W.: Training language GANs from scratch. In: Advances in Neural Information Processing Systems 32: Annual Conference on Neural Information Processing Systems 2019, NeurIPS 2019, Vancouver, BC, Canada, 8–14 December 2019, pp. 4302–4313 (2019). http://papers.nips.cc/paper/8682-training-language-gans-from-scratch

32. Mihalcea, R.: Graph-based ranking algorithms for sentence extraction, applied to text summarization. In: Proceedings of the 42nd Annual Meeting of the Association for Computational Linguistics, Barcelona, Spain, 21–26 July 2004 - Poster and Demonstration. ACL (2004). https://www.aclweb.org/anthology/P04-3020/

33. Moratanch, N., Chitrakala, S.: A survey on extractive text summarization. In: 2017 International Conference on Computer, Communication and Signal Processing (ICCCSP), pp. 1–6. IEEE (2017)

34. Myung, I.J.: Tutorial on maximum likelihood estimation. J. Math. Psychol. **47**(1), 90–100 (2003)

35. Nenkova, A., Passonneau, R.J.: Evaluating content selection in summarization: the pyramid method. In: Human Language Technology Conference of the North American Chapter of the Association for Computational Linguistics, HLT-NAACL 2004, Boston, Massachusetts, USA, 2–7 May 2004, pp. 145–152. The Association for Computational Linguistics (2004). https://www.aclweb.org/anthology/N04-1019/

36. Over, P., Dang, H., Harman, D.: Duc in context. Inf. Process. Manag. **43**(6), 1506–1520 (2007). Text Summarization

37. Papineni, K., Roukos, S., Ward, T., Zhu, W.: Bleu: a method for automatic evaluation of machine translation. In: Proceedings of the 40th Annual Meeting of the Association for Computational Linguistics, Philadelphia, PA, USA, 6–12 July 2002, pp. 311–318. ACL (2002). https://doi.org/10.3115/1073083.1073135, https://www.aclweb.org/anthology/P02-1040/

38. Pennington, J., Socher, R., Manning, C.D.: Glove: global vectors for word representation. In: Proceedings of the 2014 Conference on Empirical Methods in Natural Language Processing, EMNLP 2014, A meeting of SIGDAT, a Special Interest Group of the ACL, Doha, Qatar, 25–29 October 2014, pp. 1532–1543. ACL (2014). https://doi.org/10.3115/v1/d14-1162

39. Qazvinian, V., et al.: Generating extractive summaries of scientific paradigms. J. Artif. Intell. Res. **46**, 165–201 (2013). https://doi.org/10.1613/jair.3732

40. Ren, P., Chen, Z., Ren, Z., Wei, F., Ma, J., de Rijke, M.: Leveraging contextual sentence relations for extractive summarization using a neural attention model. In: Proceedings of the 40th International ACM SIGIR Conference on Research and Development in Information Retrieval, Shinjuku, Tokyo, Japan, 7–11 August 2017, pp. 95–104. ACM (2017). https://doi.org/10.1145/3077136.3080792

41. Rennie, S.J., Marcheret, E., Mroueh, Y., Ross, J., Goel, V.: Self-critical sequence training for image captioning. In: 2017 IEEE Conference on Computer Vision and Pattern Recognition, CVPR 2017, Honolulu, HI, USA, 21–26 July 2017, pp. 1179–1195. IEEE Computer Society (2017). https://doi.org/10.1109/CVPR.2017.131

42. Rush, A.M., Chopra, S., Weston, J.: A neural attention model for abstractive sentence summarization. In: Proceedings of the 2015 Conference on Empirical Methods in Natural Language Processing, EMNLP 2015, Lisbon, Portugal, 17–21 September 2015, pp. 379–389. The Association for Computational Linguistics (2015). https://doi.org/10.18653/v1/d15-1044

43. See, A., Liu, P.J., Manning, C.D.: Get to the point: summarization with pointer-generator networks. In: Proceedings of the 55th Annual Meeting of the Association for Computational Linguistics, ACL 2017, Vancouver, Canada, 30 July–4 August, Volume 1: Long Papers, pp. 1073–1083. Association for Computational Linguistics (2017). https://doi.org/10.18653/v1/P17-1099

44. Steinberger, J., Jezek, K.: Evaluation measures for text summarization. Comput. Inform. **28**(2), 251–275 (2009). http://www.sav.sk/index.php?lang=en&charset=ascii&doc=journal&part=list_articles&journal_issue_no=11112220#abstract_5263

45. Teufel, S., Moens, M.: Summarizing scientific articles: experiments with relevance and rhetorical status. Comput. Linguist. **28**(4), 409–445 (2002). https://doi.org/10.1162/089120102762671936

46. Vaswani, A., et al.: Attention is all you need. In: Advances in Neural Information Processing Systems 30: Annual Conference on Neural Information Processing Systems 2017, Long Beach, CA, USA, 4–9 December 2017, pp. 5998–6008 (2017). http://papers.nips.cc/paper/7181-attention-is-all-you-need

47. Wang, S., Jiang, J.: Learning natural language inference with LSTM. In: NAACL HLT 2016, The 2016 Conference of the North American Chapter of the Association for Computational Linguistics: Human Language Technologies, San Diego California, USA, 12–17 June 2016, pp. 1442–1451. The Association for Computational Linguistics (2016). https://doi.org/10.18653/v1/n16-1170

48. Wang, Y., Lee, H.: Learning to encode text as human-readable summaries using generative adversarial networks. In: Proceedings of the 2018 Conference on Empirical Methods in Natural Language Processing, Brussels, Belgium, 31 October–4 November 2018, pp. 4187–4195. Association for Computational Linguistics (2018). https://doi.org/10.18653/v1/d18-1451

49. Zhan, J., Loh, H.T., Liu, Y.: Gather customer concerns from online product reviews-a text summarization approach. Expert Syst. Appl. **36**(2), 2107–2115 (2009)

50. Zhang, H., Goodfellow, I.J., Metaxas, D.N., Odena, A.: Self-attention generative adversarial networks. In: Proceedings of the 36th International Conference on Machine Learning, ICML 2019, Proceedings of Machine Learning Research, Long Beach, California, USA, 9–15 June 2019, vol. 97, pp. 7354–7363. PMLR (2019). http://proceedings.mlr.press/v97/zhang19d.html

51. Zhou, J., Rush, A.M.: Simple unsupervised summarization by contextual matching. In: Proceedings of the 57th Conference of the Association for Computational Linguistics, ACL 2019, Florence, Italy, 28 July–2 August 2019, Volume 1: Long Papers, pp. 5101–5106. Association for Computational Linguistics (2019). https://doi.org/10.18653/v1/p19-1503

Classification of Colorectal Cancer Histology Images Using Image Reconstruction and Modified DenseNet

Tanmoy Sarkar[1]([⊠]), Animesh Hazra[1], and Nibaran Das[2]

[1] Department of Computer Science and Engineering, Jalpaiguri Government Engineering College, Jalpaiguri 735102, West Bengal, India
{ts2150,animesh.hazra}@cse.jgec.ac.in
[2] Department of Computer Science and Engineering, Jadavpur University, Kolkata 700032, West Bengal, India
nibaran@cse.jdvu.ac.in

Abstract. Colorectal cancer is one major cause of cancer-related death around the globe. Recent breakthroughs in deep learning have paved the way to apply it for the automation of histopathology images as a tool for computer-aided diagnosis of medical imaging. Here we have presented a novel state of the art classification model for classifying the colorectal histopathology images into 9 classes. All the traditional approaches like texture-based classification, transfer learning etc. already has been used to achieve a state-of-the-art result, but these have some limitations. Rather than using conventional mechanisms, we have proposed a methodology that can interpret the histopathology images in a more generalized way without image preprocessing and augmentation mechanisms. A combination of two deep learning architectures i.e., an encoder unit of autoencoder module and a modified DenseNet121 architecture are used for this purpose. An accuracy of 97.2% on Zenodo 100k colorectal histopathology dataset has been reported. The presented result is better than most of the contemporary works in this domain. We have also evaluated the effectiveness of the current approach for the low-resolution histopathological images and achieved good recognition accuracy.

Keywords: Classification · Colorectal cancer · Deep learning · DenseNet · Histology images · Image reconstruction

1 Introduction

Biomedical imaging is evolving as one of the crucial tools in the healthcare system across the world. In the year 2020, an average of 53,200 deaths will occur all over the United States due to colorectal cancer (CRC) [1]. The primary challenge of colon histopathologists is to distinguish the benign from malignant disease and also categorize the diseased cells into the multiple classes which are already defined in the literature [4]. Thus, automating this process completely reduces a lot of ambiguity and time in detecting cancer. Histopathology provides a diagnosis for cancer by studying the tissues

© Springer Nature Switzerland AG 2021
P. Dutta et al. (Eds.): CICBA 2021, CCIS 1406, pp. 259–271, 2021.
https://doi.org/10.1007/978-3-030-75529-4_20

obtained from a certain suspicious portion of the human body. A lot of progress is being made in this field to achieve maximum possible accuracy in detecting the disease [4, 16, 17]. There exist numerous classification methods like SVM, CNN, KNN, logistic regression, random forest, decision trees etc. [4, 5] which are able to produce great results but still these techniques have some limitations [5].

(a) In texture-based classification models [5], in order to solve the classification task, a fixed set of texture features has been chosen to determine what type of cancer the input image holds. Those features can be fed into some convolutional neural network (CNN) based classifiers or some cluster-based classification module or other classical machine learning module. In this case, the limitation is that the model has less generalization capacity because a fixed set of textures has been chosen.

(b) The traditional models work in such a way that they cannot perform well in low-resolution images. Hence, we need to design a flexible model which can precisely work on the images having different types of resolutions.

(c) State of the art deep learning architectures also have some limitations in classifying the CRC. Generally, they perform well on object-based classification tasks but in case of texture-based classification like classifying histopathology images, they tend to overfit very quickly and have less generalization capability.

Here, a model has been presented in order to tackle solve these limitations, creating a well-generalized model which can even perform well with variations of image resolution. To achieve this goal, we have used features extracted from an image encoder and passed that features to a modified version of DenseNet121 [14] for classification. Initially, the autoencoder is trained on a subset of the main dataset for image reconstruction and later from that trained autoencoder [6], the encoder is taken for encoding the input images into important feature maps. These feature maps are then fed into the modified DenseNet121 classification block, which is a regular DenseNer121 architecture with some changes in the first few blocks of the network, hence producing a model with high generalization power capable of solving the limitations discussed earlier. In different sections, we have discussed the entire workflow in detail which includes the structure of the autoencoder and feature extraction from the encoder block of autoencoder unit, detailed structure of our modified DenseNet121 block, all the performance measures, comparison of our proposed model with the standalone DenseNet121 architecture in terms of generalization capability along with the exhibition of proposed model on low resolution images.

2 Literature Review

Deep learning has acquired demand in medical imaging research which includes magnetic resonance imaging on the brain, cancer detection of breast ultrasounds and diabetic foot ulcer classification and segmentation etc. [8]. There are varieties of research papers that survey colorectal cancer. In this section, some of them are briefly outlined in a nutshell.

Rathore et al. [9] discussed ensemble approach based on predefined set of features to detect and grade colon cancers. For performance measures the individual performances of the classifiers with the ensemble model have been compared against two colon cancer datasets. The outputs interpret that the ensemble model provides accurate results and remarkably increases the effectiveness of independent classifiers. The authenticity of this method recommends wide relevance over existing standalone classifiers, leading to precise detection tools for colon cancer specimens in patients.

The most promising accomplishment in result of DNA microarray is sampling of gene expression data between tumors from different sources. At present, designing evolutionary artificial neural nets have flourished as favored alternative of discernible ideal network. In [10], the authors proposed an evolutionary neural network that classifies gene expression profiles into benign or malignant CRC cells. The empirical output on colon microarray data exhibits effectiveness of explained model with respect to other classification models.

Urban et al. [11] created a sophisticated polyp identification and localization method which can operate in exact time. It is being observed that the occurrence of polyps in a frame with 96.4% accuracy with 0.991 AUC score by utilizing a CNN initially trained on ImageNet and next retrained on the proposed polyp dataset. Little incorporation of this model helped it to localize the polyps inside bounded regions with a significant F1 score of 0.83 with 10 ms inference time for each frame. Hence, the authors believe that, during live colonoscopy running, this methodology will need more careful examination for finding extra polyps.

Ding et al. [12] developed a model based on Faster R-CNN for metastatic lymph node detection in the patients with rectal cancer. The main goal is verification of its accuracy in medical use. The 414 patients with CRC were diagnosed in a period of 26 months and the data was collected from the six medical centers, and the MRI data for pelvic metastatic lymph nodes of every patient was recognized by Faster R-CNN. Diagnosis based on the Faster R-CNN concept was compared with pathologist and radiologist-based treatments for methodological verification, by utilizing the correlation analysis and consistency checking. Here, the proposed diagnostic method exceeds radiologists in the judgment of the disease but is not as accurate as of the pathologists.

In [5], the colorectal histology data were classified with various methods like CNN, KNN, logistic regression, and random forest. The classifier producing the most accurate results compared to other models has been taken. Convolutional Neural Network was found to be the best technique with an accuracy of 82.2%.

In [4], the authors prepared a new dataset with 5000 colorectal cancer histological images which included eight different types of tissues. For CRC, in fact, there are no promising results on multiclass texture separation. Here, the authors used the above dataset to evaluate the performance of classification for a broad range of texture descriptors and classifiers. As an outcome, they established a perfect classification strategy which noticeably outperformed conventional methods, for tumor-stroma separation and establishing an up-to-date standard for multiclass tissue separation.

In [13], the authors proposed an ANN for the classification of cancer and feature selection of the colon cancer dataset. For feature selection, the best first search technique was used in the Weka tools and the accuracy achieved was 98.4% and without feature selection, the accuracy obtained was 95.2%. Thus, it was seen that feature selection boots the classification accuracy which was based on the experiment on the said dataset.

3   Proposed Methodology

In this method, a combination of image encoding and classification algorithm is used. An encoder block from autoencoder module is trained for image reconstruction. The encoder's outcome is embedded in modified DenseNet121 architectures and used for the classification task to improve the performance compared to its traditional counter parts. More specifically, encoder is used for extracting the important activation maps of features present in the images which helps the classifier perform well without any image preprocessing and augmentation techniques.

The idea of choosing DenseNet is motivated by the vanishing-gradient problem, maximum feature propagation in forward and backward pass, stimulating feature reuse and a smaller number of parameters which has achieved SOTA accuracy in different competitive image classification tasks [14]. Due to the advantage of feature reuse in every block of the DenseNet model, the main activation maps extracted from the encoder block will remain intact throughout the whole blocks of the network and propagate properly to enhance the performance of classification task.

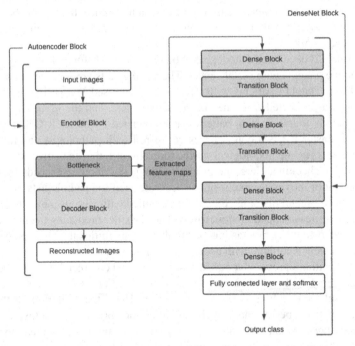

Fig. 1. Picture depicting the workflow of the proposed model.

The next section consists of dataset description where different characteristics of the dataset are described along with the dataset distribution into train, test and validation sets. After that, the image reconstruction module, in which we reconstruct the histology images using the autoencoder architecture, are elaborated. Following this, we apply classification algorithms on the encoded features from the autoencoder unit. For this purpose, the modified DenseNet121 model is used, thus classifying each image into one of the 9 categories. All these steps are discussed below in detail and a brief workflow is depicted in Fig. 1.

3.1 Dataset Description

In this task, data pertaining to the colorectal cancer was used from Zenedo dataset [2], a publicly available standard histology image dataset. This dataset is considered as the benchmark one in the field of colorectal cancer histology image data. It consists of 100000 numbers of RGB images (without color normalization) having dimension of 224 × 224 pixels at 0.5 microns per pixel. There are 9 categories of classes namely adipose (ADI), background (BACK), debris (DEB), lymphocytes (LYM), mucus (MUC), smooth muscle (MUS), normal colon mucosa (NORM), cancer-associated stroma (STR) and colorectal adenocarcinoma epithelium (TUM).

In the present work, the dataset is distributed into train, validation and test set having 80000 images, 10000 images, 9000 images, respectively. Also, an additional test set containing 1000 images are prepared and resizing them into ¼ th of their original height and width to test our model against low resolution images. Below is a depiction of original

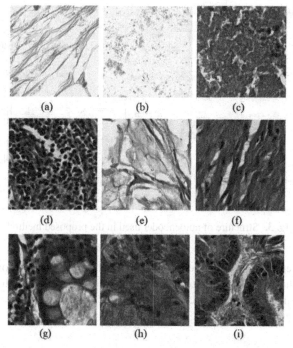

Fig. 2. Nine independent sample images of every class of colorectal cancer tissue present in the dataset are shown here. (a): adipose (b): background (c): debris (d): lymphocytes (e): mucus (f): smooth muscle (g): normal colon mucosa (h): cancer-associated stroma and (i): colorectal adenocarcinoma epithelium.

images of all the categories of colorectal cancer tissues from the above-mentioned dataset (Fig. 2).

3.2 Extraction of Encoder Activation Maps

Autoencoders, a special kind of neural networks consisting of both an encoder and a decoder part, generally used for image denoising, image retrieval, watermark removal, dimensionality reduction, anomaly detection etc. [6]. Our goal is to encode the colorectal histopathological images with the encoder, then decode the encoded data with the decoder such that the output is reconstruction of original input image. After training the autoencoder the extracted feature maps obtained from the encoder is used in classification tasks. A pictorial representation of autoencoder module is shown in Fig. 3.

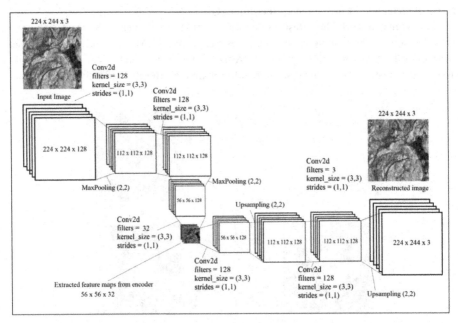

Fig. 3. Structure of autoencoder used in the proposed method.

The aim of encoding the image into a set of feature maps is to provide important information to the classification block. It helps the model for focus on to the important regions of the image needed for classification which are validated with Grad-CAM visualization later.

3.3 Classification of Cancer Cells

Coming to classification, our aim is to successfully classify 9 types of cancers present in the above-mentioned dataset. A modified DenseNet121 has been used for this purpose. DenseNet has a capability of diminishing the vanishing-gradient problem, encouraging feature reuse, and due to its smaller number of parameters the redundant features will be ignored [14].

In this network, every layer gets auxiliary inputs from all previous layers and the output feature maps from that specific layer will be passed into the subsequent layers in the entire network to ensure maximum information propagation both in forward and backward directions (Fig. 4).

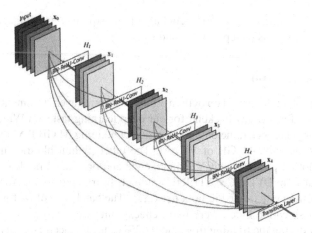

Fig. 4. A 5-layer dense block where each layer takes all preceding feature-maps as input [14].

In our use case, we have slightly changed the architecture of DenseNet121 by removing the first two convolution blocks before starting off the dense block and replacing it

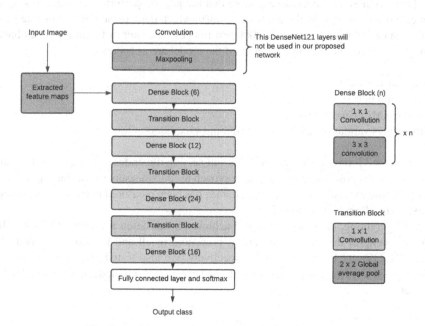

Fig. 5. Architecture of the proposed DenseNet module.

with our encoder block from our trained autoencoder. Thus, the activation maps extracted during image reconstruction will remain intact and pass through all the subsequent layers of DenseNet leading the model to higher accuracy. During training inside the classification block the weights of the encoder is being frozen (Fig. 5).

4   Results and Discussion

In this section, we have discussed in detail about the experimental setup for the model along with SOTA results to support the said setup.

4.1   Experimental Setup

The entire work is implemented on python 3.6.8 programming environment and we have used Keras with TensorFlow backend for our deep learning tasks on Windows 10 OS. Network training has been done on a workstation containing 64 GB RAM and NVIDIA RTX 2080Ti GPU with 11 GB of VRAM. The other python libraries used here are NumPy, matplotlib, pickle OpenCV. Source code and pretrained models are available at https://github.com/DVLP-CMATERJU/colorect. In training setup, Adam optimizer with 0.001 learning rate is used in both networks. The batch size of 64 for autoencoder and 32 for classification block were used, checkpoints were saved and monitored by validation loss during the training time and 97.2% of testing accuracy was achieved.

4.2   Performance Evaluation

Here, the efficiency of the proposed model pertaining to various performance measures have been discussed. In order to calculate that the generic performance measures have been calculated along with the confusion matrix which depicts the number of true predictions in each category based on 9000 test images. The four different measures have been used here for measuring efficiency of the model are as follows.

- Performance metrics
- Confusion matrix
- Grad-CAMs visualization
- Training vs validation accuracy and training vs validation loss curves

Performance Metrics Calculation. This sub-section illustrates and discusses the findings from the proposed method and the approach used to measure the performance metrics of the said method. Here, the performance has been measured in terms of accuracy, precision, recall and F1 score [17].

During training, the proposed model achieved a validation accuracy of 97.67%. In 9000 test samples the value of accuracy, precision, recall and F1 score obtained are 97.2%, 97.23%, 97.1% and 97.16% respectively. We also tested our proposed model with the 1000 low resolution images mentioned earlier and our model has achieved 97% test accuracy.

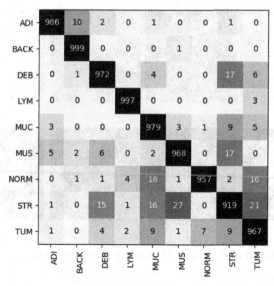

Fig. 6. Confusion matrix illustrating the result of classification on test samples.

Performance Evaluation Using Confusion Matrix. To validate the performance of classification, the confusion matrix has been used, which is demonstrated in Fig. 6 as follows:

In the confusion matrix for the proposed model, y-axis denotes the true categories of the images and the x-axis denotes the predicted categories. It therefore gives us the validation of our findings against the original categories of the images. Here, it can be demonstrated that out of the 1000 images which were of adipose category, 986 images have been correctly predicted as adipose category cells and 14 images has been wrongly categorized. Similarly, out of the 1000 stroma category images 919 have been correctly categorized. However, 81 stroma category images have been falsely categorized. Out of the 1000 lymphocytes images, we have 997 true predictions and 3 false predictions. Only 1 image among 1000 background images has been misclassified. Out of 1000 debris images, 972 are true predictions and out of 1000 mucus images only 21 have been wrongly classified. 968 images out of 1000 have been correctly classified as smooth muscle and 957 images among 1000 have been correctly classified as colon mucosa. Finally, 967 out of 1000 colorectal adenocarcinoma epithelium images have been correctly predicted.

Performance Evaluation Using Grad-CAM Visualization. Here, we have discussed the Gradient-weighted class activation mapping (Grad-CAM) [15] for our model interpretability. The goal of using Grad-CAM is to examine how the encoder is influencing the overall classification performance. Below we have provided a detailed view of the images and their corresponding Grad-CAM results showing which regions of the images were being extracted by the encoder were useful for classification task.

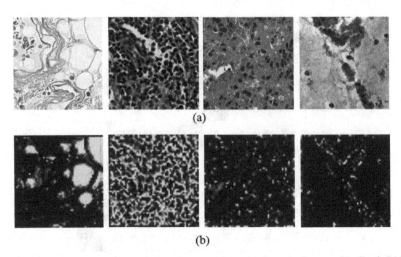

Fig. 7. (a): Show the four colorectal cancer images from the Zenedo dataset, (b): Grad-CAMs of the corresponding four images as shown in (a).

Based on the Grad-CAM visualizations shown in Fig. 7, we can clearly observe that the encoded activation maps are useful for extracting the important regions of histopathology images.

Performance Evaluation of the Proposed Model Against the Standalone DenseNet121 Model. In the present work, we have used a modified DenseNet121 architecture over its traditional implementations. Now, the concern is, can it perform better than the standalone DenseNet121 model? Below is a graphical representation of training metrics vs epochs of our proposed model against the standalone DenseNet121 model during the training (Fig. 8).

From the above graphical analysis, it is clear that the standalone DenseNet121 model overfits heavily. Fluctuation of the curves, the difference between validation accuracy and the training accuracy varying by a large margin clearly shows that the standalone DenseNet121 model overfits and fails to interpret and generalize the dataset. Conversely, in our proposed model the difference is quite consistent and small throughout the entire training epochs. It signifies that we have managed to counter the overfitting problem which leads us to achieving a generalized classification model. Also, the loss in our proposed model is small compared to the standalone DenseNet121 model. The standalone DenseNet scored 96.2% highest validation accuracy during the training phase whereas our proposed model got 97.67% highest validation accuracy. It clearly indicates the superiority of our proposed method.

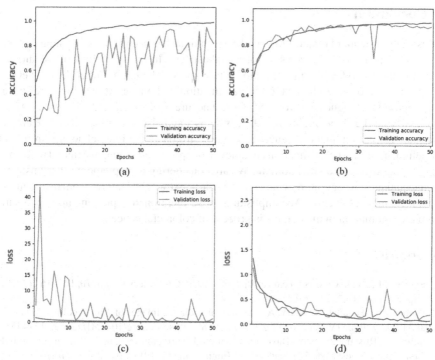

Fig. 8. (a) and (b) represents the training accuracy vs validation accuracy curves for the standalone DenseNet121 model and the proposed model respectively, (c) and (d) represents the training loss vs validation loss curves for the standalone DenseNet121 model and the proposed model respectively. In both cases the comparison is based on first 50 training epochs.

4.3 Comparative Study

In this section, a comparison of some significant works in this field with our proposed methodology is presented. This comparative analysis is illustrated below in Table 1.

Table 1. Comparison of performance metrics of some previous works and the proposed work.

Sl. No	References	Employed methodology	Testing accuracy (%)
1	Ponzio et al. [16]	Transfer learning	96
2	Urban et al. [11]	Convolutional neural network	96.4
3	L. Ding et al. [12]	Faster region-based convolutional neural network	91.4
4	Rathore et al. [9]	Multi-step gland segmentation	90.6
5	Kim et al. [10]	Convolutional neural network	90
6	Salmi et al. [3]	Naive Bayes classifier	95
7	Rizalputri et al. [5]	Convolutional neural network	82.2
8	**Proposed methodology**	**Encoder and modified DenseNet121**	**97.2**

5 Conclusion

In this study, a standard image autoencoding technique has been applied for image reconstruction of the histology images of colorectal cancer. The encoder block of the autoencoder module encodes raw images into feature space. Then, a modified DenseNet121 architecture has been implemented for classification with those extracted feature space. The proposed technique achieved a SOTA test accuracy of 97.2% and F1 score of 97.16 for classifying the above mentioned 9 class dataset and also very much effective classifying low-resolution images. Cancer-associated stroma and colorectal adenocarcinoma epithelium has lowest classification accuracy in our proposed model, we intend to further continue our research on this domain. We are considering to implement other unsupervised techniques in near future which will be able to extract the features from histopathology images more efficiently. Accomplishing above-mentioned improvements will ensure complete automation in the diagnosis process of colorectal cancer.

References

1. Siegel, R.L., et al.: Colorectal cancer statistics, 2020. CA Cancer J. Clin. **70**, 145–164 (2020). https://doi.org/10.3322/caac.21601
2. Kather, J.N., Halama, N., Marx, A.: 100,000 histological images of human colorectal cancer and healthy tissue (Version v0.1). Zenodo (2018). https://doi.org/10.5281/zenodo.1214456
3. Salmi, N., Rustam, Z.: Naïve Bayes classifier models for predicting the colon cancer. In: IOP Conference Series: Materials Science and Engineering (2019). https://doi.org/10.1088/1757-899X/546/5/052068
4. Kather, J., Weis, C., Bianconi, F., et al.: Multi-class texture analysis in colorectal cancer histology. Sci. Rep. **6**, 27988 (2016). https://doi.org/10.1038/srep27988
5. Rizalputri, L.N., Pranata, T., Tanjung, N.S., Auliya, H.M., Harimurti, S., Anshori, I.: Colorectal histology CSV multi-classification accuracy comparison using various machine learning models. In: Proceedings of the International Conference on Electrical Engineering and Informatics (2019). https://doi.org/10.1109/ICEEI47359.2019.8988846
6. Kali, Y., Linn, M.: Science. Int. Encycl. Educ. **313**, 468–474 (2010). https://doi.org/10.1016/B978-0-08-044894-7.00081-6
7. Huang, G., Liu, Z., Van Der Maaten, L., Weinberger, K.Q.: Densely connected convolutional networks (2017). https://doi.org/10.1109/CVPR.2017.243
8. Goyal, M., Oakley, A., Bansal, P., Dancey, D., Yap, M.H.: Skin lesion segmentation in dermoscopic images with ensemble deep learning methods. IEEE Access. (2020). https://doi.org/10.1109/ACCESS.2019.2960504
9. Rathore, S., Iftikhar, M.A., Chaddad, A., Niazi, T., Karasic, T., Bilello, M.: Segmentation and grade prediction of colon cancer digital pathology images across multiple institutions. Cancers (Basel) **11**, 1–16 (2019). https://doi.org/10.3390/cancers11111700
10. Kim, K.J., Cho, S.B.: Prediction of colon cancer using an evolutionary neural network. Neurocomputing. (2004). https://doi.org/10.1016/j.neucom.2003.11.008
11. Urban, G., et al.: Deep learning localizes and identifies polyps in real time with 96% accuracy in screening colonoscopy. Gastroenterology. (2018). https://doi.org/10.1053/j.gastro.2018.06.037
12. Ding, L., et al.: Artificial intelligence system of faster region-based convolutional neural network surpassing senior radiologists in evaluation of metastatic lymph nodes of rectal cancer. Chin. Med. J. (Engl.) **132**, 379–387 (2019). https://doi.org/10.1097/CM9.0000000000000095

13. Rahman, M.A., Muniyandi, R.C.: Feature selection from colon cancer dataset for cancer classification using Artificial Neural Network. Int. J. Adv. Sci. Eng. Inf. Technol. (2018). https://doi.org/10.18517/ijaseit.8.4-2.6790
14. Huang, G., Liu, Z., Van Der Maaten, L., Weinberger, K.Q.: Densely connected convolutional networks. In: Proceedings - 30th IEEE Conference on Computer Vision and Pattern Recognition, CVPR 2017 (2017). https://doi.org/10.1109/CVPR.2017.243
15. Selvaraju, R., Cogswell, M., Das, A., Vedantam, R., Parikh, D., Batra, D.: Grad-CAM: visual explanations from deep networks via gradient-based localization. Int. J. Comput. Vis. **128**(2), 336–359 (2019). https://doi.org/10.1007/s11263-019-01228-7
16. Ponzio, F., Macii, E., Ficarra, E., Di Cataldo, S.: Colorectal cancer classification using deep convolutional networks an experimental study. In: Proceedings of the 5th International Conference on Bioimaging, BIOIMAGING 2018, Part of 11th International Joint Conference on Biomedical Engineering Systems and Technologies, BIOSTEC 2018 (2018). https://doi.org/10.5220/0006643100580066.
17. Sirinukunwattana, K., et al.: Gland segmentation in colon histology images: the GlaS challenge contest. Med. Image Anal. **35**, 489–502 (2017). https://doi.org/10.1016/j.media.2016.08.008

Author Index

Printed in the United States
by Baker & Taylor Publisher Services